DR. CAT'S
HELPING HANDBOOK

A Compassionate Guide for Being Human

Dr. Cat's Helping Handbook

A Compassionate Guide for Being Human

Cat Saunders, Ph.D.

HEARTWINGS
FOUNDATION

WAIVER: Neither the publisher nor the author accepts any responsibility or any legal liability for any adverse reactions, experiences, or situations that may result from reading or using the material in this book.

Saunders, Cat

Dr. Cat's Helping Handbook: A Compassionate Guide for Being Human

Bibliography. Includes index.

ISBN 978-0-9675008-2-9

Library of Congress Catalog Card Number: 99-96530

Ten percent of the proceeds from this book will be donated to support the work of selected individuals and organizations.

For ordering information or to contact the publisher for excerpt reprint permission, please visit www.drcat.org.

This book is dedicated with love and gratitude to

IHALEAKALA HEW LEN

CONTENTS

Section Three

Section Four

Section Five

The Group as Healer:
Adding Power to the Punch 255

Section Six

Guided Meditations:
Calling the Spirit Within 295

Section Seven

Be Here Now:
What's Next? 319

ACKNOWLEDGMENTS

Since the first edition of this book took fifteen years to create, you can imagine that there are many people—living and dead—who have contributed to its journey. In the eight years that have elapsed between editions, many more deserve special acknowledgment as well. Although it would be impossible to thank everyone, I want to make a devoted effort to appreciate as many as I can. I figure this is a golden opportunity to write the best "Gratitude Cleanup List" I've ever done.

There's no way I could prioritize these people in terms of their contribution to me and to this book. Therefore, I've simply arranged them alphabetically, though in an unconventional way: by *first* name, because that's how I arrange my personal files. Thank you, all of you!

Alice Miller: Thanks for championing the rights of the child and for exposing the *poisonous pedagogy* of "for your own good" parenting. **Ammachi:** Thanks for holding and blessing this book as my "firstborn child" during darshan. Your sweet grace is a gift beyond compare. **Andrew Vachss:** Thanks for being one of my favorite heroes. Thanks for inspiring me with your courage, your creativity, your brilliance, and your undying commitment to prosecuting predators of children. Thanks also for many years of stimulating personal correspondence and for always encouraging me to stay strong and "Dance on!" **Arny and Amy Mindell:** Thanks for Process-Oriented Psychology. Thanks for your outrageous wildness, your insightfulness, your playfulness, your books, your generosity, and your love. **Bette Lamont:** Thanks for "giving me my brain back" by teaching me how to do neurological repatterning. Thanks to you, this book took only fifteen years instead of thirty! **Canelle Demange:** Thanks for deepening and strengthening my work with neurological repatterning, and thanks for being my sweet soul sister and DNA-level friend. **Carol Dillon:** Thanks for being my trusted graphic designer and Web wizard. Thanks for your beautiful cover design for this book's second edition, and thanks for being such a pleasure to work with. **Carl Jung:** Where would any of us *shadow dancers* be without you? Thanks for being so far ahead of your time that you joined the timeless ones. **Carlos Castaneda:** Thanks for bringing don Juan's teachings to the world, especially his instructions about death. **Claudia Black:** Thanks for your integrity, your sensitivity, your books, and your personal support of my writing. **Christiane Northrup, M.D.:** Thanks for your awesome books, beginning with *Women's Bodies, Women's Wisdom*, and thanks for your generous support of this book. Thanks also for being a powerful role model for me and countless others, and thanks for many years of juicy personal correspondence. **Dan Savage:** How amazing that you, the Seattle *Stranger*'s king of brutal outspokenness, were the one whose column (10/14/99) persuaded me to soften—though only slightly—my words against circumcision in this book. Thanks! **Dave Matthews:** Thanks for staying real in the midst of fame and fortune. Thanks for inspiring me in more ways than you will ever know, and thanks for your cover of "Time of the Season," which is one of my favorite songs to dance to every morning when I get up. **David and Doreen Tanenbaum:** Thanks for

helping me get started in private practice in 1985, and thanks for believing in me as a writer. **David Young:** Thanks for loving me with the purity of a child's heart, for being a respectful and compassionate editor for my work with *The New Times*, and for believing in me and my writing. Thanks for being an unconditionally loving and faithful friend—a true soul brother. **Deborah Koff-Chapin:** Thanks for advising against independently publishing this book because you knew how hard it would be—and once I decided to go for it anyway, thanks for supporting me every step of the way. Thanks for SoulCards and Touch Drawing, and thanks for your wisdom and your love. **Deverick Martin:** Thanks for publishing my writing in *The New Times* and for bringing my work to the Internet. Thanks for your generosity, your honesty, your devotion to growth, and your undying love. **Don Johnson:** Thanks for being one of the first to donate to this book's publication, and thanks for having such a good heart. **Donia Alawi:** Thanks for your publication donation that came from out of the blue and made me cry. Thanks for being my longtime friend and my favorite "nutrition guru." **Dr. Cat's Helping Handbook:** Thanks for being my ally, my teacher, and my taskmaster supreme. You have worked on me in ways that made me laugh, cry, swear, and ultimately, surrender to you as a living being with a will of your own. Thanks for giving me the privilege of stewarding your journey. **Elisabeth Kubler-Ross, M.D.:** Thank you for your courage and commitment in helping people overcome fear and denial in the face of death. **Eric Berne, M.D.:** Thank you for developing the elegantly simple mad/sad/glad/scared model of responsible emotional communication, which helped me overcome manic-depression. **Every client, student, and workshop participant:** Thanks for being my teachers, all of you! **Fredric Lehrman:** Thanks for being one of my top-ten mentors of all time. Thanks for your Renaissance elegance, your humor, your brilliance, and your menagerie of dragons. **Gabriele Rico:** Thanks for your books about writing and the creative process, because they gave me valuable tools and precious encouragement along the way. **Grady Gray:** Thanks for your role in my dance with infinity! **Greg Ostergaard:** Thanks, Ace, for those wild and wonderful years as co-therapists in the early 1980s. Thanks for seeing an advertisement for one of my workshops in 1985 and for asking me, "So when does the book come out?" This is it!

'Ihaleakala Hew Len: Thanks for teaching me Ho'oponopono (along with Morrnah Nalamaku Simeona) in 1985—the same year I began writing this book. Thanks for modeling self-care and 100% personal responsibility, and thanks for teaching me that the only honest way to help anyone is to work on *myself*. **Irwin's Cafe (Seattle):** Thanks for being my partner's (John's) "home away from home" for great food and camaraderie, and thanks for being a major player in my book giveaway service project with hundreds of gift copies donated to your patrons, one by one. **Jackie McNamara:** Thanks for coming into my heart the moment we met—and thanks for staying there. Thanks for being such a devoted and faithful assistant for my classes, and thanks for being a true friend. **jill frey:** Thanks for being the one who first put *Dr. Cat's Helping Handbook* into digital form. Thanks for being a top-notch human being, a wonderful "little sister," and a dear friend. **Joe Rahn:** Thanks for being there for me like a steady drumbeat for nearly 30 years as part of my true spiritual family. I miss you since you died. **John Giovine:** Thanks for believing in me and my work even when your own faith faltered. Thanks for giving so generously of your time and energy (including "green energy") toward the creation of this book, and thanks for coming up with such a great title: *Dr. Cat's Helping Handbook*. Thanks for being my partner and my true companion, and thanks for giving me the opportunity to hone my character and become a better person through loving and being loved by you. **John Eric Rolfstad:** Thank you for your courageous and compassionate work as Director of People's Memorial Association, providing gentle and humane options for end-of-life care. Thanks also for giving away my books at PMA's Annual Meeting, and most of all, thanks for your friendship. **John Travolta:** Thanks for helping to teach about death in your movies *Phenomenon* and *Michael*. Thanks, too, for playing that wild rascal-angel Michael, because a dream told me that your character in that movie is the angel for this book. **Julia Cameron:** Thanks for *The Artist's Way*, not only because it helped me as a writer and an artist, but also because that book was one of the models I used in developing the design for this book. **Kenyth Freeman:** Thanks for an amazing first meeting at an autopsy in 1974. Thanks for being my friend and core member of my true spiritual family. Thanks for being one of my top-ten best mentors, who introduced me to many of the disciplines that became essential parts of my life. **Kris Estes:** Thanks for giving me the experience of having a benefactor during some very lean years when your generosity brought me to tears many times. Thanks for being such a dear friend, and thanks for being my compatriot and ally in the land of physical challenges. **Krysta Gibson:** Thanks for being the founder of *The New Times* and for being my first publisher. Thanks for believing in me as a writer, and thanks for your encouragement during this book's embryonic stages. **Laura Davis:** Thank you for all your books, especially *The Courage to Heal* and *I Thought We'd Never Speak Again*, both of which are masterpieces. Thanks also for your warm personal support of this book. **Leanne Garn:** Thanks for your invaluable feedback during this book's early drafts, and thanks for your generous financial and moral support. Thanks for your extraordinary friendship and your commitment to 100% personal responsibility. **Leslie Heizer:** Thanks for gracing my life in a million ways since that fire walk in the Cascades in 1984. Thanks for introducing me to Process Work and special thanks for helping me mine the gold in my shadow. **Lucia Capacchione:** Thanks for turning me on to Summit University and the inimitable Mel Suhd, so I could experience a humane and rewarding doctoral program. Thanks also for your three questions for compassionate caring (included in this book's chapter called "My Personal Rules of Respect"). **Marc Allen:** Thanks for coming close to publishing the original edition of this book through New World Library, and thanks for *not* publishing it, because that helped me step up to the plate. **Marcella Hunter:** Thanks for being the person who opened my eyes to the power of privilege. **Marie Hanthorn:** Thanks for your skillful computer work for the first edition of this book, and thanks for being a kind and spirited friend. **Marilyn Milos:** Thanks for your loving friendship and thanks for your incredible courage in the fight against involuntary circumcision through NOCIRC. Here's to the day when involuntary circumcision for *both* sexes is a thing of the past! **Marla Greenway:** Thanks for being my best friend, my twin flame, and my inspiration. I treasure your brilliance and your beauty, your humor and your wildness, your courage and your strength, your wisdom and your warmth. The original manuscript for this book brought YOU to me, which I'm sure is one reason I wrote it! Thanks for your undying support, and thanks for being my favorite pen pal of all time. **Martha Vallely:** Thanks for being my first private practice client in 1985 and for not caring who knows that. Thanks for growing with me, for breaking boundaries with me, for sharing dreams and shamanism and poetry and painting with me, and for knowing that the only real healing is the healing that happens through love. **Mary J. Getten:** Thanks for understanding the highs and lows of independent publishing from firsthand experience, and thanks for being a wonderful pen pal and a gifted animal communicator. **Melvin Powers:** In 1987, I called you—a publisher of best sellers—and you personally took time to brainstorm with me about how to turn my ideas into a book. Thanks! **Mel Suhd:** Thanks for your unwavering encouragement to follow my own truth. Thanks for mentoring me through my doctoral odyssey at Summit University, and thanks for extending your loving support long after I graduated. You are one in a million! **Michael Harner:** Thanks for believing in this book from the first time you saw an early manuscript in 1992. Thanks for being my favorite shaman, who always taught me to listen to my own shamanic teachers and power animals (in nonordinary reality) over and above anything you or anyone else said. Thanks for helping me journey past the point of my death, because that experience changed my life forever. **Michael Tomlinson:** Thanks for your playful letters, your hilarious stories, and your devotion to growth. Thanks for modeling courage and integrity in the challenging world of independent publishing, and thanks for giving *Dr. Cat's Helping Handbook* such a wonderful endorsement. **Mitch Marder, D.D.S.:** Thanks for your honesty, your skill, your humor, your friendship, and your generous "dental work donations" toward the publication of this book. Thanks also to your staff—especially Flo Pierce—for their kindness, and thanks for giving away hundreds of copies of *Dr. Cat's Helping Handbook* through your office as a longtime supporter of my book giveaway service project. **Morrnah Nalamaku Simeona:** Thanks for bringing the updated Ho'oponopono to the world and to me. I am eternally grateful! **M. Scott Peck, M.D.:** Thanks for your concept of "healthy depression" from *The Road Less Traveled*, because it gave me heart in the midst of dark times. Thanks for your deep understanding of the shadow, your exquisite book about death (*Denial of the Soul*), and your encouragement of my work. **My shamanic teachers and power animals in nonordinary reality:** Thanks for being there with me every step of the way, for guiding me with patience and grace, and for calling me "Bozo" with such love. *New Times* **readers:** Thanks for all your letters and messages of support. Thanks also for the occasional hate letter, because I think that old adage is true: *"If you don't have enemies, you aren't doing anything."* **Nina Brauer and BookSurge:** Thanks for doing such a great job on the second edition of *Dr. Cat's Helping Handbook*. Compared to my brutal experience with the original edition, working with BookSurge was a joyride! **Nirmala (Martha) Russo:** Thanks for being my precious soul sister and compatriot all these years. Thanks for believing in me as a writer, and thanks for *knowing* (long before I did) that this book *had* to be independently published. **Peg Price:** Thanks for teaching me Eric Berne's mad/sad/glad/scared model because it helped me overcome manic-depression; it helped me teach hundreds of clients and workshop participants how to become friends with their feelings; and it can now help even more people through its inclusion in this book. **Peter Shalit, M.D.:** Thanks for saving my life (literally) and thanks for being such a great ally in helping me navigate the wild and sometimes challenging world of conventional Western medicine. Thanks to your wonderful staff as well—especially J. Steve Mayo—for their warm support. **Philip Brautigam:** Thanks for contributing your prodigious skills to the original production of this book. **Ram Dass:** Thanks for being one of my top-ten mentors of all time. Thanks for your humor, your gutsiness, and your willingness to use every aspect of your life—including your stroke—to "hold the door open" for others. **Renee Locks:** Thanks for our sweet and mysterious connection, and thanks for saying *yes* when I asked if you'd do some Brush Dance cards with one-liners from *Dr. Cat's Helping Handbook*. Your art and calligraphy are gifts to us all. **Rhonda Dicksion:** Thanks for joining Krysta Gibson as her editor for *The New Times* during the years when you two stewarded its growth. Thanks for helping me hone and develop my writing, and thanks for all the laughs—and your great cartoons! **Rich Haag:** When you were my favorite professor in the Landscape Architecture Department at the University of Washington, you told me that you spent only 10% of your time designing, even though you owned one of Seattle's most successful landscape architecture firms. Thanks for your honesty about that, because it catalyzed my change of majors to psychology. Quite literally, this book may never have happened without you. **Robert Koch:** Thanks for being my favorite Vedic astrologer, my "death buddy," and my soul brother. Thanks for many years of invaluable personal and professional guidance, and thanks for laughing about things with me that I can laugh about with no one else. **Robin Norwood:** Thanks for your groundbreaking book, *Women Who Love Too Much*, because it's been a lifesaver and one of my most important teachers about compassion for the self. **Robyn Brode:** Thanks for your incredible indexing and proofreading skills. Thanks also for saving me from some "beginner's mistakes" in the original design of this book. **Rodger Webster:** Thanks for sharing your beautiful understanding of forgiveness, which I included in this book. **Rose De Dan:** Thanks for coming to my rescue with your graphic skills during a crucial stage in the final weeks of this book's original production. Thanks for your kindness and your integrity, and thanks for being my shamanic prayer buddy. **Rusty Palmer:** Thanks for being my single most important family systems mentor. Thanks for your awesome perceptivity, your ruthless compassion, and your radical humor. You still ride around on my shoulder when I work with clients. **Sally Giovine-Kerr, Bob Kerr, and the Giovine-Kerr clan:** Thanks for all the lessons—gentle and fierce—and thanks for the love and laughter. **Sandra Ingerman:** Thanks for being my soul retrieval mentor and my longtime compatriot. Thanks also for the soul retrieval you gave me, because it helped me write this book with all of me present. **Sandy Fox:** Thank you for your friendship, your depth of spirit, your devotion to peace, and your generous PR work in my behalf. **Shadow teachers:** Thanks for tempering me on the anvil of pain, for helping me burn off karma, and for teaching me that the nucleus of my fear always holds a nugget of gold. **Sondra Ray:** Thanks for teaching me so much about the breath, for helping me discern deep levels of family patterning, and for encouraging me to *go for it* as a writer. **Steven M. Hall, M.D.:** Thanks for being my personal physician, my colleague, and my friend. Thanks for helping me keep going in the midst of nonstop physical challenges, and thanks for being a "country doc" as well as a shaman-healer. You're the best! **Steven Spielberg:** Thank you for all your movies—and in light of its turning-point contribution to my reworking of "The Anger Primer" chapter, thanks especially for *Saving Private Ryan*. **Susan (Tulp) Lien:** Thanks for your helpful suggestions, your computer skills, and your loving patience with my crazy-exhausted "mother-bear energy" during the final rounds of production for the first edition of this book. You rock! **Sy Safransky:** Thanks for keeping *The Sun* alive in the face of all odds. Your courage and your persistence as a publisher and a writer are an inspiration to me. **Tony Robbins:** Thanks for your *Personal Power* tape program. Thanks for your indomitable spirit, your understanding of neuroassociations, your outrageous humor (I love the one about the live crickets), and your commitment to helping people give wings to their dreams. **Vicki Marie Haynes:** Thanks for teaching me the basics of writing when I was fourteen. **Vicki Noble:** Thanks for your wonderful Motherpeace Tarot, and thanks for your powerful work with shamanism. Thanks for your humility, your insightfulness, and your support of my writing. **Warren, Gerd, Adriane, and Scott Saunders:** Thanks to all of you, my blood family, for giving me the perfect foundation of experiences from which to write this book. Thanks for all your teachings—shadow and light, mysterious and mundane. My love and gratitude for each of you is immeasurable.

Anyone I've knowingly or unknowingly forgotten:
Thanks for everything!

PREFACE:
WHAT THIS BOOK IS NOT

Many of the ideas in this book are offered as a counterbalance to the age-old maxim that you must put others first. While this "others first" perspective may be valid for some, it can give rise to a host of maladies—both personal and global—if it is overemphasized to the point of self-neglect. Because this book flies in the face of certain prevailing attitudes, I'd like to say up front what this book is *not,* to defuse some of the criticisms that inevitably arise when mainstream beliefs are challenged.

This book is *not* a permission slip to focus only on yourself. Be sure to read the introduction carefully.

This book is *not* intended for those who already focus too much on their own navels. Such people could stand to pay more attention to others.

This book is *not* saying that inner work is more important than outer work. Both are important and both are necessary for balance.

This book is *not* a treatise on the relative worth of psychology as compared to politics, feelings as compared to thoughts, or meditation as compared to activity. Every milieu and modality is valid in its own time and place.

This book is *not* a substitute for working on yourself with the help of a mentor who can call you on your stuff. It's easy to fool yourself into believing that you're enlightened if you only work on yourself alone.

This book is *not* meant to be used in place of medical, psychiatric, psychotherapeutic, or other professional advice. You have the right to experiment with any of my suggestions, but you are completely and legally responsible for your choices and actions, no matter what I say or don't say in this book.

This book is *not* the whole puzzle. It's one very small piece of a very big puzzle. May it help you enjoy the mystery!

INTRODUCTION:
COMPASSION IS THE KEY

My basic message is simple: *Be compassionate with yourself and take good care of yourself.* If you do this, it will be the best gift you can give to yourself, humanity, and the planet. If you take care of yourself, no one else will have to take care of you. If you are truly compassionate with yourself, you will not be inclined to harm anyone or anything. In addition, if you see that your own needs are met, you will be in a better position to share with others, care for the planet, and serve in your own special way.

The human heart will never be satisfied with caring only for the self. You can trust that if you take care of yourself, you will naturally want to care for others. Also, if you make sure that your own needs are met, your concern for others will arise from a genuine desire to give without expectation of return. This is very different from *giving* in order to *get*.

For thousands of years, the socio-religious injunction to *put others first* has clouded the issue of self-care. After all, there will always be others, so if you put others first, who will take care of you? Will you have to rely on others to take care of you? Some folks believe that God (by whatever name) takes care of their needs, which supposedly leaves them free to care for others. How do you make sense of this dilemma?

Perhaps this question can be resolved in a way that goes beyond the polarities of putting others first or putting the self first. I believe that true compassion is actually a dance between these two polarities. In other words, I learn to care for others as I learn to care for myself, and vice versa. Therefore, a true humanitarian is someone who considers the needs of *all* people, self included. Since cultural and religious conditioning has emphasized compassion for others, this book seeks a rebalancing of polarities by championing equal rights for self-care.

Ram Dass says, "Compassion simply stated is leaving other people alone." This means allowing other people the right to *be*. I would further define compassion as the ability to let *everything* be—

You take good care of yourself. If you do, all will be beneficiaries.

IHALEAKALĀ HEW LEN

We cannot live only for our-selves. A thousand fibers connect us with our fellow men; and among those fibers, as sympathetic threads, our actions run as causes, and they come back to us as effects.

HERMAN MELVILLE

A man is rich in proportion to the number of things he can afford to let alone.

HENRY DAVID THOREAU

...the healthy, the strong individual, is the one who asks for help when he needs it whether he's got an abscess on his knee or in his soul.

RONA BARRETT

Compassion realizes, above all, that life is too brief to be stuck in any one side of the whole.

ARNOLD MINDELL

including self, other beings, and all things. To let something be, I must first be *aware* of its existence and then *accept* its existence. Thus, awareness and acceptance are two basic components of compassion.

This book can help you hone your awareness and deepen your capacity for acceptance. If you turn these skills of compassion toward yourself, your ability to love others will grow. If instead you deaden your awareness and deny yourself acceptance, your ability to care for others will likewise diminish.

One essential part of self-care is the willingness to seek (and receive) help when you need it. It's great to believe that if we all take care of ourselves, everyone's needs will be met. However, you may not always know *how* to take care of yourself. At other times, you may know how, but you might not be *able* to do it. Therefore, taking care of yourself doesn't mean you're supposed to handle everything yourself without help. Taking care of yourself simply means that you are responsible for yourself, including asking for help. This book can help you take more responsibility for yourself by encouraging you to discover, respect, and provide for your own needs.

If you don't take responsibility for yourself, all kinds of problems arise. For one thing, if your needs are not met, you may turn to addictive habits for comfort, denial of pain, numbing of feelings, or perhaps even death as an escape. Even so, addiction is not wrong. It can be used as a teacher to help you deepen your compassion, if you are willing to look underneath the compulsive behavior to discern your true needs. The first section of this book, "The Five-Minute Switch System," focuses on the challenge of transforming addictions into teachers.

The process of unraveling old habits and addictions usually unleashes a parade of emotions, as the proverbial skeletons leave the closet and stir things up. For most people, it takes a lot of practice to become comfortable with all aspects of the self, especially the parts that have been hidden away. To assist you in becoming better friends with your humanity, "The Heart of the Matter" (Section Two) offers in-depth discussions and creative techniques for working with the broad range of human emotions and experience.

"Creativity's Gift" (Section Three) continues this work with an emphasis on writing, and "Person to Person" (Section Four) provides suggestions for practicing your skills in different kinds of relationships. The fifth section, "The Group as Healer," expands the basic themes of this book into group settings, and the book closes with three guided meditations in Section Six. Finally, in "Be Here Now" (Section Seven), I've included a bibliography of the books that have played a significant role in my own thinking about compassion.

Because your development is unique in relation to others, and because your own experience will shift over time, this book was designed to be read in any direction possible, so you can follow your heart in working through it. Because of this nonlinear approach, you may find some of the basic information repeated here or there to make the chapters more self-contained.

As you explore the ideas and suggestions in this guide, take what's right for you and let the rest go. There is no right way or wrong way to use this book. There is only your way—and your way is best for you.

If I am not for myself, who will be for me? But if I am for myself alone, why am I?

HILLEL

The

Five-Minute

Switch System:

Breaking

Addiction's Grip

SECTION
ONE

THE FIVE-MINUTE
SWITCH SYSTEM

The purpose of the Five-Minute Switch System is to break the automatic response quality of addictive behavior. By addictive behavior, I mean not only substance addiction, but also addiction to compulsive ways of thinking, feeling, or acting. For example, people who never struggle with overindulgence in substances such as food, drugs, or alcohol may struggle with overindulgence in relationships, sex, or work.

Here's my definition of addiction: **An addiction is anything that stands in the way of total awareness and acceptance of yourself, others, and the world.** In the introduction, I explained how awareness and acceptance are the two basic components of compassion. Therefore, an addiction is anything that stands in the way of being fully *compassionate* with everything and everyone, including yourself.

You can test this definition in your own life by using it to determine whether or not something is an addiction for you. In considering a particular habit, ask yourself: "Does this habit make me less aware or less accepting of myself, others, or the world around me?" The trick in answering this question is to be fully honest. Sometimes an addiction can seduce you into believing it actually increases your awareness and acceptance, when in fact an unbiased observer would say the opposite. It's easy to fool yourself. What's that old joke? Denial isn't just a river in Egypt. I'll say more about this in a moment.

Addictive behavior is not bad or wrong. In fact, it's a common human experience. Generally speaking, human behavior is determined by two basic tendencies, both of which are hard-wired into our brains because they support survival. One is the tendency to move away from pain. The other is the tendency to move toward pleasure. Obviously, this description is a gross oversimplification. However, if you're really honest about the motivation behind any of your choices or actions, I bet you'll discover that everything boils down to the pursuit of pleasure or the avoidance of pain. If you're embarrassed about being so primal and predictable, don't worry.

Habit is habit, and not to be flung out of the window by any man, but coaxed downstairs a step at a time.
MARK TWAIN

The first principle is that you must not fool yourself—and you are the easiest person to fool.
RICHARD FEYNMAN

Everyone is primal and predictable!

From the Wall Street money marketer to the voluntary simplicity advocate to the indigenous farmer, everyone is playing the same game. We're all moving away from whatever causes us pain and toward whatever brings us pleasure. Even the saints of the world, who continually minister to the needs of others, are doing exactly what brings them the most pleasure. The most selfless humans are acting in the most selfish ways! It's just that they associate pleasure with the act of helping others.

What's interesting about the pleasure-pain principle is that different people associate different things with pain and pleasure. The very thing that delights one person may totally distress someone else. For instance, I grew up in a family that valued self-discipline, so it's actually pleasurable for me to do certain things that other people avoid. For example, I like to exercise every day, and I don't feel good if I skip it. In contrast, I know people who struggle to get out for a ten-minute walk.

Another interesting thing about the pleasure-pain principle is the way it relates to addiction. In most cases, addiction involves a dance between pain and pleasure. For instance, an alcoholic may turn to alcohol to avoid some underlying pain, which may or may not be conscious. Once the alcohol is consumed, it usually brings some level of pleasure, even if the pleasure is only experienced as the absence of pain. After a binge, though, there is usually some degree of pain (i.e., hangovers, upset relationships, or other unfortunate consequences of drunken activity). This often stimulates the person to drink again to numb the physical or emotional pain, so the vicious cycle begins anew.

My own past addiction to marijuana illustrates a similar dynamic. Although the reasons for my addiction were many and complex, it all boiled down to the pursuit of pleasure and the avoidance of pain (emotional pain). In many ways, marijuana brought me extreme pleasure. It helped me feel more *connected* to my body, to my creative passions, and to the wonders of the world. Many times, I joked with friends that marijuana was my antidote for a severely repressed upbringing. It was my ally and my teacher, my comfort and my friend.

On the flip side, however, many years of daily dope smoking brought me considerable pain. Not only did it affect my emotional stability and cloud my perceptions, it also hurt my body. Marijuana debilitated my immune and respiratory systems, my adrenal glands and liver, and my connective tissue. So great was my hunger for its *high* that I kept using it long after it began to cause immediate and

Discipline doesn't have to be about restriction, it can be about freedom, it can be about openness, it can be about more rather than less.

BATYA ZAMIR

Love is the only drug that works.

JOHN COIT

extreme physical distress, which lasted for days after smoking even a single toke.

This kind of destructiveness is a telltale sign of addiction. The destruction may take years to manifest, or it may appear in areas apparently unrelated to the addiction. In my case, I was particularly intrigued by the fact that marijuana weakened my connective tissue, yet it helped me *feel* more connected. Ironically, the connectedness I sought through the drug at one level was taken away at another level. This taught me a painful lesson about addiction as a double-edged sword. It also inspired me to learn, over many years' time, how to satisfy my underlying need for *connection* in ways that were not destructive.

In offering my personal example and the example of an alcoholic, my purpose is not to delineate the intricacies of various addictions. Instead, I simply want to introduce the idea that addiction is intimately linked to basic underlying needs. Specifically, addiction arises when people respond to the pleasure-pain principle with automatic, compulsive behaviors instead of responding with consciously chosen actions.

As I said before, everyone associates different things with pleasure and pain. Although everyone avoids pain and desires pleasure, what you need may be different from what I need, depending on what we each associate with pleasure and pain. Also, two people might use the same addiction to satisfy different needs. Again, this is because needs arise from uniquely personal associations with pain and pleasure.

To show you what I mean, let me bottom-line my own deepest pleasure. My biggest *high* is to feel connected to myself and to everything in the cosmos. When I feel connected, it seems like nothing can stop me. I'm in *blaster* bliss! When I feel disconnected, on the other hand, I experience physical or emotional pain.

In my family, pleasure seeking was not valued as an end in itself. At some point, I turned to drugs to overcome my guilt about seeking pleasure. It worked temporarily, at least. Of course, I used drugs for many other reasons, but the point is, marijuana gave me a way to *instantly* feel connected to myself and to the world. It also gave me a way to assuage the pain of my emotional baggage. *Voilà!* Pursuit of pleasure and avoidance of pain all rolled into one...joint! What more could I ask?

As it turned out, I decided to ask for a lot more. As I gradually let go of my habit, I used it as a teacher to help me understand what I needed. I paid careful attention to what happened before, during, and after smoking marijuana. I turned myself into a science

The most instructive experiences are those of everyday life.
FRIEDRICH NIETZSCHE

If you're not doing something, it's because you associate more pain with doing it than not doing it.
ANTHONY ROBBINS

experiment, and I collected data. I kept tabs on my needs and desires, my body and my emotions, and my sense of connection or disconnection (see "The Three-Day Window" for more about this).

Over time, I discovered what marijuana was giving and what it was taking away. Eventually, I began to associate more pain with smoking it than with not smoking it. Please understand that this was not about judging the habit. I'd long since abandoned the need to control my behavior by assigning some arbitrary set of morals about drugs. After all, marijuana had helped me survive when I had no better coping skills. Rather than make it wrong, I used my addiction to learn about myself. Marijuana was a crutch, but it enabled me to walk until I could stand on my own.

I don't know what you'll discover when you examine your own compulsions. I hope that you won't make yourself or your habits wrong (see "Addictions as Teachers"). Instead of blame or criticism, I encourage you to *explore* your addictions. You can start by considering the following questions. What is your highest pleasure? What is your deepest pain? What do you need in order to experience pleasure in your life? What do you need in order to feel safe in relation to pain? How does your habit satisfy your need for pleasure? How does it help you avoid pain? Can you imagine other ways to satisfy your desire for pleasure? Do you know any other ways to deal with pain?

The point is *not* to get rid of your natural human tendencies to pursue pleasure and avoid pain. The point is rather to examine how you can meet these needs in ways that are constructive and enlivening, as opposed to destructive and deadening. Will you attempt to satisfy your underlying needs through automatic responses (addictions) that bring temporary relief, without concern for long-term consequences? Or will you choose to satisfy your underlying needs through creative actions that provide both short- and long-term benefits? The choice is yours. Unfortunately, many people live their lives on automatic pilot, without ever realizing that they can make conscious choices about how to respond to their basic needs.

Once you're fully at choice about an addiction, you are no longer addicted. However, determining whether you are truly at choice is no simple matter. This is usually a long process. Within this process, there is lots of room for denial and lots of room to fool yourself about whether or not you're really making conscious choices. Compulsion has a way of creeping in, disguising itself in a thousand different ways, and making you think you're in control when it's really the addiction that's running the show.

What's holding her back drives her on.

OSIP MANDELSTAM

Any time choice seems to be cut off, illusion is operating.

DEEPAK CHOPRA

The Five-Minute Switch System provides a balanced approach for healing compulsive habits by combining the discipline of focus with the openheartedness of a nonjudgmental stance. The basic idea is to catch yourself just as you are about to do something you consider addictive. At that point, stop whatever you are doing for five minutes, and do something else. That's it. In both the *Beginner's Version* and the *Advanced Version* of the Five-Minute Switch System (see below), it doesn't matter what you do during—or after—your time-out. The point of your break is simply to give yourself a chance to interrupt the automatic response cycle.

When you first begin using the Five-Minute Switch System, don't worry about whether or not you do your addiction after the time-out. Again, the purpose of the break is to create a space for you to become more aware of what you're doing. Even addictions need your awareness and acceptance! See if you can set your judgments aside, and give yourself permission to do or not do your habit after the allotted time-out.

By focusing on the *moment of choice* instead of focusing on the addiction, you open the way to increased awareness. This is important, because *awareness* can help you change the automatic quality of your response to underlying needs. In other words, the problem is neither the addiction nor the underlying need. Instead, the problem is a lack of awareness. Without awareness, it's difficult to experience, accept, and satisfy your underlying needs in ways that support you without hurting you. On the other hand, if you act with awareness, you can take care of yourself in ways that increase your well-being without taking anything away.

He who mounts a wild elephant goes where the wild elephant goes.

RANDOLPH BOURNE

To conclude, here are three versions of the Five-Minute Switch System:

Beginner's Version

1. Catch yourself just before you do a habit that you consider addictive.

2. Take a five-minute break by setting a timer or by noting the time on a clock or watch.

3. During the time-out, do anything other than your usual habit. Check out the remainder of this section if you want some ideas about what to do.

4. At the end of your break, either do or don't do your habit, with as little judgment as possible.

Advanced Version

Follow the same directions as in the Beginner's Version, except gradually increase the length of your breaks by five-minute intervals until you are doing thirty-minute breaks.

Veteran's Version

When you can easily interrupt the addictive cycle by at least thirty minutes, the next step is *always* to choose *not* to do your habit afterward, instead of leaving it open-ended. Work with whatever feelings come up. Use the tools you already have, or experiment with the ideas and techniques offered in this book.

If your time-out explorations help you see how to meet your underlying needs in more constructive ways, act on what you've learned once your Switch System break is over. If you're not sure what to do, follow your first hunch. Trust your intuition to lead you to your next step.

The greatest learning occurs when you're practicing diligently and seem to be getting nowhere.

GEORGE LEONARD

THE COMPASSIONATE THOUGHT GAME

When you pause for a five-minute break, imagine the most compassionate thought you could have about yourself. Play with this thought for a few minutes, and see if any images come to mind. Can you see yourself and your situation right now with accepting eyes and a tender heart?

If you have trouble feeling compassionate toward yourself, pretend that you are one of your best friends—or perhaps a favorite sweetheart, a companion animal, a special teacher, or a saint. When you have switched perspectives, imagine that you are looking at yourself through his or her eyes, the eyes of someone who unconditionally loves and accepts you.

Practice having this feeling of compassion for yourself until it becomes second nature. After you've mastered it in small ways, extend this kind-hearted perspective to situations where you may be judging yourself in other ways. Remember that five-minute breaks can be used not only for substance or behavior addiction, but also for addiction to compulsive ways of thinking.

Personally, I can usually recognize my most compassionate thought by noticing my body's reaction. When such a thought enters my mind, my body relaxes, and I may literally breathe a sigh of relief. Find out how *your* body feels when you have compassionate thoughts, and then cultivate those thoughts. When you treat yourself with openheartedness, you will naturally treat others in the same way. Kind thoughts are contagious. Spread them around!

In each of us, there's a lot of softness, a lot of heart. Touching that soft spot has to be the starting place. This is what compassion is all about.

PEMA CHÖDRÖN

REACH OUT—
YOU'RE NOT ALONE

There are many Twelve Step programs available, which help millions of people ease the pain and isolation of addiction. Although my own path of healing took other routes, I respect the contribution of these groups. One common characteristic of many Twelve Step programs is the use of *sponsors*. As I understand it, a sponsor is a fellow group member who acts as a support person to help you work with the recovery principles of your particular organization.

For this simplified version of the sponsor concept, you can ask a friend to be your designated buddy. Then when you take a five-minute break, use the time to call your friend. Once you make the call, feel free to say whatever you like if you simply want to connect. However, if you want to go a little deeper, try the suggestion in the following paragraph. By the way, if your call is answered by a phone machine or voice mail, you can still proceed, as long as you're sure your friend will be the only one who hears your message.

If you use addictive behaviors or substances to deal with emotional pain, try making a one-sentence expression of your bottom-line feeling. You might say *I hurt*, or *I'm really sad*, or *I'm overwhelmed with anxiety*, or whatever else fits for you. See if you can hold the truth of your simple statement without going into details. If you think this sounds easy, I challenge you to try it.

It took me years of work before I could say *I hurt* without going into long explanations to justify my pain. Clients of mine have also said that they find it difficult to bottom-line their pain in one sentence, without any embellishment. Many people have been shamed for expressing or having pain. If you say *I hurt*, others may accuse you of wallowing, which is considered disgusting. In our society, there is great confusion about the difference between self-disclosure and self-pity.

Even in therapeutic settings, I've often had to reassure clients that I will not shame them for expressing pain. Obviously, wallowing does exist, and some people do get stuck in self-pity. In my experience, however, most people can barely take a step into their pain without judging themselves to be wimps. The truth is, an honest expression of pain is not shameful; it's an act of courage.

Because many people do not understand the dynamics of shame, it's very important that you choose your buddy carefully, so you don't get shamed again, on top of whatever shame you already have. When you call your friend during a time-out to say *I hurt*, ask your buddy to respond gently and simply. For example, she or he could say, "Thanks for telling me," or "I'm glad you trust me enough to tell me when you hurt." If your friend can hear you without trying to change or fix your pain, that's the best. A kindly tone of voice is also helpful.

Next time you catch yourself craving an escape when emotional pain arises, reach out to your buddy instead. As with all five-minute breaks, you can still turn to your addiction afterward. But first, reach out. Who knows? You might choose to do something different after a good dose of support.

I look for someone who will understand my need without taking me for a beggar.
RAINER MARIA RILKE

THE COIN
FLIP METHOD

The Coin Flip Method works like this: When you find yourself about to do whatever you think is addictive, stop and flip a coin. If it turns up heads, you do the habit. If it's tails, you pass. That's it. The less you think about it, the better. The idea is to inject some *conscious* spontaneity into your life, as an antidote to *compulsive* spontaneity (the kind that happens automatically). Remember, the purpose of the Five-Minute Switch System is to focus on your awareness, not on your addiction.

If one of your compulsions is to think about everything excessively, you can use this method to push that compulsion to the point of absurdity and thereby transform it. In other words, exaggerate the Coin Flip Method by using it constantly. No kidding! Loosen up the controlling part of your personality by delegating your authority to a silly little coin.

If you're like me, you may be humbled by the Coin Flip Method because it quickly reveals how attached you are to a particular habit. For example, you might find yourself flipping the coin again and again until you get the answer you want. Interesting, huh? Notice how you feel when you get heads and when you get tails, in terms of the consequence of saying *yes* or *no* to your addiction.

Do you get mad when the coin flip says you *can't* have what you want? Do you think the technique is great fun when you get a *yes*—and stupid when you get a *no*? Do you turn the coin into a tyrant and rebel against it? Are you compassionate with yourself no matter what feelings come up when you flip the coin? Whatever your experience, try to keep your sense of humor. Stay focused on the quality of your awareness.

If you use this technique regularly, you might switch some of the compulsive energy from your addiction to the act of coin flipping, which is a curious phenomenon. If this happens, you may discover that the real issue is compulsiveness. In other words, addictive *energy* is the trickster, not the addiction itself.

Thus, it's the *relationship* between you and your addiction that holds the power. The Coin Flip Method merely helps you learn more about this relationship.

If you want to increase your humility, try using this method in front of your friends. For instance, if you have a cigarette habit, you could say, "Excuse me, I need to flip a coin right now to see if I'm going to smoke." If anyone asks about it, just say that you're practicing a new form of spiritual detachment. That should raise a few eyebrows.

Break a habit. Do something that makes you feel insecure.

PIERO FERRUCCI

BANK ON
YOURSELF

M any years ago, a former colleague of mine (whom I'll call Bill) admitted that he had a problem with alcohol. He knew he wasn't willing to give it up entirely because he loved beer. However, he also knew that if he drank more than two beers a week, alcohol became a problem for him. Based on this knowledge of himself, he devised a creative and self-accepting system for managing his habit.

Obviously, if Bill had wanted to explore his addiction more fully, he could have completely let go of it. This, in turn, would have helped him discover the feelings and needs masked by the alcohol. However, Bill's choice was to keep drinking beer within strict limits that allowed him to maintain a reasonably functional lifestyle. The point is, abstinence doesn't work for everyone, nor does it work for every kind of addiction. In addition, some people don't want to do core-level addiction work.

If you do want to go deep in your work with compulsion, it's okay to gradually release your habits over time in whatever way feels safe for you. If you force an addiction to stop prematurely— before you know how to satisfy your underlying needs in other ways—your addiction will probably just change form. For example, smokers may become overeaters if they stop their cigarette habit without addressing the underlying issues.

Obviously, if you've taken an addiction to the point of imminent self-destruction, or to a point where you are hurting others because of it, you may need to stop the addiction before it stops you. Many addictions can be explored while you are still in the process of releasing them. However, if you feel confused about the seriousness of your level of addiction, it may be wise to seek competent professional counsel to sort out your perceptions. Denial can be difficult to spot without the help of an outside perspective.

With that said, here's the method Bill used to keep his addiction under control. For every day that he was alcohol-free, he paid himself two dollars. He also paid himself two dollars on the one day a week

You can't solve a problem on the same level that it was created. You have to rise above it to the next level.

ALBERT EINSTEIN

that he drank two beers, as long as he stayed within that self-imposed limit. If he ever fell back on his agreement, he didn't punish himself; he simply didn't pay himself.

Bill kept track of these payments on a private calendar designed specifically for this purpose. Occasionally, he deposited whatever he'd earned in a separate account at the bank. The final stipulation of his contract was that he had to use the money to purchase something special for himself. Since most of Bill's money was used to support other members of his family, this last part of the deal was particularly attractive to him.

Even though Bill's system included a reward, it's important to understand that he was not abstaining from alcohol just so he could buy himself a present. Rather, he was abstaining because he felt better—and his life worked better—when he was alcohol-free. The reward was simply frosting on the cake.

In my early thirties, I used Bill's method to help me heal some ingrained food habits that were left over from fifteen years of anorexia. Obviously, total abstinence from food is not an option for most of us, so food addiction can be particularly challenging. After the worst of my anorexia was over, I no longer starved myself, but I still struggled with some old eating patterns and food fears. Like my former colleague with the alcohol habit, I had come to know the intricacies of my own addiction quite well, since I'd been anorexic for so long.

For my own bank account system, I devised a list of specific foods and eating activities. Then I decided how much I would pay myself for progress in each category. For example, I paid myself a dollar for eating a few more bites than usual at a meal. If I ate foods that were scary for me, I paid myself a little more. At the top of the anxiety column, I paid myself twenty-five dollars for doing what for me was the most unpleasant food scenario at that time: sharing a meal with my folks. Despite the fact that I'd long since left their home, having dinner with them resurrected old family patterns of guilt, expectation, and control. Needless to say, this was not conducive to good digestion.

After a few months on the plan, I had to stop because I was making so much money I couldn't afford to keep paying myself. It worked! The system also scored a victory over anorexia, because it provided small rewards along the way and a big reward at the end. This helped me learn to associate more *pleasure* with eating. The system made it safe for me to focus on my little successes, and there was no punishment for the times I chose addiction over awareness.

He who knows that enough is enough will always have enough.

LAO TSU

Never allow perfection to stand in the way of improvement.

ANONYMOUS

True life is lived when tiny changes occur.

LEO TOLSTOY

In your five-minute breaks, perhaps you could devise your own *Bank on Yourself* account. You could use this account to reward yourself for consistent use of the Five-Minute Switch System. Or you could give yourself a certain amount of money each time you *don't* do your habit after the break. If you have a complex addiction, maybe you could develop a plan similar to mine, although this would require time outside your five-minute breaks to figure out the details.

Anorexics aren't the only ones who have trouble giving themselves pleasure. In fact, one of the paradoxes of addiction is that there is often something *underneath* your habit—something you are denying yourself—which would actually bring you far greater pleasure. Whatever the case, you may never know what your addiction is hiding until you begin to let it go. Do as much as you can with your five-minute dips into greater awareness, and remember to *bank on yourself*.

WHAT'S YOUR BOTTOM LINE?

Sometimes when I find myself stuck in a habit, I notice similarities in the situations that trigger it. If I can remember to take a few minutes to tune in to how I really feel, I often discover that the addictive behavior is not what I need at the deepest level. Whatever I truly need is what I call my *bottom line*.

Next time you do a five-minute breather, determine your bottom line. That is, figure out what you truly need in that moment. You can get to your bottom line by asking yourself questions like these: If I wasn't going to do my addiction right now, what would I do instead? What do I really need right now? What do I actually want? If I could do anything in the world right now, what would I do?

When you listen to your deepest self, give yourself complete permission to discover whatever you *think* you need, without judgments or conditions. For example, if you think you need a million dollars, so be it. It's not helpful to edit your thoughts about what you need, based on what you think is possible. Don't censor your desires and don't deny your needs.

If you're afraid you don't deserve what you want or need, consider the possibility that *deserving* and *not deserving* are beside the point. As an analogy, think about a flower. Is it wrong for a flower to soak up the sun, fill the surrounding air with its fragrance, and drink in all the nourishment it needs from the earth? A flower doesn't worry about whether or not it *deserves* light, space, and nourishment. In fact, the more a flower's needs are met, the more it benefits itself and everything around it. The same is true in relation to you.

I used to think I should censor my needs based on what I thought was socially, politically, or spiritually correct. If something didn't meet these criteria, I tried to repress the need. Guess what? *Repressed needs feed addiction.* Big time! To help me heal this pattern of denying personal needs, I once consulted a devotee of the spiritual master known as Babaji. This particular devotee was a woman whom I regarded as being ethically and morally advanced.

Whatever is true for you is the most important thing. To hell with the rest of it.

SUSAN CHERNAK MCELROY

Humans are the only creatures who are too hard on themselves. Dogs loll. Birds roost. When cats get tired, they sleep; when they're hungry, they eat. Mostly they lay in the sun and yawn. There's a lesson there.

TAD BARTIMUS

After explaining my tendency to judge personal needs, I asked for her advice. First she laughed mischievously, then she replied, "Cat, the fulfillment of every desire leads you closer to God. If you wanted a red Mercedes, I would tell you to go after the red Mercedes. After you satisfy that desire, you'll just want something else…and then something else…and something else after that. Eventually you'll get bored with the material stuff, but you have to satisfy the lower needs before the higher needs present themselves. Don't worry about it! Follow your heart's desire, and trust that your heart will lead you to God."

Ram Dass says the same thing in a different way. He gives the analogy of a teenage boy who spends his whole childhood collecting baseball cards by the hundreds. Baseball consumes his life. Then along comes puberty, and something inside of him shifts. Suddenly he is talking about girls and cars. His baseball cards gather dust in the corner. He doesn't have to force himself to give up baseball cards when he becomes interested in girls and cars. Rather, his desires simply change as he matures.

The point is, desire is not wrong. It's actually an effective internal mechanism that helps you follow your heart and take care of your needs. People get in trouble with desire only when they try to strangle it, contort it, or ignore it. Desire is an innocent human experience, like hunger. If I listen to hunger and respond appropriately, it helps me stay alive. If instead I ignore hunger's simple message, or if I confuse it with emotional messages, hunger can become a tyrant instead of a servant. Desire works the same way.

Go ahead and feel whatever you feel, desire whatever you desire, and need whatever you need. When you meet your needs as they are, without judgments or conditions, they can evolve naturally in a way that supports your spiritual growth. *It's not necessary to pit your spirituality against your humanity.* Therefore, when you ask yourself, "What's my bottom line right now?" be sure to give yourself the freedom to need or want absolutely anything.

When you've got this mastered, see if you can take one more step during your five-minute breaks. That is, if your bottom line reveals a need for something you can satisfy in the moment, go for it! If what you want is not immediately available, spend your time-out considering how to make it possible, then put your plan into action as soon as you can. If what you need seems out of reach, relax for five minutes while you imagine yourself having, being, or doing whatever your heart desires. See it, smell it, taste it, hear it, and feel it as vividly as possible. For a few minutes, forget about *deserving* and play with *imagining*.

Tell me to what you pay attention and I will tell you who you are.

JOSÉ ORTEGA Y GASSET

That man is richest whose pleasures are cheapest.

HENRY DAVID THOREAU

Thus, you can use your five-minute breaks to discover how your addiction is covering up a bottom-line need. When you act compulsively instead of honoring your true needs, it's like putting a bandage on a deep wound. The skin may stick together on the surface, but total healing cannot occur all the way down. In other words, an addiction is like a bandage: It shows you where there's a wound from having a need that has not been fully addressed.

Somewhere underneath those bandages and wounds lies the bottom-line truth about your needs. For five minutes here or ten minutes there, you can practice responding to your deepest needs, one step at a time.

To find the good life you must become yourself.

BILL JACKSON

FIVE MINUTES
TO TAKEOFF

This is an advanced version of "What's Your Bottom Line?" Imagine that you have exactly five minutes left to live. What would you do with your time?

DO IT
NOW.

THE BRUTAL TRUTH

Since addiction work is difficult for most people, I purposely try to "sneak in the back door" at the House of Compulsion because the front entry may be blocked by years of accumulated defense mechanisms. Denial, resistance, and boatloads of unprocessed feelings may stand in the way of change. However, while I generally recommend a gentle *back door* approach to healing addiction, there are times when this isn't enough.

Sometimes when you need to break a stubborn impasse, there's nothing like a cold dip in the icy waters of Brutal Truth. Be forewarned, however, that this particular exercise is most effective at the Advanced and Veteran levels of your work with the Five-Minute Switch System, because it generally requires more than a few minutes of time. If you need to refresh your memory about the Advanced and Veteran versions, they're described at the end of the first chapter in this section.

Before I go any further, let me assure you that when I talk about you confronting the Brutal Truth about your addictions, I'm talking about you facing *your own* truth about them. I'm not talking about you allowing others to impose their opinions on you without your permission. In pursuing your own understanding of the Brutal Truth, then, I trust you to know when it's right for you to do the exercise offered in this chapter. Don't take a dip in those icy waters unless you're ready, willing, and able to withstand the jolt. This is supposed to help you, not hurt you.

The first step in telling yourself the Brutal Truth about your addictions is to set the stage by creating an *envelope of kindness*. First, find a place to write where you will be free from interruption. Take a few moments to tune in to your heart. Ask yourself if it's a good time for you to face your fears about a specific addiction that has been bothering you. If it's not a good time to proceed, don't!

If you get the go-ahead, ask yourself what you need before you begin your truth-telling. Find out if there's anything you can do

In the end, only kindness matters.

JEWEL

now to increase your safety and comfort, knowing you're about to confront some *shadow* aspects of your character. For instance, you could surround yourself with soothing music. Or you could arrange a phone check-in with a good friend for later, so he or she can give you a dose of support to help you *warm up* after your icy dip into Brutal Truth.

If you're not an experienced *shadow dancer* (i.e., if intense feelings are scary for you), I also suggest that you set a timer the first few times you do this exercise. Limit your dips to ten or fifteen minutes, then build up your time gradually. It's smart to go slow with addiction work because when you start messing around with your *habitual rituals*, you'll stimulate all the repressed feelings and needs that lie hidden beneath the armor of compulsion.

For now, I'll assume that you've created an envelope of kindness and you're ready to dig in. Begin by thinking about your addictions. Remember my definition of addiction (from the chapter called "The Five-Minute Switch System"): **An addiction is anything that stands in the way of total awareness and acceptance of yourself, others, and the world.**

Using this definition or one of your own, select one of your most troublesome addictions to examine now. When you're ready, get some paper and a pen, and start writing down the Brutal Truth. That is, write down everything that you *don't* like about your addiction. Write down everything that *disgusts* you about it.

If you really want to go for the jugular, write down everything that you absolutely *hate* about your addiction. Write down what you hate about all the ways it causes pain in your life (despite its short-term pleasures). Write down what you hate about how your addiction hurts your body, your mind, your emotions, your work, your creativity, your relationships, your dreams, your passions, your sexuality, your spirituality, your safety and the safety of others, and your overall goals in life.

As you continue writing, stay tuned to your envelope of kindness. Stop writing if you lose the ability to hold your hate as a mere part of the whole. If you start seeing the Brutal Truth as the *whole* truth, you've gone too far. If you get stuck there, you might want to turn to the chapter called "Addictions as Teachers." It can help you broaden your viewpoint again.

Remember that this exercise is about getting clear. It's not about masochism or melodrama. Maintain a warrior's perspective on your truth-telling, or don't do it at all. The point is to turn your hate into an ally, not a bludgeon.

If you have trouble with the word *hate*, consider this: Sometimes hate is simply a passionate offshoot of love. Now obviously, that's an intense statement and a lot of people will be offended by it, so let me give you a few examples. I *hate* rape because I *love* respect. I *hate* child abuse because I *love* children. I *hate* war because I *love* peace. I *hate* environmental degradation because I *love* Mother Earth. As you can see from these examples, this kind of hate can be honored alongside love, because they both simply reflect the depth of my passion in different ways.

Please don't misunderstand me. I have no place in my heart for hate that shows up as bigotry, intolerance, and other forms of prejudice against people or other beings. I reserve my hate, such as it is, for rebellion against certain *ideas* or *actions*. Yes, this means that I make judgments about things, not in terms of blame or make-wrong, but in terms of discerning the best course of action for myself.

For instance, I hate the taste of avocados and therefore choose not to eat them, but this doesn't mean that I think avocados are wrong! This is the point that some people miss when they get carried away with *judging judgment*, or decrying all forms of hate: They forget that if you can't make judgments, you lose your capacity for *discernment*, and if you forfeit your ability to hate, you lose the full spectrum of your *passion*.

I realize that at the "big picture" cosmic level, everything is perfect and I couldn't possibly improve the universe, even though this universe currently includes things I hate such as rape, child abuse, war, and environmental degradation. Let's face it, though, I don't hang out at the cosmic level all the time. While I try to remember the overall perfection as I go about my life, I'm also aware that I live in a mundane, physical world of duality. This world requires me to take a stand and to choose a course of action. Even the choice of *inaction* is a choice that cuts a path.

Thus, I encourage the judicious use of judgment in order to facilitate choice, and I advocate the compassionate use of hate in order to harness the power of this primitive emotion. Hate can be especially helpful when you must make choices that require extreme levels of motivation. Let me explain.

Basically, everyone makes choices according to two primal motivating factors: the urge to move away from what causes pain, and the urge to move toward what brings pleasure. As I mentioned in the Five-Minute Switch System chapter, these two primal responses are hard-wired into our brains because they support survival.

If you think about these basic urges, it's not hard to see how *helpful* forms of hate and love can arise from these two natural

Let us be kinder to one another.
ALDOUS HUXLEY

I reserve my hatred, such as it is, for racism, child abuse, animal abuse and other injustices.

JENNIFER JAMES

tendencies. The question is: How much awareness do you have when you choose *what to move away from* and *what to move toward?*

Arny Mindell says, "Know what you're doing and do it!" Thus, I'm asking you to write down everything you hate about your addiction so you can *know what you're doing* in regard to it. If you can't bring yourself to look at what you hate about your addiction, you won't be able to take full advantage of this powerful source of motivation. This is the high side of hate: You can use it to ignite your passion to move away from whatever causes you pain. In this way, hate can be your ally when you're ready to choose out of addictive behavior.

Of course, some people won't even face what they love about their addictions because this, too, can reveal uncomfortable feelings and the unflattering desire *not* to take responsibility for one's actions. I call this desire *unflattering,* because most people are embarrassed to admit their attraction to the experience of *spacing out, numbing out,* or *checking out.*

Don't get me wrong. There's nothing inherently wrong with wanting to *go unconscious* now and then. However, even this can be done with awareness, as paradoxical as that sounds. Unfortunately, most people reach for their habitual rituals at the first sign of distress, without thinking about it. More often than not, they may not even be consciously aware of their discomfort before they automatically turn to their favorite addiction. Does any of this sound familiar?

As hard as it may be for people to face what they love about their addictions, it may be even harder to face what they hate about them. This isn't only because people have difficulty with the word *hate.* It's also because if people face what they hate about their compulsive behavior, they might be motivated enough to stop doing it.

While this may seem like a positive thing, it's not so positive to the part that doesn't want to change. This is particularly true if change means letting go of comfortable habits and stepping into more responsibility and more freedom. As long as people stay on automatic, they can avoid the responsibility that comes with greater freedom of choice. Never underestimate the power of addiction and its flip side, the fear of freedom! The combination of these two forces can keep even the best of us stuck in self-destructive habits for years.

If you still can't bring yourself to look at what you hate about your addiction, then perhaps you can work with what you *fear* about it instead. Write about how you're afraid that your habit might be detrimental to your physical health, your mental clarity, your

The change of one simple behavior can affect other behaviors and thus change many things.

JEAN BAER

emotional balance, your career, your creativity, your night dreams and your day dreams, your sex life, your spirituality, your safety and the safety of others, and your ability to move forward with your goals.

For example, are you scared that the strange pain deep in your body might be some awful disease that has come from doing your habit? Then write it down. Are you afraid that your friends have been avoiding you lately because your addiction is getting in the way? Write it down. Are you concerned that you aren't getting ahead in life because multiple compulsions are keeping a damper on your energy? Write it down. Write it *all* down. Be specific. Tell the truth as if your life depended on it—because maybe it does.

When you're done writing about your fear (or your hate), take some time to reflect on what you've learned about yourself and your addiction. Jot down a few summary notes. Congratulate yourself for your courageous truth-telling, and remember to *seal up* your envelope of kindness by doing something actively supportive for yourself once you've finished the exercise. Then, when you're ready, step back into your everyday life, and see how your dip into the Brutal Truth changes the way you act.

...don't confuse intuition with impulsiveness. Just because you're using intuition doesn't mean you throw your head out the window. Think about the end result of your decision. The wounded gut often encourages us to ignore consequences. The wise gut knows that a good choice will still be a good choice if we sleep on it.

DANEEN SKUBE

Ritual: Are You Addicted or Aware?

Everyone has personal rituals. People have rituals for eating, sleeping, bathing, dressing, working, exercising, making love, and filling time. These are the kinds of rituals that *Webster's* would define as "customarily repeated acts." They aren't necessarily the same as conscious ritual. While habitual rituals may provide comfort in a world largely beyond our control, they can also put you to sleep. How conscious are you each time you eat an apple? Brush your teeth? Take a shower? Watch television? Crawl into bed? Have an orgasm?

If you want to become increasingly aware, you can use even the most mundane habits to cultivate greater mindfulness. As I mentioned in the introduction to this section, you can focus on your attachment to any activity, feeling, relationship, or situation in order to increase your awareness. Typically, human life involves some degree of struggle with attachment. One solution to this struggle is to replace destructive, unconscious attachments with conscious, life-supportive ones.

Spiritual texts from all over the world tell stories of holy people who were once drunkards or addicts, before they turned their attention to God. Similarly, Twelve Step programs help people shift their focus from addiction to something more expansive, such as a Higher Power, a spiritual path, or simply a love of life.

Someone once said that all addiction is a cry for God. For me, this means that all addiction is a cry for *connection*—a connection to self, to others, and to the mystery of life. As a human being, I can answer this cry for connection with addictions that provide a temporary fix, or I can seek out deeper, more long-lasting forms of support and satisfaction.

Conscious ritual is one way that I can creatively respond to my need for connection. With compassion for my human tendency toward attachment and familiarity, I use rituals to celebrate these tendencies in positive ways, instead of denying them. Simply put, conscious ritual is the practice of *form*. It's a way to create an experience of order within a constantly changing universe.

Years ago, in an interview with *The Sun,* master drummer and storyteller Michael Meade described this practice as:

> *...doing something repetitively so that it tends to have a solid form. Wildness without form is very dangerous, and that's another reason people don't like it. When the rains hit the desert, you might get wildflowers, but you might get flash flooding. One can delight your soul and cause an eruption of feeling and energy, and the other can kill you. So wildness has those two directions. A form makes it into something that can be worked with.*

Although Meade was not talking about addiction versus ritual, his words describe the difference between the two. Addiction provides a *compulsive* way to deal with the raw power of wildness, which has the potential to destroy me. In contrast, ritual—the practice of form—offers a safe way to channel the energy of this wildness through the vehicle of *awareness*. Ultimately, if I let my addictions run my life and lull me into unconsciousness, I go toward destruction. When instead I choose my habits and create my rituals with awareness, my life can blossom like Meade's wildflowers in the rain.

In healing my addictions, I've often designed rituals that satisfy my underlying needs, while simultaneously transforming my habits' destructive qualities. For example, in helping myself out of anorexia and bulimia, I decided to approach my food attachments with compassion instead of criticism. Gradually, I found small ways to celebrate my food attachments in ways that increased my awareness.

Eating disorders are extremely complicated illnesses that have spiritual, physical, neurological, emotional, familial, and cultural roots. Over the years, I explored as many of these factors as possible. In the process, I sought ways to honor the wildness of my body with all its sensations, feelings, passions, and needs. Contrary to the popular misconception that anorexics don't like food, I was actually obsessed with it. However, food also terrified me.

As I worked with the complex factors underlying my eating disorders, I slowly learned how to ritualize eating in a way that was supportive instead of destructive. For example, I used elegant bowls for my vegetables and crystal goblets for my juice. When I ate dinner,

> *Too much awareness, without accompanying experience, is a skeleton without the flesh of life.*
>
> ANAÏS NIN

> *Habit is either the best of servants or the worst of masters.*
>
> NATHANIEL EMMONS

The solution to my life occurred to me one evening while I was ironing a shirt.

ALICE MUNRO

The best way to make your dreams come true is to wake up!

KABIR

I lit candles and played soft music. As I chewed the food, I offered prayers and asked for help in assimilating the meal. With small rituals such as these to accompany my deeper healing work, my food fears slowly dissipated. Bit by bit, I was able to become more fully present with the experience of eating.

As you can see, the difference between conscious ritual and addiction is simple. Conscious ritual increases awareness; addiction decreases it. Thus, it's possible to use your compulsive habits to become more conscious merely by shifting your perspective and by paying more attention to what you're already doing. On the other hand, you can use ritual to purposely develop greater mindfulness and understanding. In either case, the focus is on awareness.

If ritual is already an important part of your life, you can use your five-minute breaks to perform rituals that you already know. If the concept of ritual is new for you, perhaps you could use your time-out to invent a simple ceremony in the moment. As a third alternative, perhaps you could use the time to begin reading one of this book's other chapters about ritual, such as "The Resolution Prayer," "The Fire Ceremony," and "The Talking Circle."

Every moment offers a window of opportunity for ritual because every action gives you a chance to ask yourself, "Am I addicted or aware?" One way to use this question ritualistically is simply to sit with it for five minutes and consider what it means to you. When you're ready to go beyond the Five-Minute Switch System, you can use this question as a mantra. Let it help you stay awake—truly awake—all day long.

THE INNER DANCER

During your five-minute breaks, turn on some music and *move!* Don't worry about how you look. Just *move.* If your little finger is the only part of you that moves, that's good enough. If all you can move are your eyelashes, then do an eyelash dance.

Any way you dance is the perfect way to dance. Let your body lead you in any direction. Feel the music. *Be* the music. Follow the first sensation that catches your awareness, and let it spread until your whole body is dancing that sensation. Listen to your whims. Sway to the rhythm of your heart.

If you're shy, imagine that you're alone in the middle of a forest meadow, dancing with the grass and the wind. If you're a performer at heart, pretend that you're dancing for an audience of ten thousand adoring fans.

Dance your favorite animal, your favorite flower, or your favorite rock star. Dance your joy, dance your rage, dance your fear, dance your grief. Imagine that you are REALLY BIG and dance the planet. Imagine that you are *really small* and dance an electron. Dance the Milky Way—or dance the space between the stars.

However you dance, dance your own dance. Do it with *all* of you!

Life without music would be a mistake.

FRIEDRICH NIETZSCHE

Watching the World

This culture could use a few more people looking out the window!

RAM DASS

To do nothing is sometimes a good remedy.

HIPPOCRATES

One of my favorite forms of meditation is to sit and stare out the window. This is also one of the most difficult forms of meditation for me because my upbringing overemphasized work and productivity. For many years after leaving my parents' home, I never let anyone catch me doing nothing. I was so well trained that it was even hard for me to do nothing when I was alone! Yet I've always noticed that *doing nothing* generates abundant creativity for me.

My favorite role models, cats, watch the world all the time, without apology. They watch the world as if they are drinking in every nuance of movement, every shape-shifting dance of wind, every passing scent, and every whisper of sound. I admire their quiet awareness and their undying curiosity.

In your five-minute breaks, position yourself like a cat in front of one of your favorite windows. If it's warm enough to have the window open, so much the better. Get comfortable and open all your senses. Don't read or eat or catch up on your correspondence. Just let yourself stare into space, allowing your eyes to move freely from one focus to the next, without effort. In addition, try this meditation without music or the radio, so you can *watch* with your ears, too.

If it's hard for you to do nothing, treat your window meditations as a vital counterbalance to our culture's workaholic madness. Imagine how much better the world would be if everyone took the time to slow down. If that's still not enough encouragement for you to do nothing, consider Lao Tsu's words from *The Tao Te Ching:*

> *The sage does less and less*
> *Until there is nothing left to be done.*

FREE BREATHING

Do you ever notice that you're not breathing? People hold their breath in all kinds of situations. They stop breathing when they're upset, when they exert themselves, or when they concentrate. If you want to learn more about breathing, notice when you stop. Then simply begin breathing again.

Air is the body's primary form of nourishment. Even though we can survive without food and water for long periods, we can't go without air for very long at all. The more fully and freely you breathe, the more you can increase your life energy and your overall well-being.

Fitness experts and spiritual masters alike sing the praises of breathing. Breathing may be physical, but it's also mystical. The breath can be used to transform consciousness, just as it can be used to rejuvenate the body.

During your five-minute break, find a comfortable place to sit or lie down. For these few minutes, *breathe*. Play with your breath if you like. Do some form of breath work, if you know one. The important thing is to keep breathing. When you get done breathing in, breathe out, and when you get done breathing out, breathe in. This may sound simple, but if you can do this continually for five minutes without losing your awareness, congratulate yourself.

If you want to go a little deeper with this, let your awareness focus more intently on the rhythm of your breath. Let your breath become one long, circular, connected breath. If you feel a gap between the inhale and the exhale, or between the exhale and the inhale, find a way to gently close the gap.

Relax and let your rib cage open like a flower to the sun. When you allow your chest to expand, notice how atmospheric pressure brings the air rushing in, without any effort on your part. Inhaling is an act of *receiving*. As you breathe in, feel the spaciousness around your heart. Give your heart lots of room to pulse and pump freely.

When you exhale, it's not necessary to push or control your breath. Don't try to force all the air out of your lungs. Simply allow

The first step toward creating a sense of personal power is conscious breathing.

IYANLA VAN ZANDT

Time is breath.

G. I. GURDJIEFF

your breath to tumble out like a waterfall. When you are done breathing out, open your rib cage again—*as softly as a butterfly opens its wings*—and let the air come flowing in naturally. If you forget what you're doing, that's okay. When your focus returns, resume your connected breathing.

This kind of breathing is only one of many forms of breathing. There is no right way to breathe. Breathing techniques have many different purposes. The one previously described can be used to increase energy and aliveness. If you don't want to do this kind of breath work, simply watch your breath as it is, without trying to change it. This can be transformative in itself.

Whatever style of breathing you choose, feel free to get carried away. If you can't remember why you started your time-out in the first place, that's okay. In fact, it's great! Either way, you'll give yourself an extra infusion of oxygen, which is to say, an extra infusion of *life*.

Soul Massage

When is the last time you gave yourself a massage? Do you always wait for someone else to give you bodywork? How about using your own hands? Granted, there are some places you can't massage yourself, and besides, there's nothing like a pair of expert hands to reduce you to a mound of mush. However, you can get your touching needs met more regularly if you give your own body plenty of tactile attention.

In your next five-minute breather, how about giving yourself a mini-massage? Maybe you could give yourself a foot rub. Maybe your face, neck, or belly could use some strokes. Whatever feels good, do it! The more pleasure you give yourself, the less you'll want to do anything that hurts you. Giving yourself a massage may not seem like a big deal, but it's an act of self-care that registers at the cellular level. Think of all the amazing things your body does for you each day. How about thanking it with your hands?

When you give yourself a massage, imagine that you are touching a deeper level of your being. Imagine that you can feel your *emotional* body as tangibly as you feel your skin, your muscles, and your bones. If feelings come up as you touch your body, do what you can to let them move within you and through you. If sounds come, let them out. If you feel like singing, sing. If you start to laugh, cry, rage, or shake, let that happen, too.

As you massage your body, imagine that you can go even deeper. Imagine that you can touch your *soul*. As you rub your muscles, be very gentle, as if you are massaging the sacred essence of your being. Consider that there may be no real difference between body and spirit, except perhaps a variation in density or a variation in the speed of vibration.

These days, quantum physicists are reluctant to draw hard lines between energy and matter. As you touch your body, remember that you are touching a moving mass of energy. Even when you're lying still, your atoms are dancing wildly! See if you can caress them with your hands.

The strongest, surest way to the soul is through the flesh.
MABEL DODGE

The Heart

of the Matter:

Making Friends

with Yourself

SECTION
TWO

How to Be
Seriously Silly

Foolishness is a valuable quality to cultivate. However, some people who grew up in difficult families may end up taking life a little too seriously. Those who have adopted this stance probably have every right to be serious, coming from situations that were anything but funny. Some serious types never crack a smile, while others go to the opposite extreme and yuk it up all the time, wearing grins on their faces no matter what they're feeling.

This chapter offers some suggestions for shifting an overly serious perspective by injecting a little humor into the mix. In no way is this intended to deny the pain and fear that often underlie excessive seriousness. However, some people become so focused on their pain that they forget the healing power of laughter. Believe it or not, humor and pain can be great traveling companions on the road to self-discovery.

Whatever the source of your seriousness, it may take practice for you to lighten up. If you think you can't lighten up, try the "Pretend Method." My longtime friend, Joe Rahn, taught me this method years ago. We used to play it whenever one of us was down in the dumps. For example, if I was feeling depressed and I'd done as much crying or raging as I could, Joe would suggest that I just *pretend* as if I felt fine and act accordingly. The funny thing is, somewhere along the way of *acting* as if I felt fine, I would actually start *feeling* fine.

If you can't imagine how you would act if you felt fine, then imagine how others might act if they felt fine, so you can use their behavior as a model. If you think it's phony to act differently than you feel, consider this: If I really tune in, I notice that I always have every feeling happening somewhere inside of me. It's only my focus of attention that shifts.

Sometimes I focus on a particular feeling because I feel more comfortable with it. I may also favor a particular emotion because I believe it will get me more attention. Some families give more attention to the jolly person, others to the sad or angry one, and still

The only security we have is in our ability to fly by the seat of our pants.

BRAD BLANTON

We are what we pretend to be, so we must be careful about what we pretend to be.

KURT VONNEGUT, JR.

What you focus on determines how you feel.

ANTHONY ROBBINS

The most wasted day is that in which we have not laughed.

SEBASTIEN CHAMFORT

Without whimsy, none of us can live.

THEODOR SUESS GEISEL
(AKA DR. SEUSS)

others to the scared one. What was true in your family? What is true in your life now?

You may be in for an interesting ride if you decide to explore the relationship between your feelings and your behavior. Again, I'm not advocating denial of feelings, nor am I advocating inauthentic behavior. Instead, I'm suggesting that you learn to play with your behavior while you stay in touch with *all* of your emotions, not just the one that is most apparent. You are always at choice about your actions, no matter how you feel.

In learning to be seriously silly, it's great to start small. Experiment with letting yourself merely *feel* foolish. Think back to a time when you were totally embarrassed, then watch the memory in your mind's eye while you keep your compassion actively engaged. If the memory is initially painful, pretend you are watching an actor in a movie. With gentleness, see if you can expand the narrow focal point of your *personal* pain until you can see the wider perspective of the *situational* humor. When you can review this memory-movie and laugh about it, you'll know you're making progress in recovering your foolishness.

One of my favorite role models for foolishness is Dr. Patch Adams. Patch is a world-famous physician, a peace diplomat (he calls it "nasal diplomacy" because he wears funny noses), and a founder of the Gesundheit Institute. He and his generous colleagues have given away free medical help to thousands of people. In addition to his humanitarianism, Patch is well known for his outrageous apparel and his abundant supply of masks, hats, and props. He shares these props with other people in order to encourage laughter and general rowdiness. He calls himself a *ha-ha-holic*, and he knows the value of making a fool of himself in public.

One of Patch's suggestions for lightening up is to wear your underwear on the outside of your clothes. When I first heard him say this at a lecture, I almost fell out of my chair laughing. In the back of my mind, I couldn't help but see my straight-laced mother's reaction to such a stunt. By the way, Patch didn't say you have to go out in public with your underwear on the outside, although I bet he has. Instead, you can start small and be ridiculous in the privacy of your own home.

One of my favorite spiritual teachers, Ram Dass, is another good source for antidotes to seriousness. Since the late seventies, Ram Dass and a group of his friends have worked together in creative ways to do world service through an organization called Seva Foundation. Seva, which means "to serve" in Sanskrit, was born out of their desire to relieve suffering in the world. While their world work helps them to grow spiritually, they also try to have a good time as they focus on such deadly serious projects as the eradication of blindness, refugee survival, emergency health care, and homelessness.

Fortunately, Seva members are as committed to humor as they are to helping. At their board meetings, for example, they have a rule about not getting too somber. Anyone who uses the word *serious* has to put on a pair of Groucho Marx glasses—those big, black, horn-rimmed glasses with the rubber nose and the fake moustache. Following their example, perhaps you could keep a pair at your house. In fact, you might want to keep a second pair on hand, in case you have visitors.

If you ever get dangerously serious, maybe you could don a pair of Groucho Marx glasses while wearing your underwear on the outside of your clothes. If that's not enough to loosen you up, here are a dozen more quick and easy ideas to help you shake off the doldrums.

A man needs a little madness or else he never dares to cut the rope and be free.

NIKOS KAZANTZAKIS

1. Sing like an opera star.

2. Dance like a maniac.

3. Collect your favorite cartoons from newspapers and magazines. Glue them into blank books, and keep them handy for when you have a *serious attack.*

4. Paint your face or cover it with stick-on stars. Go to a public place with your decorated face, and watch other people react. Carry some extra paint or stars with you, in case anyone else wants to join the fun.

At the height of laughter, the universe is flung into a kaleidoscope of new possibilities.

JEAN HOUSTON

5. Fingerpaint. Get real messy while fingerpainting.

6. Paint your body (be sure to use nontoxic paints). Paint a painting with your body on a huge piece of heavy paper, or use your body to paint someone else's body (with permission, of course).

7. Put your shoes on the wrong feet, and put your clothes on backward. Go over to a friend's house, and act as if there is nothing unusual about how you're dressed.

8. *Imagine* yourself walking naked through a roomful of your most conservative relatives.

You will do foolish things,
but do them with enthusiasm.
COLETTE

Even the gods love jokes.
PLATO

9. Find a magazine full of important celebrities, and alter their appearance. Draw moustaches on them, blacken in a few teeth, frizz out their hair, add tails or horns, or draw incongruent sexual appendages on their bodies. Write in funny captions. Share your artistic creations with a friend, or do the drawings together.

10. Make funny faces in a mirror. Make funny faces with a friend. Make funny faces with a whole group of people. Take pictures and give prizes for the weirdest face.

11. Blow bubbles in the park. See what—or whom—you attract.

12. Look at yourself in a mirror and start laughing for no reason. Practice chuckling, giggling, and howling your head off. Keep it up for at least five minutes. If you can keep it up for ten minutes, you're probably a Zen master. If you can do it for twenty minutes, you may be a candidate for sainthood.

For those of you who think it's a waste of time to be ridiculous, please be careful. Your face may be in danger of cracking from the strain. For those of you who know the value of humor, I encourage you to go forth and make a fool of yourself with gusto!

ARE YOU A DOORMAT?

Do you ever feel like a doormat? If you let people walk all over you, or if you have a hard time standing up for yourself, you probably know what I'm talking about. There are a million paths that lead to doormat behavior, but this chapter won't delve into that. You'll have to look elsewhere to explore the roots of victimhood, martyrdom, apathy, and oppression. Here, I simply want to offer a few techniques for identifying and working with the doormat syndrome.

If you want to understand this syndrome, it helps to know something about doormats. The most obvious thing about doormats is that they maintain a *very* low profile, so they won't bother anybody. More precisely, doormats welcome anyone who wants to step on them, stomp on them, wear muddy shoes on them, wipe you-know-what on them, or discard them if they become displeasing in any way. Doormats take whatever they get. Since doormats never complain, no one worries about hurting them.

Do any of these descriptions sound familiar? During my own doormat years, I would speak up for myself occasionally, but it wasn't the norm. At some point, my doormat behavior began to happen with greater regularity and intensity. When someone specifically used the word *doormat* in relation to me, I knew it was time for some heavy introspection.

Being the overly responsible type, I figured that I wouldn't be acting like a doormat so often unless I was working out some kind of victim pattern. I'm not saying that I was responsible for the way other people treated me, only that I had some part in the system. In other words, the doormat syndrome was *my* pattern, and it was up to me to change it. I knew it was useless to blame the people who were walking on me. After all, when people walk on you, you can either blame them for doing what comes naturally in the presence of a doormat—or you can stand up for yourself and prevent it from happening.

I myself have never known what feminism is. I only know that people call me a feminist whenever I express sentiments that differentiate me from a doormat.

REBECCA WEST

You might as well fall flat on your face as lean over too far backward.

JAMES THURBER

If you hide your true self and feelings from others so they will like you or approve of you, then the person they like and approve of is not really you.

WILLIAM FREY

I had to learn to say no before I could learn to say yes.

PEG PRICE

Saying no conveys the message "I'm living my life." Don't wait until you have ten minutes to live to say it for the first time.

BERNIE SIEGEL

If you have a lot of anger, grief, or shame about being a doormat, you may want to avoid your pain rather than work toward healing it. This is why I often bring up the subject of addiction when I talk about the doormat syndrome. The humiliation of doormat behavior is certainly not the only kind of pain people seek to alleviate through addiction. However, when people feel as if they've been walked on, it's easy for them to turn to a familiar habit for comfort.

For example, have you ever come home from work feeling trampled because you didn't speak up about something important? Have you ever been blue because your lover or your friend treated you badly, yet you said nothing? Have you ever let authority figures (your boss, your parents, your therapist, your doctor, your landlord) talk you into doing things that didn't feel right for you? These are only a few of the numerous ways you might find yourself caught in the doormat syndrome. Unfortunately, such situations can be triggers for addictive behavior.

Of course, it's not wrong to seek comfort when you hurt, even if you turn to an addiction. However, if you want to overcome tendencies toward doormat behavior, pay attention to the times when you seek out your favorite habit. Whether you turn to alcohol, drugs, cigarettes, coffee, food, work, television, nonstop people, or anything else, find out if there is a connection between your *habitual rituals* and a feeling of disempowerment.

In addition to using addiction to alert you, you can also watchdog the doormat syndrome by paying attention to your relationship with conflict. If you tend to say nothing in order to keep the peace, or if you have trouble saying *no* to people, you may have some doormat tendencies.

If you're a conflict avoider, take heart. There are many ways to overcome the fear of standing up for yourself. In a moment, I'll give you one technique for transforming this kind of fear. The trick is to keep practicing. Doormat behavior is a pattern, and patterns are created by repetition. It takes intention to get out of a rut, and it takes repetition of new behaviors to cut a new groove.

Here's a body-oriented technique for shifting the doormat syndrome. This exercise exaggerates the doormat experience in order to bring you face to face with any victim tendencies you might have. When you feel the full force of doormat behavior *in your body*, it's pretty disgusting. Fortunately, you can use your disgust to help you act in more empowering ways (see "The Brutal Truth" for more about this).

When you're ready to experiment with this technique, begin by choosing a space where you feel safe. You can work alone, with a trusted friend or coach, or with a support group. It's helpful if you can practice this technique immediately after you have a doormat experience, but you can also use it anytime, spontaneously, if you can access memories of past victimhood.

First, think about a situation in which you felt *walked on*. Next, imagine yourself in that situation as a doormat—an actual doormat. In fact, *act* like a doormat right now by lying down on the floor, flat on your face. Imagine that someone is walking all over your back while you say nothing.

Try this while lying face down, and then try it face up. When you do it face up, *see* all the people who have ever walked on you. *Feel* them walking on you with their grimy, stinky shoes. *Listen* to their comments as they scrape the dirt from their soles off on your face. In short, imagine them *using* you while you say nothing.

When you can really *see, feel, hear,* and even *smell* them doing this, add to the experience by saying these kinds of statements out loud: "Thank you for walking on me! It feels so good to be used! Let me lie a little flatter so you don't have to lift your feet so high!" You get the idea. Keep this up until you feel thoroughly disgusted. Do it until your sense of self-worth comes welling up, until you can no longer tolerate the doormat position.

When you get to this point, stand up. I mean, actually stand up! Let the visceral experience of your burgeoning self-respect *force* you to get up off the floor. Stand on your own two feet, and let your personal power electrify every cell of your body. Imagine that you are all lit up like a lightning bolt, with fire in your eyes and sparks flying out from your fingertips. Breathe continuously as you imprint this experience on your nervous system.

As you stand there glowing with self-esteem, take a moment to reflect once again on your doormat memory. See if you can imagine your old victim pattern as a distant cloud on the horizon while you continue to feel the energy of your lightning-bolt self-respect pulsing through your veins. Keep your feet planted firmly on the ground, and keep your gaze focused upward and outward.

As you revisit that old doormat image, consider this. Were you ever mortally afraid to question authority, displease someone, or put yourself first? Did these kinds of situations ever make you tremble or shake or cry? Did they ever make you nauseous or weak in the knees? Were you ever afraid that you'd be struck dead by lightning if you didn't do as you were told?

If any of this fits for you, then recall the intensity of that fear while you *keep breathing*. Stay fully aware of your fiery self-respect. If the fear threatens to overwhelm your confidence, take a few

I cannot give you the formula for success, but I can give you the formula for failure: Try to please everybody.

HERBERT BAYARD SWOPE

It's a funny thing about life; if you refuse to accept anything but the best, you very often get it.

SOMERSET MAUGHAM

moments to connect more strongly with the lightning bolt of personal power that forced you to get up off the ground. When you can fully identify with the lightning bolt—and see the fear as a dissipating cloud far off on the horizon—then you're in a good place to stop.

Now here's the paradox. If you were ever afraid that you'd be struck dead by lightning for not doing as you were told, guess what? You've *become* the lightning! You've claimed the power of the force that you feared, and you've used it to annihilate a pattern that was no longer serving you. By going all the way into your doormat behavior, you have transformed it. This is one of the universal principles of change. When you take one polarity to its extreme, it shifts. Although there's no telling exactly how the shift will manifest, change is inevitable once a polarity is exhausted.

Once you've mastered all the different parts of this technique, try practicing it mentally. Then, when a potential doormat situation arises, you can let the *visceral memory* of your lightning-bolt experience help you act in empowering ways. If this isn't enough to do the trick, you can redo the *physical* exercise again later when you're alone, to reinforce your progress.

Here's the bottom line: If you feel like a doormat, don't take it lying down! Some people won't like it when you stand up for yourself, but anyone worth having around wouldn't want you any other way.

No one can make you feel inferior without your consent.
ELEANOR ROOSEVELT

THE ANGER PRIMER

T his is a how-to chapter about anger. Of all the feelings people have, anger is the most misunderstood, mistrusted, and misdirected. It's not hard to see the effects of irresponsibly expressed anger in the world. If we are to survive as humans, much less evolve, anger must be given careful attention and deep respect. Since a partial understanding of anger can be dangerous, I recommend that you read this entire chapter before you experiment with the suggestions offered here. All aspects of anger work are important. None should be neglected or ignored.

Anger is one of God's greatest gifts.

DALE TURNER

Some people think that enlightenment means not feeling or expressing so-called negative emotions, such as anger. I disagree. In my opinion, there are no negative human emotions. To me, an evolved human is someone who knows how to *be human*—someone who can feel and express all feelings in responsible ways. That last part is the key. Problems do not stem from having feelings, but from being irresponsible with them.

Anger is not wrong. In simple terms, anger is a primal signal that you are feeling blocked from getting what you need or want. Understood in this way, anger is obviously a valuable emotion. When you feel blocked, anger helps you identify the impasse, and it motivates you to remove the block or to change direction. This applies whether the impasse arises from your own unresolved issues or from external factors that affect your personal, familial, or community well-being.

At its physiological base, anger can stimulate the *fight-or-flight* response. This response is hard-wired into the brain, and it's designed to support your survival. The power of this primal response can also be harnessed to support collective survival. That is, anger can contribute energy to fight for ideals, overturn social injustice, or rebel against oppression. In this way, anger may transcend the personal and provide fuel to change the world.

Despite these individual and collective advantages of anger, people are often scared of it. In fact, a lot of people have asked me

Anger is a reaction to injustice and falseness, it gives us the courage to right wrongs, and it is not "sinful" as long as we use it to help ourselves or others.

LYNNE FINNEY

Very few children are accepted when they are angry. What the parents need to learn then is that natural anger only lasts for fifteen seconds. Then it's over with and they are ready to move on. But if you are not allowed to be angry and, even worse, if you get spanked, punished or reprimanded, then you will become Hitlers, small and big Hitlers, who are full of rage and revenge and hate.

ELISABETH KÜBLER-ROSS

how to *get rid* of their anger. While I respect the fear that generates this request, I don't think it's possible or desirable to get rid of any feeling. If you got rid of your anger, for example, you might also lose the passion that can spur you toward personal, interpersonal, or global change.

This chapter focuses on personal and interpersonal anger work, though the same principles of responsibility and respect apply to all areas of life. Even if you choose to use the fiery energy of your anger to fuel outer world action, I still recommend that you learn and practice the principles of solitary anger work. Individual work can help you sort out which aspects of your rage require private resolution, which call for interpersonal negotiation, and which demand that you take action in the world.

A Simple Model for Feelings

In 1971, when I was seventeen, a chaplain-counselor at my university asked me what I did with my anger. I told him I didn't have any anger. Noting my obvious state of denial, the chaplain gently guided me to go deeper. First he taught me how to recognize when I was frustrated or upset. Over time, I began to see that these kinds of feelings had anger at their root. Because the chaplain was so accepting, he made it safe for me to come out of denial.

Once I got permission to feel, I was hooked. Emotions were scary, but they were also exciting! It wasn't long before I was pursuing active anger work with Gestalt and Bioenergetics therapists. The young woman who "had no anger" was suddenly beating pillows and screaming profanities in safe, structured situations. So much for denial.

Although it may seem like I became fast friends with anger, it would be more accurate to say that my relationship with anger has always been quite challenging. For me, anger requires constant vigilance and ongoing care, because its primal force can still terrify me. Rage is like fire. I get better at handling it, and sometimes I even enjoy it, but I never forget that rage—like fire—can do great harm if it burns out of control.

Out-of-control anger may show up as verbal attack, psychological violence, withdrawal of love, or physical abuse (such as spanking, hitting, or destruction of property). Many people have only experienced anger in one or more of these irresponsible forms of expression. As a result, they may consider all anger to be abusive.

If this sounds familiar, take heart. Anger does not have to be abusive, but it usually takes a lot of reeducation to make anger safe.

One of my favorite tools for working safely with anger—and with all feelings—comes from a school of therapy called Transactional Analysis (T.A.), which was originated by Dr. Eric Berne. Since 1981, when I first learned this method from my dear friend Peg Price, I've often credited it with helping me to overcome my fear of feelings, especially my fear of anger. I used to think that if I expressed my anger, it would either kill me or level the world. I know this is a common belief.

The T.A. model showed me a way to experience and express emotions in small, structured increments. Basically, it breaks down feelings into four main categories: mad, sad, glad, and scared. The purpose of this simplicity is not to deny the endless shades and subtleties of emotion. Rather, it's designed to help you *bottom-line* your feelings so you can work with them more easily.

Before I say more about the intricacies of responsible emotional expression, let me give you the basic form developed by Eric Berne. Take a few moments to try it out, if it's new for you. As you speak or write the following sentences, fill in the blanks as spontaneously and truthfully as you can.

*I'm mad that*_____.
*I'm sad that*_____.
*I'm glad that*_____.
*I'm scared that*_____.

Continue cycling through these four statements until you feel complete for the moment. If the intensity of a particular feeling surprises or shocks you, don't worry. You don't have to feel that way until the end of time! Each statement is in present tense for good reason. Feelings move and change like the weather. Thus, this model allows you to make a *weather report* of your emotional *skies*.

As you practice with the sentences, there may be a particular feeling that repeatedly draws a blank for you. If this happens, pause for a moment and breathe into your belly. See if anything occurs to you. If not, continue to the next sentence. Repeat this process with each round, always holding an opening for the hidden emotion to surface. It's okay if it takes months or years to get in touch with feelings that are scary for you. Take your time.

In addition to using the T.A. model to do an inventory of your feelings in general, you can also use it to explore a specific feeling. For example, you can repeat the *I'm mad that* statement over and over, filling in the blank with one angry thought after another until you're finished.

Imagine that we conjure up a world that is safe for mothers and daughters.

LOUISE BERNIKOW

Spanking is a parental temper tantrum. You can't teach children to gain control of their impulses by losing yours.

KYLE PRUETT

Aside from using the mad/sad/glad/scared format for solitary use, you can also use it with another person. The beauty of these four statements is that they keep you focused on yourself, instead of on the other person. Even if you think someone or something else has triggered your emotions, the truth is, your feelings arise from *within* you. For instance, no one can *make you mad*. Your anger is your anger, so it's up to you to take responsibility for it.

Ask Permission and Be Responsible

Before you share your feelings with another person, there's an important preliminary step. That is, *ask permission* first. For example, if you're angry, you could ask the other person if he or she would be willing to listen to your anger for a mutually agreed-on period of time, as long as you promise to be responsible about it. Afterward, you could offer to reciprocate by listening. If you're both old hands at responsible communication, you can abbreviate the way you ask permission, but I still recommend that you do it. I'll say more about this in a moment.

If both of you agree to proceed, remember that when one person speaks, the other person *only* listens. This benefits both people. If you're the one who's talking, it's validating to be fully heard without someone else jumping in to comment or steal the focus (see "The Basics of Listening"). On the listener's side, it's the T.A. model's respectful *I* statements that make the difference. That is, it's easier to listen without interrupting if the other person isn't blaming you.

Another important tip is to describe your anger in terms of *situations*. Obviously, if someone else's actions are involved in triggering your anger, you might refer to that person when you express your feelings. As much as possible, however, describe the person's *actions* as opposed to the person's *character*. For example, it's better to say, "I'm mad that our dinner was ruined because I waited two hours for you," instead of saying, "You're such a jerk and you're always late and when are you going to get your act together anyway?"

It may seem silly to ask permission before expressing anger, and it may feel contrived to use structured statements. However, I'd wager that any awkwardness you feel will be more than offset by your enjoyment of newfound levels of respect. Even still, if you continue to struggle with this style of emotional communication, perhaps you could think of it as a foreign language.

When people begin learning a foreign language, they usually feel stiff and awkward at first. The same is true when you're learning

Responsibility means not blaming anyone or anything for your situation, including yourself. It is the ability to have a creative response to the situation as it is now.

DEEPAK CHOPRA

emotional responsibility. Initially, the process of asking permission and using a stylized form may feel uncomfortable and phony. Like any new language, the trick is to keep practicing until it feels natural.

Anger, Abuse, and Personal Rights

Some people don't want to admit that what they do with their anger is their choice. There are people who want you to feel guilty or ashamed if they're angry with you. They may expect you to *fix* whatever they think you did *wrong*. Some people even believe that if you *make them mad,* then it's your job to take whatever sort of anger they want to dump on you.

Please don't fall for that one, because it's a manipulative trap that leads to abuse. What's my definition of abuse? **Abuse occurs when someone uses another person to meet a need in a way that harms, coerces, or devalues the other person.** You can read more about abuse in "The Dilemma of Forgiveness" and "Disrespect and Subtle Abuse: Watch Out for These Characters."

For now, rest assured that it's not your job to listen to other people's anger unless you are truly willing and interested. Of course, if the other person is important to you, you might miss out on some deep levels of intimacy if you refuse to hear any kind of anger, even if it's responsibly expressed. True intimacy requires emotional honesty, and emotional honesty includes all feelings. Even still, anger can be volatile, so it deserves all the respect you can give it.

If you're on the receiving end of anger, you have the right to ask others to communicate about their anger in a way that feels safe for you and at a time that works for you. After all, your willingness to listen is a *gift,* not an obligation. If your needs are discounted, or if someone *demands* that you listen, I'd encourage you to avoid the inevitable fireworks that might ensue. In such cases, feel free to beat a hasty retreat!

If you ask people to couch their anger in respectful terms, or to wait until you're ready to listen, they may become even angrier. They might call you *controlling* or some other more offensive name. However, there's a difference between controlling others and taking care of yourself. Decide for yourself which is happening, and make your own choices about whether to keep listening to another person's anger if you don't feel respected.

If you question the idea that you have rights in regard to other people's anger, consider an extreme situation. Do you believe that domestic abuse victims have no rights? Do you believe that if they are beaten, they must have *had it coming*? Do you think it's their

No person in the world ever attempted to wrong another without being injured in return—some way, somehow, sometime.

WILLIAM GEORGE JORDAN

job to take whatever they get, since attackers often blame them (the victims) for the abuse? Do you think it's the victims' obligation to be whipping posts for their tormentors?

Assuming you see my point, I hope you will take care of yourself every time you are faced with another person's anger, even if you believe you played a role in triggering it. No matter what you've done, the other person is still responsible for his or her anger. Don't join the escalation by lying down like a doormat or by standing unprotected like a whipping post. Respect yourself by refusing to tolerate anything less than respect from others.

Along with mutual respect, another essential right in regard to anger is the right to withdraw. You have the right to withdraw from any situation, whether you are the person expressing anger or the one listening to it. In addition, you have the right to withdraw without being pursued, attacked, or shamed for it.

If I'm the angry one, I may want to withdraw in order to think, beat pillows, pray, or call a friend for counsel. On the other side, I may wish to withdraw from someone who is angry if I'm feeling too vulnerable, if I'm not feeling respected, or if I simply want to do something else at that time.

By the way, if you need to withdraw, it may be helpful to express your willingness to talk later. On the other hand, if you find yourself being abusive or if you are feeling abused, you might not have enough time to make a graceful exit. In this case, get yourself some space *fast*. My best tip? Take a brisk walk *alone* for at least twenty minutes. This will give the fight-or-flight wiring in your brain a chance to cool down.

If a walk is not an option, you could put on some headphones and dance. If you don't want to walk or dance, then take a long shower or a bath, or simply lie down and breathe into your belly. Whatever you do, do something *supportively* physical for at least twenty minutes. For more help with extreme rage, turn to the chapter called "STOP! LOOK! LISTEN! An Emergency Plan for Anger Overloads."

Here's a good guideline to remember: **Expressions of anger enter the realm of abuse when people cease to care about their own or other people's well-being.** It's never okay to disregard anyone's needs or feelings just because you're angry. Therefore, when you express anger, stay aware of your responsibility to be mutually respectful. Active respect prevents abuse, because it keeps you attuned to your own and the other person's well-being. Of course, it takes practice to be angry and respectful at the same time, but it is possible.

Believing ourselves to be possessors of absolute truth degrades us; we regard every person whose way of thinking is different from ours as a monster and a threat and by so doing turn our own selves into monsters and threats to our fellows.

OCTAVIO PAZ

When in doubt, take a bath.

MAE WEST

The truth is, responsible anger is actually a *gift*. At its best, clearly expressed anger is simply a communication that your boundaries have been overstepped or that you're not getting what you need (remember, though, that it's no one else's job to give you what you need). When you express your anger with love, it can tell another person more about you. In this way, anger may be seen as a statement of your desire to be known and, therefore, to be more intimate with the other person.

Obviously, this kind of anger is different from anger that is used to attack. If you're angry, ask yourself if you want the other person to know you better or if you want to attack (i.e., criticize, condemn, punish, or shame). If it's attack you're after—whether it's physical, psychological, or psychic—I would advise you *not* to communicate with the other person until after you've done some anger work on your own.

Hatred is a normal human feeling, and a feeling has never killed anyone.
ALICE MILLER

Physical Anger Work and Quiet Alternatives

So far, I've suggested some basic techniques for verbal expression of anger. To round out your repertoire, I'd like to make some recommendations for expressing anger in a *physical* way when you're by yourself. I believe that the energy of anger (or any strong emotion) can get *stuck* in your body if you don't find ways to move and express this energy.

Expression always involves *movement*, even if it's only movement of thoughts. Of course, it's possible to shift blocked or repressed feelings merely by working with your thoughts. However, I advocate emotional expression that honors *all* levels of experience, including the primitive, passionate, physical level.

As I mentioned earlier, anger often stimulates a fight-or-flight response from deep in the brain. Though modern life doesn't usually require that you actually fight or flee, I still think it's helpful to somehow honor your body's primal need for movement when this response is triggered. That's why I recommend a brisk walk, a wild dance, or some deep belly-breathing when you're enraged. If you want to get even more physical, keep reading.

I will tell you what I have learned myself. For me, a long five or six mile walk helps. And one must go alone and every day.
BRENDA UELAND

Fight-or-flight energy can be channeled into other activities besides anger expression, just as sexual energy can be transmuted for other purposes. However, most people who struggle with anger aren't interested in transmutation; they just want some basic, mundane support. Those who seek to spiritualize their anger are often the same people who believe that anger is shameful, dangerous, or unevolved. Again, the goal here is not to get rid of anger, but to become friends with it by learning how to make it safe.

Anger is a defense of your uniqueness and individuality. In the Bible it's called righteous indignation. So if you don't like the idea of getting angry, it's okay to get righteously indignant.

BERNIE SIEGEL

In the early 1980s, I worked with a wonderful movement therapist named Margaret, who helped me overcome my terror of anger. From the start, she could see that I was afraid to feel anger in my body, despite the fact that I'd been exploring anger consciously for years. With great patience, she instructed me to do ten- or twenty-second dances of my anger until gradually, over two years' time, I was able to stay with the experience of anger for several minutes without getting terrified. Eventually I discovered the exhilaration that can come with the full-out expression of rage, so long as it happens within the context of a safe and structured environment.

Although I advocate physical anger work, some people may never feel comfortable with the sounds and movements associated with it. If this is true for you, give yourself permission to do whatever kind of anger work feels safe. If you respect your style of expression as it is, you may eventually feel safe enough to experiment with more intensity. However, if your best efforts toward full-out anger work remain at the level of silent acknowledgment of your feelings, that's okay.

This might be a good time to talk about *quiet* forms of anger work. Quiet expression can be useful in situations where it's not appropriate to make noise, for whatever reason. It's also helpful for those who feel traumatized by loud sounds. Last of all, quiet anger work is valuable for people who simply want to enlarge their *tool pouch* of expressive techniques.

Here's one powerful way to experience anger in your body without making any noise. Sit quietly, breathing continuously, while you silently say *yes* to the full force of rage in your heart. While you do this, let your mind run wild through every possible fantasy of anger. Observe these thoughts and images without judgment, and without any intention to act them out.

I call this kind of meditation "watching the parade." Although it's true that thoughts can be used to hurt others, that's *not* what this exercise is about. This exercise is about *witnessing* your human passions and vulnerabilities without trying to change them. That's all. If you can hold anger in your heart with full awareness and acceptance, you will be performing a minor miracle for yourself and for the world.

Rage is like a wounded child. It needs your love. It does not need to be shamed, blamed, criticized, sanitized, brutalized, or denied. It needs what every wounded child needs: to be *treated* respectfully and to be guided toward *acting* respectfully. Rage isn't anger gone bad. It's anger that has not been honored, so it got louder. Treat your rage tenderly and help it find *safe* expression.

In addition to the rage meditation, there are many other forms of anger work that are quiet, yet very physical. For example, clay-play and drawing are great ways to actively channel your *fire*. I like to have a handy stash of plasticene or earthen clay, Play-Doh, crayons, drawing paper, colored pens and pencils, fingerpaints, glitter, glue, multi-colored construction paper, rubber stamps, and ink. Who says you can't have fun with anger?

One of my favorite techniques is to do *inwardly* wild, *outwardly* quiet anger work by playing loud rock music through headphones while dancing my rage. I can punch and kick up a storm, like Arnold Schwarzenegger. Unlike his movies, however, I don't make any noise and nobody gets hurt.

Violence, Pacifism, and War

No anger primer would be complete without addressing the worst-case scenario of violence and rage, namely, war. Therefore, I want to talk frankly about the fight-or-flight response that goes beyond *personal* anger to *collective* survival. First, I'll tell you how I make sense of violence and war. Secondly, I'll explain how I make peace with my pacifist tendencies, so they don't tyrannize all my other principles. Last of all, after sharing my position on these difficult subjects, I'll encourage you to explore your own relationship with violence all the way down to its most terrifying, enigmatic, primitive core.

Years ago, I read an interview with the Dalai Lama, who is a deeply compassionate man and a paragon of pacifism. Even he, the Dalai Lama, said that if he had to cut off one of his fingers to save his hand, he would do it.

Around the same time, I saw a television interview with Elie Wiesel, noted author and survivor of the Nazi Holocaust. The interviewer asked him a hypothetical question: If he could have killed Adolph Hitler, would he have done so? Wiesel said *yes*. I'll never forget that.

How can a couple of pacifists talk about doing violence to themselves or to others? Isn't that hypocritical? Not in my book. *Webster's* defines pacifism as "the opposition to war or violence as a means of settling disputes." I think it's possible to be *opposed* to violence, and yet find yourself called to use it in extreme situations when all else has failed.

Like it or not, violence is part of nature and it's a part of human nature. Frankly, our puny human outbursts—and even our wars— are minor in comparison to earthquakes, volcanoes, sunspot

Just as we are taught to read, to write, to paint, or to sing, we should be taught how to deal with conflict—from childhood. That is where a culture of nonviolence must begin, with the children.

SATISH KUMAR

Even warfare [can be conducted] out of compassion. Destruction is much less.

DALAI LAMA

There is too much of what I call "violent pacifism" in the world today. People preach peace and unconditional love while shooting at other drivers on freeways, ignoring the needs of their loved ones, stepping on their colleagues at work to get to the top, and killing forests and animals that get in the way of their desires or their profits.

LYNNE FINNEY

Sometimes the absence of anger can be the problem. Tolerance and apathy in the presence of evil may make us victims, or even instruments of evil.

DALE TURNER

eruptions, and supernova explosions. Nature is full of violence! It dances at every level of existence.

Conception, for instance, is a violent act. The sperm *violates* the integrity of the egg in order to merge with it and create life. Another more obvious act of violence is eating. All of us, vegetarians included, must kill to survive. As Thich Nhat Hanh says in *Present Moment, Wonderful Moment:*

> *This plate of food, so fragrant and appetizing, also contains much suffering.*

It's futile to deny that violence is necessary for life. It makes more sense to be aware of this fact and to be responsible in relation to it. Unfortunately, there is so much fear of *irresponsible* violence that all violence is often judged to be wrong. As a result, many people think that part of their own primal nature is wrong—the part that could kill if one's life is threatened.

No part of human nature is wrong, even the violent or destructive part. Everyone has the *capacity* to be violent and destructive. Everyone! One of my heroes, Elisabeth Kübler-Ross, tells the story of Golda, who survived Maidanek, one of Hitler's most notorious death camps. Kübler-Ross visited Maidanek after World War II, in the hope of gaining some understanding of the horrors committed there.

Seeing Maidanek firsthand only bewildered Kübler-Ross. She wondered how anyone could treat fellow humans with such absolute cruelty. In the midst of her ruminations, Kübler-Ross was approached by a woman named Golda. Golda understood Kübler-Ross' inability to comprehend the brutality, but she said that any of us would be capable of committing such atrocities if we had been raised in Nazi Germany. "There is a Hitler in all of us," Golda said simply.

I agree with Golda. In fact, the people who scare me most are those who think they have no violent streak, no capacity for cruelty, and no potential for rage. These people are probably not ascended masters; they are more likely in denial. Their *anger burner* may not be functional, and their survival instinct may be disconnected, but that doesn't mean their potential for violence is nonexistent. It probably just went *underground*.

The trick with angry, destructive, or violent thoughts is to know what to do with them. Obviously, you'll get in a lot of trouble—morally, socially, legally, and karmically—if you *act out* your violent thoughts by hurting yourself, others, or the environment. I am NOT advocating that. Instead, I'm suggesting that you learn to *be with* any thoughts or feelings that horrify or repulse you. I even recommend that you find safe and responsible ways (such as those outlined in this chapter) to express these scary thoughts and feelings. The point is, if you can find it in your heart to accept the *little Hitler* within, you'll be doing your part to mitigate the collective buildup of this powerful shadow force.

It may sound paradoxical, but even as I work to accept the Hitler *within*, I may draw boundaries and take a stand against a Hitler (or any other tyrant) in the *outside* world. I like to believe that if everyone did their part to process their own cruelty, this cruelty would not need to appear in colossal forms that threaten us all. However, I'm a realist and I try to work with *what is*, even as I work toward *what can be*.

Therefore, in the matter of real-world tyrants, there may be times when my response to violence is based on practical survival needs in the midst of a global community where everyone is *not* doing the hard inner work necessary to make peace with their own shadows. To put it bluntly, I will take the pacifist route as long as I possibly can, utilizing all the resources at my disposal to keep myself and others safe. In the end, however, I would kill to survive. It's intense for me to make that statement publicly, because so many people will misunderstand or take my words out of context. Therefore, I'd appreciate your patience in allowing me to explain this position more fully.

As much as I hate war, I can understand World War II because it was about saying *no* to a real-world tyrant (Hitler), who had gotten so out of hand that the entire human race was threatened by his insanity. Ultimately, this is the highest purpose of anger: to say *no* when survival is at risk.

I make sense of the need for a collective response to Hitler—even a violent collective response—by thinking about it in individual terms. As an individual, if someone threatens my life, I will do everything possible to negotiate, disable my attacker, or run away (not necessarily in that order). If all else fails, however, I would kill to defend myself. I've been in enough life-threatening situations to know that this is true about me. Although I'm a pacifist by nature, there's an even deeper part of my nature—an older, instinctual part—that brings with it the capacity to kill. Ironically, the animal wisdom that ensures my survival would also allow my pacifist self to survive along with it!

For years, I tried to *spiritualize* everything. I didn't want to make room in *my* universe for any kind of violence, responsible or otherwise. In this version of starry-eyed pacifism, I would shake my

To survive it is often necessary to fight, and to fight you have to dirty yourself.
GEORGE ORWELL

Only very lowly and late have men come to realize that unless freedom is universal it is only extended privilege.
CHRISTOPHER HILL

As long as you knock and judge and criticize anybody, you are responsible for a Hiroshima, Nagasaki, Viet Nam, Maidanek, or an Auschwitz.

ELISABETH KÜBLER-ROSS

Whatever you say about God you should be able to say standing over a pit full of burning babies.

ELIE WIESEL

Every gun, every warship, every rocket signifies a theft from those who hunger and are not fed, those who are cold and are not clothed.

DWIGHT D. EISENHOWER

head in disgust at those who raised their fists or dropped their bombs. I thought such people were unevolved, when in fact it was I who needed to grow up.

At some point, I got more connected to my animal self, and I started thinking more deeply about the paradox of peaceful life, in terms of how much violence it takes to support survival. I would contemplate the words of Elie Wiesel or think about Hitler, or I'd consider the time someone tried to rape my best friend at knifepoint. What happens to my pacifism when reality—RIGHT NOW—presents its opposite? Do I turn the other cheek or do I fight?

I've told you my answer to that question. What's yours? For my part, if I would fight to save my life, how can I judge a country that fights to defend itself? Don't get me wrong. I rarely find any country's reason for war to be worthy of blowing thousands of people to bits. However, my idea of a stupid reason might be someone else's idea of *survival.*

This doesn't mean I *condone* war. That would be like saying I condone hell. In point of fact, I hate war. If it were up to me, I'd destroy *all* the guns and the bombs and the weapons of mass destruction. However, it's not up to me, so I make do with reality. The reality is, large-scale war is uniquely human. Have you ever wondered about that?

What if war is part of the human condition, the way peaceful coexistence is part of it? *Can you work for peace even if you must make peace with war?* What if there are bigger forces that play themselves out through our individual and collective experiences? *If you are only a pawn in the game, can you still find the courage to take a stand?* What if we humans are as curious about death and destruction as we are about life and creation? *Can you accept and celebrate the apparent contradictions of your humanity?*

When I was in the process of adding this section to the Anger Primer, something happened that intensified my writing experience. On August 7, 1998, terrorists bombed the American embassies in Kenya and Tanzania, killing 257 people. Two weeks later, on August 20th, Americans bombed several sites in Sudan and Afghanistan—a response that many people on all sides (including me) regarded as an act of terrorism in its own right.

When my country dropped those bombs, I stopped working on this new section. I knew what I needed to say about violence, but I was afraid to take a stand. I knew that hard-core pacifists would judge my acceptance of the *fighter* position, and I knew that warmongers would judge my advocacy for peace. Eventually I realized that extremists of either position can be equally blind. Even pacifists can become tyrants if they refuse to acknowledge the value of the opposing position. What if everyone could make room for both positions—and for everything in between?

Consider this: What would have happened to the Jews if no one had sacrificed their lives to stop Hitler's genocide? Could it be that one of the purposes of the fighter position is to preserve the lives of pacifists? And could it be that one of the purposes of the pacifist position is to inspire those who are willing to die? The point is, human existence is rarely black or white. Sometimes life is messy and complicated and confusing.

After several days of sitting with these thoughts, I noticed that I still hadn't returned to my work on this section. I was agitated and angry. I knew something was trying to be born in my writing, but I didn't know how to birth it. In the midst of this turmoil, I had an intuition. Steven Spielberg had just released his three-hour movie, *Saving Private Ryan*, about World War II. Although I usually avoid violent movies, I had a sense that his movie would break my impasse and help me finish this section on violence, pacifism, and war.

I'd read many reviews of *Saving Private Ryan*, and I knew that World War II veterans were themselves impressed by Spielberg's accurate depiction of the horrors they endured. Since I knew the film would be an excursion into hell, I made a plan. My intention was to *breathe continuously* and to keep my eyes, ears, and heart open, no matter what. I succeeded, but it wasn't easy. By the time I left the theater, I was overcome with grief and shock. My legs were so shaky that I could barely walk, and I couldn't bring myself to speak for the rest of the night.

There is really no way I can describe Spielberg's movie, except to say that he has done the world a great service by showing war in all its messy, complicated, confusing, and excruciatingly gory detail. As far as I'm concerned, those who criticized *Saving Private Ryan* as if it was merely some pro-war, good old boys' story, missed the point entirely. War may be unavoidable sometimes, but it's nothing to cheer about. Even victory is hollow, because war requires so much bloodshed, so much loss of life, and so much destruction. I think Spielberg did a fine job of showing the truth about war.

When his film opened to its brutal half-hour portrayal of the Normandy massacre (D-Day), I wanted to throw my arms around every veteran alive and say THANK YOU. I wondered how I could ever honor all those men (and in this case, it usually was men) who carried their butchered buddies on their backs, forced themselves to blow other men's brains out, and kept going even when they felt their own bodies splintering and splattering and suffocating in blood.

How can a Hitler, or some other murderer, appear in this world? I don't think any single theory can account for this phenomenon, and I think it's a mistake to try to reduce it to being brutalized by your parents or having grown up in some horrible situation....

JAMES HILLMAN

Wars don't end. Their effects may trail off as time passes, but what would have been is always different afterward, and for people who live through them, individual life is forever an aftereffect.

JERRY LARGE

The writer in me knows only one way to express my gratitude to those who suffered: *by using the freedoms those soldiers fought to protect.* Think about it. I wouldn't be writing this—and you wouldn't be reading it—if America didn't have freedom of speech and a free press. Rivers of blood have been shed so that I may speak my heart to you now.

It's tempting to deny the high cost of freedom. Those of us who have enjoyed relative ease (compared to the rest of the world) may prefer to forget the violence that birthed our comfort. It's difficult to stay conscious of all the napalmed babies, the missing limbs, and the bombed-out neighborhoods as I sit down to dinner. How on earth can I keep going when I remember the true price of peace?

Ultimately, war is mysterious, the way pain and death and life are mysterious. Acknowledging this mystery, the best I can do is figure out where my own heart is leading me, and then take a stand. I stand on the side of peace, even if I must fight. Where do you stand?

A Plan for Responsible, Solitary Anger Work

You may wonder how I can make a transition from collective violence to personal responsibility. In the midst of a discussion about war, it may seem trite to speak about inner work and the respectful expression of anger. However, I have a deep-seated belief that *personal* responsibility is actually the best defense against *collective* brutality. If you can't make peace in your own heart, how can you bring peace to the world?

Of course, peace is a *process*, which means that it includes a whole spectrum of activity and inactivity. The process of peace includes inner work and outer work, turbulence and stagnation, hopelessness and faith. The rest of this section will tackle one part of this process—the part that involves you making peace with your rage, your destructive tendencies, and your capacity to kill. If you can turn these monsters into allies, it will help the whole world.

Here's an analogy. Let's say that everyone in your neighborhood has a couple of lions. Let's also say that one family doesn't feed their lions, and they don't take care of the lions' other basic needs, such as movement and exercise, stimulation and play, and social interaction. Before long, these neglected lions are going to get hungry and restless. At some point, they might even get out and go looking for what they need. If they do, no one else in the neighborhood will be safe. Now, a couple of loose lions would be bad enough, but what if no one in the neighborhood takes care of their lions?

One solution to this dilemma would be to round up all the lions and destroy them, but some of us like lions. Besides, a lot of us know that you can't kill *wildness*. If you destroy one manifestation of wildness, it will only show up somewhere else. Therefore, a better solution would be to help everyone learn how to care for their lions, so they don't wreak havoc on the neighborhood.

Thus, my five-step plan for solitary anger work is like meat to the lions. If you keep your lions fed, they won't be as likely to cause harm. It's your job to take care of your lions, and it's my job to take care of mine. This is essential. Every person is responsible for their own primitive passions.

Too much of the animal disfigures the civilized human being, too much culture makes a sick animal.
CARL JUNG

I know I've already presented a lot of material in this primer. I truly appreciate your willingness to consider the ramifications of anger. If you can hold all these ideas in your awareness without distress, then the rest of this chapter will probably be easy for you. On the other hand, if you're struggling with some of the concepts presented here, the following five-step plan may be a bit challenging for you. Even still, it can give you a chance to integrate the principles of this chapter by allowing you to explore them in a firsthand, experiential way.

My plan for responsible anger expression was developed over two decades of work on my own and with hundreds of clients. Each phase of the plan is briefly stated and then described in detail. At the end of this chapter, the five steps are listed again as a summary.

Phase One: Lay the groundwork.
Understand the basic dynamics of anger before beginning solitary anger work. Then choose a time, a space, and a method of expression.

The first part of this primer provided some general information about the dynamics of anger. Anger education is crucial because it can help you avoid abuse—of yourself, others, or the environment. In addition, anger education can help to dispel some of the fear and shame that is often associated with this powerful emotion. Information can help you understand the primal purpose of anger, and hopefully, this understanding will deepen your acceptance of it.

True anger of the moment gives the self permission to say "no." Then "no" becomes the gentle voice of love.
EMMANUEL

Once you feel comfortable with your knowledge of anger, the next step is to hone your style of expressing it. Education is useless unless you practice what you learn, so the second part of Phase One sets the stage for *action*. To begin this part, choose a time, a space, and a method of expression. Be sure to find a time and a space that allow you to work without disturbing other people or animals.

Generally speaking, this will require you to be alone somewhere if you plan to make a lot of noise.

If you live with people who aren't bothered by intense emotions, you may only need to ask their permission before starting your work. However, many people are traumatized by angry sounds, even if the anger has nothing to do with them. Animals can also be frightened by anger work. Please remember that it's abusive to impose your emotional eruptions on others. Respect the needs of those around you.

If you live in the country, you can go out in nature to do your work (read on for more information about respecting the environment). In the city, you have to be more creative, unless you have a private space at home where you can work without disturbing others. One cityscape where you can usually make noise is underneath busy freeway bridges. However, if you want to vent your frustrations under an overpass, make sure no one else is around. This isn't just for other people's sake; it's for yours, too. Someone might misunderstand your intentions and report you to the police!

Another idea is to use your car as a private space for anger work, but if you do, drive somewhere and *stop*. DO NOT DO ANGER WORK WHILE DRIVING! It's too easy to get carried away, lose your driving awareness, and cause an accident. There are already enough irresponsible drivers who hurt themselves and others in deadly fits of road rage. Play it safe when you drive. Cars can be lethal weapons.

After selecting an appropriate space and time for your work, the next step is to choose your method. Several suggestions were offered earlier in this chapter, mostly in terms of quiet techniques. Obviously, silent expression doesn't require such careful attention to time and space. Even still, I recommend that you follow through with all the steps outlined in this plan, whether you choose to make noise or not.

If you want to do actively physical forms of anger work, many therapists suggest the use of soft bats and pillows so you don't get hurt. I like soft objects for anger work, but frankly, they're not always enough for me. Sometimes I need to be a little more violent— responsibly violent, that is. I'm a staunch advocate of careful safety precautions. In the next phase, I'll say more about violence in regard to anger work. For now, take a moment to consider what kinds of physical expression would suit your personal style.

Three of my favorite techniques for physical anger work are: beating a huge pillow with the flat face of a tennis racket (it makes a great sound); smashing discarded Volvo hoods with a pointed sledgehammer (I always use safety goggles and gloves for protection);

Anger repressed can poison a relationship as surely as the cruelest words.

JOYCE BROTHERS

and best of all, using boxing gloves or a wooden bat on a punching bag (it hangs in my house for easy access).

Another idea comes from a former client. At the time, she was just beginning to experiment with physical anger work, but she knew exactly what she wanted to do. She wanted to break dishes. She also wanted me to join her, so she'd feel more comfortable. We set up a safe space in a garage, put down a large drop-cloth, and threw the dishes against the concrete wall. I must admit, it was a rush! My client's decision to break dishes was symbolic, too, because she was recovering from an eating disorder. The humor of her choice was an added bonus.

If you have trouble thinking of ways to express your anger physically, ask a friend for ideas, talk to a counselor, or try an anger workshop taught by someone who knows how to *move* anger responsibly. Some possibilities might include seminars that use breath work, Bioenergetics, Gestalt, movement therapy, process work, or psychodrama.

If you do choose a workshop, be sure to check out the facilitator(s). The facilitator's personal integrity is often more important than the technique. An unethical or incompetent instructor can turn a valuable method into a weapon. On the flip side, a good teacher can elevate the usefulness of almost any technique.

Phase Two: Show respect for all concerned.

First, ask permission from the space and from all objects you intend to use for anger work. Next, set a clear intention that your work will be done only to express your feelings, not to hurt others.

Phase One described the importance of finding a time and a space that allow you to do anger work without disturbing other people or animals. In this phase, go a step further into responsibility by *asking permission* from the space and from any objects you want to use. This may sound ridiculous, but I'm dead serious.

As a shamanic practitioner, my perspective is all-inclusive: *Everything has consciousness.* Therefore, I do my best to respect so-called inanimate objects as well as animate beings. For instance, I talk to the Volvo hood, punching bag, pillow, or whatever else I want to use for my work. Silently or out loud, I explain that my anger has nothing to do with them. Then I ask for their permission, and I extend my appreciation (in advance) for the use of their physicality. If I get a sense that something isn't right, I won't proceed. If I feel agreement from all concerned, I go forward.

If this sounds silly, consider the way many tribal cultures show respect for all levels of life. For example, they *tune in* to plants and

I never work better than when I am inspired by anger. When I am angry I can write, pray and preach well; for then my whole temperament is quickened, my understanding sharpened, and all mundane vexations depart.

MARTIN LUTHER

Kindness is more important than wisdom, and the recognition of this is the beginning of wisdom.

THEODORE ISAAC RUBIN

If we could read the secret history of our enemies, we would find in each man's life a sorrow and a suffering enough to disarm all hostility.

HENRY WADSWORTH LONGFELLOW

ask permission before taking any part of a plant for medicinal use. It's also traditional in many tribal cultures for hunters to make supplication to the spirit of an animal before killing it. In essence, they ask the animal to make the ultimate sacrifice for the benefit of the tribe. In return, the people give not only their gratitude, but eventually, they give their own lives back to the circle of life.

Traditional native cultures understand that people are part of the web of life and one day, the remains of their human bodies will nourish the plants. The plants, in turn, will feed the brothers and sisters of the animals that are killed today to sustain the tribal community. Needless to say, this kind of respectful connection to the cycle of life is all but missing in modern industrialized societies.

Thus, if you have trouble with this part of the anger plan, I encourage you to look beyond your awkwardness and see the deeper implications of respecting all levels of existence. What if everyone treated plants, animals, and the environment with high regard? It would seem that any awkwardness you might feel about *asking permission* is a small price to pay for showing more responsibility. By the way, if you're worried about looking stupid when you talk to inanimate objects, don't worry. No one will be watching you!

When you ask permission from the objects and from the space, pay attention to your body. If your body *contracts* after asking, take it as a *no*, and then look for another time or place to do your work. If your body *relaxes* after you ask permission, take it as a *yes* and go ahead. Don't get obsessive about whether or not you're doing this perfectly. Trust your intuition, act on it, and keep practicing. The more you trust your intuition, the stronger it will grow.

If you can't quite bring yourself to ask permission of inanimate objects, at least follow through with the other part of Phase Two. That is, set a clear intention that your anger work will be done solely to express your feelings, not to hurt anyone or anything. You can state this intention out loud, or if you're shy, you can vow it silently. Either way, this intention is *essential* to responsible anger work. It provides a psychological and spiritual boundary to accompany your physical boundaries regarding appropriate time and space.

The intent to express feelings is very different from the intent to harm. It's more than possible to hurt others by directing your angry thoughts toward them with malefic intent. You can also hurt others if you're in denial of your anger because if you're oblivious to it, you can't take any precautions to acknowledge and express it responsibly. I'd much rather be around someone who is cleanly expressing anger, as opposed to someone who is *leaking* it all over the place.

If you consciously want to harm another person—or if you're so wrapped up in yourself that you don't notice or care how you affect others—there may be something in your background that needs attention. Generally speaking, people do not mistreat others unless they themselves were mistreated in some way. Even still, past abuse does not justify bad behavior in present time. Those who find themselves inadvertently or purposely inflicting harm (through thoughts, words, or deeds) would be wise to seek professional counsel. Although it's difficult and painstaking work to heal past wounding while taking responsibility for present-day actions, this work can be made easier with good professional support.

Phase Three: Blow off some steam.

Within the confines of your chosen space, with the necessary safety precautions in place and with your intention set, proceed now into the full, uncensored expression of your anger. As you move your anger, remember to keep breathing.

Assuming that you've laid the groundwork and created safe boundaries, this third phase encourages you to go full blast into your rage. Some people find this part troublesome, because it can trigger a lot of shame, fear, guilt, and grief. It may also bother those who believe that primal emotions are distasteful, or who think that there is no difference between expressing angry feelings and actually hurting someone. There is a *big* difference.

Everyone I know has violent thoughts at one time or another. Whether or not anyone admits this is another matter. As I said earlier in this chapter, violence is a part of human nature. If you object strongly—perhaps even violently—to this idea, then you've proved my point. Personally, I can't imagine that anyone will ever succeed in excising the *capacity* for violence from human nature. It's far too valuable a component of the biological mechanism for survival.

If you've done enough work to become comfortable with your fight-or-flight instinct, and if you understand how this instinct can intensify the force of your anger, then you're ready for this next phase. With your boundaries and intention clearly demarcated, it's time to go for it. By the way, Phase Three makes one small but important exception to the *do no harm* rule. That is, you might choose a style of expression that includes the destruction of some object (see Phase Two).

Although it may seem contradictory to profess respect for an object and yet destroy it, I'd like to call your attention back to the example of traditional native cultures, where tribal members would both honor a plant or animal and yet sacrifice its life for food, medicine, clothing, or

Freedom is what you do with what's been done to you.
JEAN-PAUL SARTRE

When you don't admit or acknowledge anger, the results are depression, apathy and self-destructive behaviors.
DANEEN SKUBE

shelter. Similarly, if you've asked permission to wreak havoc with a cast-off car hood, or if you've created the space to break dishes or to rip apart a phone book, then Phase Three is the time to follow through.

During this uncensored phase, give yourself permission to swear and stomp and punch and yell and rampage. Let yourself entertain any horrible, violent, or blaming thought that crosses your mind. Try not to judge yourself for any of it. Remember that this is the uncensored phase of the five-part plan, and that you have done everything possible to set the proper boundaries—both physically and spiritually—to allow free expression of your anger within the confines of your safe space.

If your upbringing was repressive, don't be surprised if your parents (or some other authority figures) show up in your imagination when you start going for it with your anger. These inner figures might try to get you to stop. This kind of interruption is probably inevitable if the Anger Primer flies in the face of everything you've been taught. If something like this happens for you, just tell the images to back off. You could even add them to your anger work and blast them to bits—in your imagination, I mean! As an alternative, you could encourage these images to leave their repression behind and join you, figuratively speaking, for a round of creative rage. It's quite possible that no one ever gave *them* permission to vent!

If you feel inspired by all this talk about physical anger work, but you don't think you have enough anger to do Phase Three, let me encourage you to try anyway. Once you begin moving your body—especially major muscle groups in your arms, shoulders, chest, and thighs—old anger memories are likely to surface spontaneously. This is perfectly normal, and it's a testament to the *physical* power of emotions.

Nothing on earth consumes a man more completely than the passion of resentment.

FRIEDRICH NIETZSCHE

Every time you *stuffed* your anger in the past, the energy of that feeling had to go somewhere. That *somewhere* might be your body. Your cells may have a backlog of accumulated sparks of rage. An angry fire may be smoldering beneath the surface, whether you can feel it or not. The good news is, you can move the stuck energy of those feelings now, a little at a time, with regular anger work.

If you've denied your feelings for years, or if you happen to be going through a frustrating period in your life, it may be helpful to do a few minutes of physical anger work every day for a while. Consider it your daily *emotional workout*. If possible, find a way to bring creativity and humor into your efforts, because if you enjoy the work, you'll feel safer and you'll be more likely to keep doing it.

If physical anger work terrifies or overwhelms you, you may

have been traumatized by rage in the past. On the other hand, extreme fear or overwhelm may simply be signals that you're not breathing fully. Either way, *slow down the process* and do your work in smaller increments. Also, make sure that you breathe deeply and continuously while doing emotional work, even if you're working quietly.

If you start crying while doing anger work, take some time to be with your tears. Grief and anger are often mixed in layers, so when you begin to peel off the layers, you may go back and forth between these two emotions. This is more the norm than the exception. Whatever you experience, I encourage you *not* to analyze the content of your feelings during Phase Three. Do this uncensored part of the plan with as little thought as possible. Let your feelings wash over you like a crashing surf. Ride the waves until you feel complete or until you get tired, whichever comes first, and then move on to Phase Four.

I imagine one of the reasons people cling to their hates so stubbornly is because they sense, once hate is gone, they will be forced to deal with pain.

JAMES BALDWIN

Phase Four: Clean up your act.

Repeat your intention that no one be harmed by your anger work. Next, express appreciation for all the objects involved, and ask that the energy of your emotions be safely dissipated. Finally, cleanse the space in your own way.

After you've completed the uncensored phase, I recommend that you reinforce your original intent to *do no harm*. Whether you speak this intention out loud or simply repeat it inwardly, the words you choose are not as important as your sincerity.

The next step in Phase Four is to express appreciation for everything that played a role in the expression of your feelings. Personally, I like to thank the space and all the objects I used to do my work. I may even (inwardly) thank the people or the situations that helped to trigger my rage. I also like to thank my body. Again, if you feel silly talking to inanimate objects, you can simply hold a sense of appreciation in your heart for all the things that helped you experience and express your feelings.

Finally, be sure to do whatever's necessary to clean up and safely dissipate the energy of your emotional work. For example, you can ask the earth, the universe, your higher self, God/dess, nature, the spirits, or whatever you wish to dispel any psychic residue that lingers from your efforts. To clear the air in a literal sense, you can burn sage or incense. If you're indoors, you can also open the doors or the windows to let in fresh air. Be a good camper, and leave the place better than you found it. Your thoughtfulness will make all the difference.

Phase Five: Rest and reflect.

Take some time after your anger work to quiet your body and your mind. Consider your experience, and notice what you've learned from it.

Anger work can be energizing, draining, or neutral in effect, depending on a thousand different factors. No matter how you feel afterward, it may take a few minutes for you to return to everyday awareness, since passionate feelings can induce an altered state. It's not a good idea to drive immediately after anger work. In addition, it would be wise to wait a while before reconnecting with others.

During your rest period, reflect on whatever happened during the uncensored phase of your work. Perhaps you had an *aha* experience, or maybe you uncovered a memory that begs for new understanding. Perhaps you remembered a time when you mistreated someone, and you realize the need to make amends. As you reflect, notice how your body and your emotions led you to new levels of awareness.

With practice, you can learn your own limits in terms of how to pace the phases of your anger work. The process will be different every time, because you are different every time. Tune in to your body, follow your hunches, and be open to surprises.

Recap of the Plan

The Anger Primer is now complete. To reinforce the ideas in this long and detailed primer, I've listed the main points in the following chapter, "Hot Tips: Anger Primer Highlights." In conclusion, then, let me restate the five phases of responsible, solitary anger work.

Phase One: Lay the groundwork.

Understand the basic dynamics of anger before beginning solitary anger work. Then choose a time, a space, and a method of expression.

Phase Two: Show respect for all concerned.

First, ask permission from the space and from all objects you intend to use for anger work. Next, set a clear intention that your work will be done only to express your feelings, not to hurt others.

Phase Three: Blow off some steam.

Within the confines of your chosen space, with the necessary safety precautions in place and with your intention set, proceed now into the full, uncensored expression of your anger. As you move your anger, remember to keep breathing.

Ever wonder why someone doesn't try softer?
LILY TOMLIN

The best politics is right action.
MAHATMA GANDHI

Phase Four: Clean up your act.

Repeat your intention that no one be harmed by your anger work. Next, express appreciation for all the objects involved, and ask that the energy of your emotions be safely dissipated. Finally, cleanse the space in your own way.

Phase Five: Rest and reflect.

Take some time after your anger work to quiet your body and your mind. Consider your experience, and notice what you've learned from it.

Celebrate your anger in safe, constructive ways. Dance it. Draw it. Sculpt it. Scream it. *Move it!* Find a hundred different ways to be with it. Above all, honor it as one expression of your passion to live full-out. Your anger wants the best for you and for everyone. Give it your best in return.

With love, even the rocks will open.

HAZRAT INAYAT KHAN

Hot Tips: Anger Primer Highlights

1. Anger is often misunderstood, mistrusted, and misdirected, but it is not wrong.

2. There are no negative human emotions. All your feelings are valuable, including anger.

3. Anger is a primal signal that you are feeling blocked from getting what you need or want.

4. Anger helps you identify whatever is blocking you (including internal blocks), and it motivates you to overcome the impasse or to move in another direction.

5. Anger can stimulate the brain's fight-or-flight response, which is designed to support survival.

6. Sometimes anger isn't only a personal experience; it may also provide fuel to work for change in the world.

A Simple Model for Feelings

7. Dr. Eric Berne (Transactional Analysis) developed a simple model for identifying feelings according to four main categories: mad, sad, glad, and scared.

8. Berne's model can help you to bottom-line the essence of what you're feeling, so you can work with your emotions more easily.

9. Use responsible *I* statements to express your feelings, especially your anger.

10. "You make me mad" is never true. No one can *make you* feel anything.

11. There is *always* more than one way to respond to any given situation. Anger is never the only choice.

12. You are responsible for your anger, no matter what.

13. Physical assault, emotional violence (shame/criticism/control), verbal attack, and withdrawal of love are all examples of irresponsibly expressed anger. Irresponsibly expressed anger is *abusive* anger.

Ask Permission and Be Responsible

14. Ask permission before telling another person about your anger. Don't proceed without permission.

15. Listening is a *gift*, not an obligation.

16. When someone is talking with you about feelings, don't interrupt unless you feel disrespected.

17. When you are talking, ask others not to interrupt unless they feel disrespected.

18. When expressing anger, describe your feelings in terms of situations (as much as possible).

19. If you must mention another person in relation to your anger, describe your feelings about the person's *actions*, not the person's *character*.

20. Initially, you may feel awkward when you ask permission and use *I* statements to express anger.

21. Treat emotional responsibility like a new language, and keep practicing until it becomes second nature.

Anger, Abuse, and Personal Rights

22. Here's my definition of abuse: **Abuse happens whenever someone uses another person to meet a need in a way that devalues the person being used.**

23. It's not your job to listen to another person's anger, and it's not another person's job to listen to yours. Listening must be voluntary.

24. If you won't listen to *responsible* anger communications, you'll miss out on deep levels of emotional intimacy.

25. Emotional honesty includes anger.

26. If you're on the receiving side of anger, you have a right to ask that it be communicated in a way that feels safe for you and at a time that works for you. However, don't use this right as a means to control or manipulate others.

27. It's abusive for people to force their anger on you whenever and however they want, without regard for your needs. The same is true in reverse.

28. Respect yourself and request respect from others in all exchanges. Don't be a whipping post.

29. In an angry exchange, both parties have the right to withdraw without being pursued, attacked, or shamed.

30. If you need to withdraw from an angry exchange, you can always talk again after both parties cool down.

31. Anger can become abusive when one person ceases to care about the other person's well-being.

32. Anger and compassion can coexist in an open heart at the same time.

33. Responsible anger is actually a gift.

34. When expressed with love, anger can tell another person more about your needs.

35. If you're angry, ask yourself if you want the other person to know you better or if you want to attack.

36. If you want to attack, do *not* tell the other person about your anger until you've worked with the angry feelings on your own.

Physical Anger Work and Quiet Alternatives

37. Angry feelings can get *stuck* in your body if you don't find ways to move and express these feelings.

38. Expression always involves movement, even if it's only movement of thought.

39. Solitary anger work may be enhanced by safe, responsible, physical expression.

40. Physical anger work is one way to honor the body's primal fight-or-flight response.

41. Repeated repression of anger and its fight-or-flight response can cause stress to the body.

42. To free up the powerful force of angry feelings, develop a repertoire of techniques for solitary anger work, so you can match the technique to the situation.

43. Some people may never feel safe with sounds and physical movement in anger. It's okay to express anger *quietly*.

44. Go slow with anger work, and get help when you feel scared or overwhelmed.

45. A supportive professional can help you feel safer with anger.

46. Give good attention and expression to all the layers of emotion that you discover while exploring your anger.

47. Creativity and humor can add depth and dimension to your work with anger.

48. It's okay to have fun while you do anger work!

Violence, Pacifism, and War

49. To face the full ramifications of anger, it's important to explore your feelings about the worst-case manifestation of violence and rage, namely, war.

50. It's possible to be opposed to violence, and yet find yourself called to use it in extreme situations when all else has failed to ensure survival.

51. Everyone has violent or destructive tendencies. The trick is to know what to *do* with these tendencies.

52. What if war is part of the human condition, the way peaceful coexistence is part of it? *Can you work for peace even if you must make peace with war?*

A Plan for Responsible, Solitary Anger Work

53. Personal responsibility is the best defense against collective brutality. If you can't make peace in your own heart, how can you bring peace to the world?

54. Make peace with your rage, your destructive tendencies, and your capacity to kill. If you can turn these monsters into allies, it will help the whole world.

55. You can use my five-step plan for responsible anger expression to explore and integrate the principles listed here (see "The Anger Primer" for details).

STOP! LOOK! LISTEN!
AN EMERGENCY PLAN
FOR ANGER OVERLOADS

Sometimes anger strikes with such intensity that all your best intentions fly out the window. In such cases, it's good to have an emergency plan already in place. Since extreme rage can short-circuit higher brain functions, I recommend a plan that's so simple a child can remember it. In fact, my plan comes straight out of childhood.

When I was a kid learning to cross the street, I was taught three words: *STOP! LOOK! LISTEN!* The message was everywhere. Adults drummed it into my head. It was even painted in crosswalks on roads.

When you're full of rage, it's the same as if you're standing at the edge of a busy street. The street is like your mind, with angry thoughts rushing around like cars speeding by in all directions. You may want to get to the other side of the street—or to the other side of your anger. However, if you don't keep your wits about you, you might get hurt or cause others to be hurt.

STOP! LOOK! LISTEN! These three words can bring you back to your senses, and they can help you prevent unnecessary pain. I'll give you a few pointers for working with them.

First, when you're possessed by anger that threatens to burn out of control, *STOP!* No matter what you're doing when anger hits, stop doing it! Then *do something else.* Since anger stimulates the fight-or-flight response, it's particularly helpful to do something *physically* active, as long as it's harmless for all concerned. If you need ideas, consult "The Anger Primer." One good option is to take a long, brisk walk by yourself.

After you've stopped doing whatever you were doing and replaced it with something more actively supportive, the next step is to *LOOK!* If you want to cross a busy street, you don't just look straight ahead. You look in every direction. The same thing applies when you're angry. Don't keep looking at whatever or whomever you believe is triggering your rage. In fact, I recommend against that, because it tends to reinforce your association of anger with that person or thing.

When a person begins to yell during an argument, it is a tip-off that he is unsure of himself.

ANN LANDERS

Instead, look in some other direction. If you're with someone, you might announce that you're breaking eye contact for emergency reasons, then go ahead and do it. Look up at the ceiling. Look down at the floor. Look out the window. Better yet, go outside and look up at the sky. Watch the clouds or the stars for fifteen or twenty minutes—and then look inside your heart. Move your eyes around in their sockets. Look up, look down, look around, and look within. *LOOK!*

Last of all, *LISTEN!* If you're still with someone else, and you believe that person was a factor in your rage, then keep quiet now. Listen carefully to whatever he or she wants to say, as long as it's stated responsibly (if not, go for a walk). Listen as if your life depends on understanding every nuance of the other person's position. Listen as if you care, because if you act as if you care, it may help you reconnect to the fact that you do care. After all, if you didn't care, you wouldn't be angry, right?

Now, whether you're with someone or by yourself, take your listening to another level. First, tune in to all the sounds around you. Notice how much you were missing while anger stole all of your attention. Turn your listening skills inward now, and see what happens next.

Focus on your breathing. Listen to the sound of your inhale, your exhale, and your inhale once again. Listen to the sound of your blood pulsing through your veins. Now get really quiet, so you can hear the wisdom of your heart. I bet your heart has something to say about the true source of your distress.

There you have it: my simple three-word plan for anger overloads. *STOP! LOOK! LISTEN!* Program your mind to flash these words repeatedly in the event of explosive rage. If you can remember these three words, they can help you safely navigate the dangers on the street of anger.

I couldn't quite bring myself to call this chapter, "STOP! LOOK! LISTEN! SNIFF!" However, that's what I would call a complete emergency plan for anger overloads. Here's how it works.

Sometime when you're not angry, find a specific smell that calms you. For some people, this might be a whiff of vanilla; for others, it might be the scent of a pine bough or a sprig of cedar; for still others, it might be the aroma of rose oil or fresh lavender. Whatever you like to smell, keep it handy.

Take long walks in stormy weather or through deep snow in the fields and woods, if you would keep your spirits up. Deal with brute nature. Be cold and hungry and weary.

HENRY DAVID THOREAU

If you can be patient in one moment of anger you will escape one hundred days of sorrow.

CHINESE PROVERB

If you find yourself in the midst of an anger overload, run for your favorite smell and give it a whiff. If you're going through a period where you're experiencing a lot of rage, you might even want to keep a source of this calming scent in your pocket for easy and immediate access.

Once you've got the source of your favorite scent under your nose, begin by sniffing it in short breaths, keeping time with your heartbeat or your breath, both of which are likely to be rapid if you're enraged. As you continue to inhale your favorite aroma, let your breathing deepen naturally. Let it slow down, bit by bit. Don't force anything. Just try to get as much of your favorite smell as possible. Focus on that.

No doubt you can guess some of the hidden bonuses of this extra tip. First, it allows you to change your focus from distress to pleasure. Second, the act of inhaling an aroma forces you to breathe, which can help you integrate your emotions. Last of all, the sense of smell is the most primitive of the five senses, and it originates deep within the brain. If you flood that part of the brain with pleasure, it may help to quiet the intense neural activity in the fight-or-flight circuits of your brain.

Next time your rage goes over the top, let your nose lead you back to center. It's very simple.

STOP! LOOK! LISTEN! SNIFF!

GUILT COULD MEAN
YOU'VE DONE
SOMETHING RIGHT

People think I'm crazy when I say their guilt could mean they've done something right. Obviously, this flies in the face of everything Mom taught. What's the deal? First of all, it might help to define terms before I get into specifics. There is a big difference between guilt and shame. Basically, you might feel ashamed if you feel bad or wrong *as a person*, whereas you might feel guilty if you believe your *actions* were bad or wrong. The next chapter, "How to Love Your Shame," deals with the former situation, when your *personhood* is in question.

This chapter deals with guilt, the experience of feeling distress about your *actions*. In the same way that I differentiate between shame and guilt, I also like to make a distinction between two different kinds of guilt. One kind is what I call "Should Guilt," which arises when you break *someone else's* rules about how *they* think you should act. The other kind I call "Good Guilt." Good Guilt is usually triggered when you break one of *your own* rules. This gets tricky, of course, because sometimes other people's rules feel right for you, so you adopt them as part of your own code of honor. I'll say more about this special case in a moment.

All of us grow up within the context of cultural, familial, political, economic, and socio-religious codes of conduct, not all of which agree with each other. From this background of diverse standards, each of us pieces together a personal code of ethics, which reflects our individual perceptions of *right* and *wrong* behavior. Whether or not there is an *ultimate* right or wrong, I honestly don't know. I do know that societies tend to organize around specific codes of conduct, and most individuals develop their own personal codes as well.

The point of this chapter is not to discuss the validity of personal or collective standards of behavior. Instead, my intention is to acknowledge that such standards exist, and that people may experience guilt when they deviate from these standards. A person who never experiences guilt may be lucky, emotionally dead,

Selfishness is not living as one wishes to live; it is asking others to live as one wishes to live.

OSCAR WILDE

You've got to have something to eat and a little love in your life before you can hold still for any damn body's sermon on how to behave.

BILLIE HOLIDAY

enlightened, severely brain-damaged, or sociopathic, depending on that person's situation and your point of view. Whatever the case, a guilt-free existence is probably more the exception than the norm. Like it or not, guilt is a common experience. Rather than avoid or deny the discomfort of guilt, I recommend that you take a more proactive approach to it.

Both Should Guilt and Good Guilt can be used to advantage. The first step is to *notice* when you're feeling guilty and *acknowledge* it for what it is. The next step is to determine which kind of guilt you're experiencing. To do this, ask yourself the following question: "Did I break *someone else's* rules about how they think I should act—or did I break *my own* rules?"

Again, if you feel guilty because you have transgressed someone else's concept of what's right, I would call your experience Should Guilt. On the other hand, if you feel guilty about breaking your own code of ethics, I'd call it Good Guilt. Last of all, if you feel guilty about breaking other people's rules that have become part of *your own* moral code, I'd call this Good Guilt as well.

For me, Good Guilt is a valuable signal that I've broken my own code of honor. It stimulates me to make *course corrections* to alleviate the discomfort of guilt. For example, my personal ethics require me to tell a close friend if there is something bothering me about our relationship. If I withhold this kind of information, I may experience some degree of guilt. Although I always reserve the right to work inwardly with the issue for a while, eventually I will tell my friend about it. In the end, our relationship may benefit from this truth-telling, but my primary goal in speaking up is to stay straight with myself. In this way, Good Guilt is my ally.

Believe it or not, Should Guilt can also be an ally. In fact, if you feel Should Guilt, you can rejoice, because it could mean you've done something *right!* Let me explain by telling you a story about a former client, whom I will call Sophia. Sophia was a talented artist, an accomplished and respected teacher, and a deeply compassionate woman. She was also severely debilitated by anorexia and bulimia, she was a survivor of sexual abuse, and she grew up in a family that was extremely critical, controlling, and manipulative.

Because Sophia had been wounded in so many ways, and because anorexic families tend to devalue the self, Sophia found it excruciatingly difficult to act in her own behalf. Unfortunately, Should Guilt played into this system perfectly. Should Guilt felt so awful that Sophia would usually *kiss ass*, rather than face the guilt that inevitably arose when she broke a family rule.

By your stumbling, the world is perfected.

SRI AUROBINDO

With lots of encouragement, Sophia gradually came to see that Should Guilt was not necessarily bad. Yes, it was a sign that she had broken a family rule, but it was also a sign that she had succeeded in standing up for herself. Although her family didn't like it when Sophia broke the rules and stood up for herself, *she* liked it. Therefore, she realized that if she could learn how to work through her Should Guilt, she could use it to her advantage. The trick was to consistently resist the pull backward into old family patterns by moving forward into more self-respect.

The question is: How does anyone work through those uncomfortable feelings of guilt? First, it's important to realize that one reason guilt feels so awful—and one reason it's so difficult to process—is that it's actually a muddy mix of multiple emotions. Working with guilt is like wrestling an octopus: All those emotional tentacles grasp and pull and twist you every which way! If you could just deal with one arm at a time, maybe you could come to grips with it more easily.

To this end, I've developed a plan for working with the unwieldy creature called guilt. The plan works for Should Guilt as well as for Good Guilt. To help you remember it, I've arranged the five steps according to the letters in the word *G-U-I-L-T*.

"G" stands for "GO THE DISTANCE." This simply means that when you come up against a mountain of guilt, it may take some effort to move it. However, the more thoroughly you process guilt each time it arises, the easier it will be to work through it next time. Mountains of guilt can be turned into molehills, which you can then step over, but this usually takes commitment and persistence.

"U" stands for "UNDERSTAND THE ISSUES." Guilt is very complex. As mentioned earlier, guilt has roots in all kinds of personal, familial, cultural, political, religious—and sometimes ridiculous—rules. A basic understanding of guilt can come from reading this chapter. In addition, you may wish to explore the roots of your own personal brand of guilt. If you want to accelerate your work with guilt, write or speak about it publicly, then watch to see how many opportunities arise to assist you in experiencing every kind of guilt imaginable!

"I" stands for "INTEGRATE THE FEELINGS." One reason people have trouble feeling, expressing, and releasing guilt is that it's not a bottom-line feeling. By this I mean that guilt does not fall into one of the basic categories of mad, sad, glad, or scared (see "The Anger Primer" for more information). In contrast to these four primal feelings, guilt is often a combination of all these feelings.

Men are afraid to rock the boat in which they hope to drift safely through life's currents, when, actually, the boat is stuck on a sandbar. They would be better off to rock the boat and try to shake it loose, or, better still, jump in the water and swim for shore.

THOMAS SZASZ

Saying no can be the ultimate self-care.

CLAUDIA BLACK

Working with a mass of undifferentiated feelings is like trying to form words from a pile of building blocks coated with slime. Imagine how much easier it would be to make words from clean blocks that have been neatly separated into stacks of the same letter.

If you want to work with guilt, I recommend that you *bottom-line* your experience into the four basic feelings mentioned above. To do this, write or speak your feelings by using the following statements, cycling through them again and again until you feel complete.

*I'm mad that*_____.
*I'm sad that*_____.
*I'm glad that*_____.
*I'm scared that*_____.

Here's an example from Sophia's work with guilt: "*I'm mad that* my family taught me always to take care of others instead of myself. *I'm sad that* I deny my needs. *I'm glad that* I'm learning to stand up for myself. *I'm scared that* I'll never be able to say *no* to my mother without feeling guilty."

If you want to go deeper than this verbal process allows, you might want to get more physical and more creative. Put on some music and dance your feelings, or try drawing or sculpting them. Find out what happens if you *get physical* with guilt. Movement is a good antidote for obsessive emotions.

"L" stands for "LEVEL THE FIELD." Guilt involves feeling regret about your actions. Leveling the field means doing whatever it takes to clear away the debris—physical, emotional, or spiritual—left in the wake of regrettable actions. If you're working with Should Guilt, you may only need to remember that you are the final authority about how you should act. Therefore, if you experience guilt for breaking rules you don't actually support, don't dismay. Instead, congratulate yourself for your courage.

On the flip side, if you're experiencing Good Guilt as a result of breaking your own code of honor, you may need to clean up your *outer* actions in addition to doing *inner* work. In this case, leveling the field might include apologizing to other people and making amends to correct any unfortunate consequences of your actions.

"T" stands for "TERMINATE THE TENSION." Let's say you've done all the previous steps, but dark clouds of guilt still hang over your head. This may indicate that you haven't fully cleaned up your act or that you haven't gotten to the bottom of your feelings. In either case, you may benefit from repeating the previous steps. On the other

In nature there are neither rewards nor punishments— there are consequences.

ROBERT G. INGERSOLL

hand, if you've done as much work as you can, you might be ready for this final step.

To terminate the tension, try a big dose of healthy distraction. Yes, even distraction has its place! In the past, I used addictive habits to distract myself from guilt. This isn't wrong, but addictions only provided a temporary fix. These days, I recommend more effective methods of distraction. Some of my personal *Guilt Away!* favorites are: watching funny movies, doing art, going for long walks, drumming, hanging out with a good friend, getting cuddled, praying for help, and especially, turning on loud rock music and dancing like a maniac.

That brings us to the end of my prescription for working with **GUILT**. To summarize, these are the five steps: **Go the distance. Understand the issues. Integrate the feelings. Level the field. Terminate the tension.** Take it one step at a time. Wrestle your guilt to the ground and put it to good use!

We are not all guilty but we are all responsible.

ABRAHAM JOSHUA HESCHEL

How to
Love Your Shame

A man doesn't learn to understand anything unless he loves it.

GOETHE

S hame is a trickster. It comes sneaking in like an icy blue fog and before you know it, you're trapped in a blinding storm of self-hate. Shame feels so awful that most of us will do anything to stop it. I don't know anyone who likes shame. In fact, most people hate it. However, hating shame won't heal it. If you want to heal shame, you have to love it to death.

Before you become nauseated at the thought of loving your shame, consider this: I'm not suggesting that you must *like* your shame. Liking relates to enjoyment; love is more about understanding and respect. It's not necessary to enjoy your shame, but I recommend that you understand and respect it. This chapter, then, will give you a three-part plan for loving your shame into oblivion.

Before getting into the plan, I'd like to define shame according to the simplest definition I know. That is, shame is when you think that you, *as a person,* are bad or wrong. On the other hand, guilt arises when you believe that your *actions* are bad or wrong.

I've noticed that allowing shame to run its course only seems to reinforce it. Resisting or denying shame doesn't help, either. The saying "What you resist persists" definitely applies to shame. Therefore, I recommend that you love your shame instead, the way you'd love a battered kitten you've adopted from a shelter.

Imagine that this little kitten (or puppy, if you prefer) has been abused for no reason except that its previous caretakers didn't know how to nurture the growth of a tiny, innocent being. Because of their lack of understanding, this little kitten now runs and hides from you, expecting to be punished again for doing the things kittens naturally do.

This kitten can be compared to your own childlike innocence, the part of you that may have been criticized and shamed a million times by those who were entrusted with your care. Because of this criticism, your innocence may have gone into hiding in order to protect itself. Once the shaming has become entrenched, that innocent part of you may not come out to play again unless you show it *only* love—consistently.

Like a battered kitten that can scratch your eyes out if it feels threatened, shame can also hurt you if you don't treat it kindly. If you don't believe shame can be hurtful, pay attention to what you do the next time you feel ashamed. The shame itself isn't hurtful, of course, but people tend to do hurtful things when they feel bad about themselves. Some people direct this hurtful behavior toward themselves, while others direct it outward.

In my twenties, painful memories sometimes overcame me to the point where I believed I must be bad to the core. Occasionally, I would beat my own body with my fists, as if to punish myself in agreement with those who made me wrong in childhood. Somewhere along the line, however, I realized my body was innocent. At that point, I made a pact with myself never to hit myself again, no matter how bad I thought I was. This pact led to the development of the three-part plan included here, a plan that has been shared with thousands of people through articles and workshops.

The rationale for my plan is simple: Respect shame because it is a very powerful feeling that can suck you under like quicksand. If you don't know in advance how to save yourself from quicksand, you're likely to flail yourself to death in an effort to escape. The question is: How do you get yourself out of shame once you're in it? As with quicksand, you must create a plan—in advance—and then put that plan into action once shame hits.

The first step is to feel your shame without acting on it. You can't heal anything you aren't willing to acknowledge. *Feel* your shame, *name* it, and *acknowledge* that yes, this is shame. As you explore the feeling, notice how you experience it. Do you feel it as a sensation in your body? If so, where do you feel it? Does your shame have a form, a shape, or a color? Can you smell it? Do you taste anything when you feel shame? Does it sound like anything? Do any images come to mind? What other times have you felt like this? Do you notice any common themes in these situations?

While you are feeling your shame, engage a part of you that Ram Dass calls the *witness*. It's the part of you that merely watches everything without judgment. With this part engaged, practice *being with* the feeling of shame without trying to change it. Find out as much as you can about your shame. As you explore it, notice what you want to do. Do you want to curl up and die? Do you want to run? Do you want to hurt yourself physically? Do you want to hide from everyone? Do you want to drink or eat or smoke or use drugs?

There is a luxury in self-reproach. When we blame ourselves, we feel no one else has a right to blame us.
OSCAR WILDE

Notice all these desires now with the witness engaged. *Don't act on these desires*. Simply notice and experience them.

Notice also if there are other feelings mixed in with your shame. Do you feel sadness, anger, or fear? If so, acknowledge these emotions, too. Cry or rage or scream or shake, or just sit quietly, saying *yes* to these feelings as you hold them in your heart.

Overall, the purpose of this first step is to feel all aspects of your shame without judgment and without acting in ways that take you away from it. That is, see if you can be with your shame without inflicting self-abuse, mistreating others, or avoiding your pain through addictive behavior. Automatic or compulsive responses to shame will not heal it.

After you have experienced your shame without acting on it, the next step is to tell a trusted friend about your shame. One painful side-effect of shame is that when you think you're bad, you may believe that others find you abhorrent, too. This is why shame makes people feel so isolated and alone. As an antidote, Step Two in healing shame is to stop hiding: to make a deal with yourself that you will tell at least one other person about your shame. It doesn't have to be the same person every time, but it needs to be another human being as opposed to a Higher Power, a disembodied entity, or your dog. It's fine to talk with them, too, but it's *people* we hide from, and it's *people* who provide the edge for healing shame.

If possible, tell someone about your shame while you are feeling it. If you're too scared to do this, or if the timing doesn't work, be sure to tell your friend later. As you practice sharing about your shame, it's okay to write about it in letters, and it's okay to use a friend's voice mail. The point is to tell another person in a manner that feels safe for you now, then gradually practice being more direct.

Healing is not a race. Recovery from shame has a time line of its own. All you can do is work with it, bit by bit, whenever it comes up. Sometimes I get a little cocky after I successfully overcome a huge chunk of shame, mistakenly thinking I've finally mastered it once and for all. Soon afterward, another layer of shame inevitably gets triggered, and I realize that there is always more work to do. The lessons just get more subtle. It helps me to give up on the idea of being *done*. Instead, I try to focus on whatever is in front of me.

When you choose a friend to help you with this step, find someone who truly understands shame, so you don't get shamed for having shame. A good buddy will know that the following statements are *not* helpful if you are experiencing shame: "Oh, you shouldn't feel that way! Don't be so hard on yourself! Don't you know how wonderful you are? Get a grip!"

Real friends are those who when you've made a fool of yourself don't feel you've done a permanent job.
JO PETTY

Rather than use these kinds of shaming statements, a good friend will simply listen without trying to change or *fix* what you're feeling. After you express your shame, your buddy can thank you for having the courage to tell about your shame. If it feels right, he or she can also ask you if you know what you need in that moment. If you can begin to focus on what you need, it will lead you to the last step in my plan.

After you have felt your shame and told another person about it, the third and final step is to do something actively loving for yourself. This is often the hardest step, because it goes against the general direction of shame, which is to punish yourself for being bad or wrong. For this step, it's fine if all you can do is to *not* do anything hurtful. That in itself is progress. However, the most helpful response is to do something *actively* loving for yourself in order to counteract shame's tendency toward contraction (shutting down), punishment, and isolation.

To choose a self-loving action, ask yourself what you need right now. If you want extra help with this, refer to the chapter called "What's Your Bottom Line?" For some people, a self-loving action might mean taking the dog for a walk or sitting quietly under a tree. For others, it might entail a long soak in a bath, or perhaps an afternoon nap. For someone else, it might involve a couple hours under the hood of a car, tuning the engine.

Whatever works for you, do it! Even if you don't *feel* like doing something actively loving for yourself, do it anyway. If you need more ideas about disengaging your actions from your feelings, check out the chapter called "How to Be Seriously Silly." Humor can be a godsend when you feel ashamed. Again, remember to treat your shame the same way you'd treat quicksand. What you feel like doing is not necessarily the best way to get free of the muck.

In summary, here are the three steps for healing shame: (1) feel it without acting on it; (2) tell a trusted friend about it; and (3) do something actively loving for yourself. When you work with this plan, don't expect overnight results. Shame runs deep. It takes consistent, long-term patience to heal shame. You may never become completely comfortable with it, but you can learn how to be kind to yourself in the midst of it.

If you make a commitment to love your shame, hold fast to this intention: Don't make yourself wrong for anything you do in the process of healing shame. To do so would be redundant and cruel. Shame does not heal shame! Be gentle and slow in your work with shame, and learn as much as you can about it. Perhaps you'll discover that shame, too, can be one of your most valuable teachers.

Having compassion starts and ends with having compassion for all those unwanted parts of ourselves, all those imperfections that we don't even want to look at.

PEMA CHÖDRÖN

I was born a divine jewel long since filmed with dust. This morning, wiped clean, it mirrors streams and mountains without end.

IZUKACHI

FOUR PRINCIPLES OF
EFFECTIVE APOLOGY

*To get justice, we must strive
to undo the top dog/underdog
reversals that make human
horrors endure. There is no
point exacting vengeance now,
knowing that it will be the
cause for future vengeance by
the offspring of those we
punish. Vengeance leads only
to revenge.*

DESMOND TUTU

In the spring of 1990, the *Seattle Post Intelligencer* ran a short editorial called "East German Apology." The article said that East Germany's first freely elected parliament had issued a unanimous statement that admitted Germany's responsibility for the "racial madness" and nationalism that resulted in genocide and "immeasurable suffering" at the hands of the Nazi regime.

Further, the article quoted them as saying, "We feel sad and ashamed and acknowledge this burden of German history....We ask the Jews of the world to forgive us." They offered to give persecuted Jews asylum in their country, and they offered financial compensation to Nazi victims for material losses. Obviously, no compensation could ever make up for the pain and horror suffered by victims of the holocaust. However, East Germany's apology provided a powerful move toward healing for both sides.

East Germany's statement was an example of an effective apology because it honored these four main principles: (1) it acknowledged the nature and extent of the victims' suffering; (2) it took 100% responsibility for causing the suffering; (3) it asked for forgiveness without expectation or demand; and (4) it offered to make amends and followed through on this commitment.

East Germany's apology was powerful because it was *clean*. There was no attempt to dodge responsibility, no attempt to discount or deny the victims' pain, no attempt to exact a response to its request for forgiveness, and no attempt to avoid the necessary step of restitution.

An apology such as this is good inspiration for everyday life. Whether a transgression is minor or extreme, the healing power of apology can be far-reaching and profound for both sides. Let me give a smaller-scale example by telling the story of a former client, Madeleine (not her real name). Madeleine survived a tumultuous childhood that was characterized by long-term physical, emotional, and sexual abuse. To her credit, she overcame these difficult beginnings and went on to become a professional painter, who enjoyed a happy marriage and a wonderful daughter. By the time I met Madeleine, her daughter (whom I will call Rachel) was ten.

One day, Madeleine came into my counseling office full of shame because she had hit her daughter. She said they were riding in a car together when Rachel started getting very vocal about something, including whining and actively taunting her mother while she was trying to drive. Madeleine doesn't expect her daughter to be sedate, so she let it go for a while.

Eventually, Madeleine had trouble concentrating on the road, so she asked Rachel to stop bothering her while she was driving. However, Rachel kept up her animated behavior despite her mother's repeated requests to stop. Finally, in a moment of total frustration, Madeleine got angry and slapped her daughter across the face.

As I watched Madeleine tell this story, I could see that she already realized the seriousness of her abusive behavior, so I simply asked her to tell me what happened next. She said that Rachel got very quiet, in obvious shock that her mother had hit her. Madeleine apologized immediately, and she told Rachel that no matter what Rachel had done, the slap was not okay.

After apologizing, Madeleine listened to her daughter express her anger and hurt, and she validated these feelings. When Rachel was done, Madeleine again expressed her remorse, and she asked for her daughter's forgiveness. Without dodging responsibility, Madeleine then explained to Rachel how she felt frustrated and disrespected by Rachel's refusal to honor her (Madeleine's) request for a calmer ride. Ultimately, the conflict between them had endangered their safety in the car. Even still, Madeleine made it quite clear that no matter what was going on for her, she was still out of line for slapping Rachel.

When Madeleine was finished telling me what happened, I gave her a lot of support for apologizing, for listening to her daughter's feelings, and for taking 100% responsibility for the abuse. Next, we brainstormed ideas for the future, in case a similar situation arose again. For example, Madeleine decided that she could find a place to pull over and stop the car, if she needed to sort something out with Rachel.

As a final step in her apology, Madeleine offered to make amends for mistreating her daughter. Immediately after the incident, Madeleine asked Rachel if there was anything she could do to make it up to her. Rachel asked for a special date with her mother later in the week. Madeleine readily agreed, realizing that Rachel's distracting behavior was at least partly due to a need for more attention.

When we teach children to suppress their feelings and not to cry, we do them a great disservice by robbing them of nature's adaptive responses to emotional stress.

WILLIAM FREY

A depressing and difficult passage has prefaced every new page I have turned in life.

CHARLOTTE BRONTË

*One does not become
enlightened by imaging figures
of light, but by making the
darkness conscious.*

CARL JUNG

*The worst sin toward our
fellow creatures is not to hate
them, but to be indifferent
toward them; that's the essence
of inhumanity.*

GEORGE BERNARD SHAW

The second part of Madeleine's amends came later, when she asked for my ongoing help to go deeper in unraveling the roots of her own abusive behavior. This amend would benefit Madeleine as well as her daughter, because it would help Madeleine integrate the pain of her own past, while also increasing her ability to act more responsibly in the future.

Thus, Madeleine's apology illustrated the four basic principles of an effective apology: (1) she acknowledged and validated her daughter's suffering; (2) she took full responsibility for causing it; (3) she asked forgiveness without expecting an answer; and (4) she followed through on her offer to make amends.

Madeleine's story shows how a sincere apology can ease the painful aftermath of an abusive situation. In addition to the short-term benefits of an apology, its ripple effects can continue to support both parties long after the incident itself has faded into memory. For Madeleine and Rachel, the ripple effect contributed many gifts of healing for each of them.

First, by taking responsibility for hitting her daughter, Madeleine admitted that her behavior was not appropriate. Had she said nothing, it's possible that Madeleine's remorseful feelings about her *actions* might have degenerated into shameful feelings about *herself*. This is significant in the long run, because it's easier to change your behavior than it is to change your personhood (see "How to Love Your Shame" for more information about how to heal the detrimental effects of shame).

Another ripple of healing occurred when Madeleine told another person (me) about the slap. By talking with me about the shame, she defused one of the main rules of dysfunctional families, namely, "Don't talk about the family outside the family." Also, since I gave Madeleine a lot of support for the way she cleaned up her act after hitting Rachel, she was able to put her misbehavior into perspective. Madeleine saw that while I didn't excuse the abuse, neither did I shame her for it. She made a bad mistake, but she certainly wasn't a bad person.

Of course, I knew that if I could help Madeleine feel better about herself, this would indirectly help Rachel, too. However, there are specific ways that Madeleine's apology helped Rachel quite directly. First of all, if Madeleine had slapped Rachel and then ignored her, or if she had told Rachel to shut up rather than express her indignation, it's likely that Rachel would have internalized her pain. Although it's impossible to tell if, when, or how this internalized pain might affect Rachel in the long run, I know it was definitely better in the short run for Rachel to process her feelings immediately after being hit. This is comparable to cleaning a wound right after it happens, as opposed to waiting until it gets infected.

Last of all, Madeleine's immediate cleanup actions prevented Rachel from internalizing shame along with her other emotional distress. If someone who loves you suddenly hauls off and hits you, you (as the child) might conclude that you must be *bad*. Why else would your mother hurt you? This is often the only way children can make sense of abuse. In contrast, if a parent admits fault and apologizes, the child is vindicated. Shame gets derailed because the child sees that the parent is responsible for the abuse, not her.

Thus, the story of Madeleine and Rachel demonstrates the lasting benefits of an effective apology. Even though these benefits help the perpetrator as much as the victim, many people are still reluctant to apologize when they cause pain. They seem to think that apologizing is the same as groveling. Nothing could be further from the truth.

Apology is about *taking responsibility*, which is the most powerful thing you can do. Apology is powerful because it takes guts to admit your mistake. In addition, apology is powerful because it puts you in a position to *do something* to ameliorate the harmful consequences of your mistake. Apology is proactive; therefore, it's a sign of strength, not weakness.

If you still resist the idea of admitting that you make mistakes, take this simple test: Are you human? Well then, you make mistakes. Everyone does. The question is: What do you want to do about your mistakes? Do you want to learn from them and take responsibility for them—or do you want to leave a mass of hurt feelings and damaged relationships in your wake?

If you practice the four principles of effective apology, you may soon discover that it actually feels good to admit your mistakes. What a relief to stop expecting yourself to be perfect! Look at it this way. If East Germany can apologize for one of the worst holocausts the world has ever seen, then perhaps each of us can apologize for our comparatively minor transgressions along the way.

Parents are of course not only persecutors. But it is important to know that in many cases they play this role as well, and very often without even being aware of it.

ALICE MILLER

Be assured that if you knew all, you would pardon all.

THOMAS À KEMPIS

THE DILEMMA OF
FORGIVENESS

For most people, forgiveness is a loaded topic. The word may evoke feelings of gratitude or guilt, freedom or fear, rapture or revulsion. Whatever you associate with forgiveness, I encourage you to bring your experiences to the table now. Explore your beliefs. Question them. See if they still fit for you. Most importantly, insert the possibility of *choice* into your consideration of forgiveness.

Obviously, it's impossible to be *at choice* about forgiveness unless you are free to forgive or *not* to forgive. I cherish the concept of forgiveness, and I value its impact on my spiritual development. However, I am ruthlessly compassionate when it comes to supporting everyone's right to find their own way. I don't care if every person on the planet—except one—thinks forgiveness is necessary for true healing. If that person needs to find another way, then his or her path must be equally respected.

It's not my intention to deny the power of forgiveness or to discredit those who uphold forgiveness as the ultimate goal of healing. Instead, I want to question the *tyranny* of forgiveness: the notion that anything less than total forgiveness is spiritually unevolved or morally bereft. From my perspective, it's not fair to shame people for not forgiving. How can anyone judge another person's healing? It's even conceivable that someone might need to experience a lifetime of *not* forgiving in order to learn about that. Who can say?

According to *Webster's*, forgiveness is the act of ceasing to feel resentment against an offender. Some people, for whatever reason, may never be willing or able to forgive their offenders. Does this mean they can't heal? No. In *Double Duty*, Claudia Black writes about forgiveness using the example of sexual abuse:

> *...seeking to forgive your offender is not a necessary part of your recovery. Focus on your life—not what you believe you should or should not feel about your*

There is only one good definition of God: the freedom that allows other freedoms to exist.

JOHN FOWLES

abuser....Clearly, an important goal in recovery is to have your anger with the offender no longer interfere with how you care about yourself or how you live your life. But it is unrealistic to expect yourself never to be angry again with the offender for the molestation. Some people get confused about forgiveness, particularly when they realize that their parents were also abused as children. Although that information is helpful, and can put your family experience in perspective, it does not erase the violations you experienced.

In my work as a counselor, I've noticed that some people want to jump into forgiveness long before they truly face and feel the full impact of their own wounding. As Claudia Black says, it's valuable to have compassion for those who hurt you, but this can get tricky if you're trying to work through your own pain at the same time.

Although forgiveness can be a beautiful act of grace, it can sometimes contribute to denial. Instant forgiveness—without the necessary emotional work—may be a convenient way to sidestep uncomfortable feelings. Also, when forgiveness is touted as the supreme goal of healing, people may be quick to forgive in order to prove to themselves (or others) that they are morally advanced. However, true forgiveness is not about seeking approval or avoiding pain.

Before I continue with more about forgiveness, let me restate my definition of abuse from the chapter called "The Anger Primer." **Abuse occurs when someone uses another person to meet a need in a way that harms, coerces, or devalues the other person.** Obviously, we all use each other to get our needs met, but this should be a mutually respectful experience.

No doubt there are a million gradations and subtleties of abuse. I don't offer a broad definition of this word so people can constantly accuse each other of being abusive. Instead, I purposely equate *abuse* with *disrespect* so that people will take respect very seriously. Hopefully, if people realize that disrespectful behavior is at some level abusive, they will work harder to be mindful of the effects of their actions.

To provide a lens of focus for a discussion about abuse and forgiveness, this chapter explores the issue of emotional healing in relation to parents. Of course, you can apply the same principles of healing to other people in your life. However, most people's individuation work includes an examination of childhood

We may not assume that a conventional mother produces a freaky child, any more than that a freaky child produces a conventional mother—or that a wild and woolly mother produces a normal child. The two generations cannot be tied together by a neat knot.

JAMES HILLMAN

relationships with parents or primary caregivers. Therefore, "The Dilemma of Forgiveness" concentrates on these formative relationships. Since there are strong taboos against holding parents accountable for the way they treat their children, please be forewarned that this chapter may stimulate powerful feelings for you. You may even get angry at me for stirring things up!

If you decide to work through childhood pain—assuming you had any—you may need to grapple with your caretakers' accountability for their actions toward you. This may seem obvious, but accountability is not the norm in many cultures, including ours. Parents are often accorded the right to treat their children in any way they choose. As a result, people are often reluctant to interfere with anyone else's parenting, even in cases of abuse. In many cultures, children are still regarded as chattel (property).

Unfortunately, many social and religious groups still uphold the taboo of questioning parents' treatment of children. Because of this, there is precious little support for you to examine your parents' methods of raising you without risking social, familial, or religious judgment. However, if you can't explore the truth of your own past—and thereby confront whatever pain you experienced—you may unconsciously repeat hurtful patterns of behavior that you learned early in childhood. On the other hand, if you can face—and find compassion for—the roots of your own hurt, it's less likely that you will repeat the cycle of abuse.

You may notice that I did *not* say that forgiveness is the only way to stop repeating patterns from the past. Forgiveness can help, but again, it's not necessarily the only way to heal. Whether or not you seek and find forgiveness, it's essential to make peace with your own woundedness, because compassion for your own pain will increase your ability to be compassionate with others. Let me illustrate this with a story.

Years ago, I read an article about a couple who gave birth to a baby boy who was neurologically incapable of experiencing pain. The parents struggled to keep their son safe, because he literally could not tell when he was hurt. A few years after his birth, the couple wanted to get pregnant again, but they were concerned about having another child with the same disability.

Despite the odds against it, the couple gave birth to a second child with the same neurological disorder. At that point, they had the incredible task of attending to the safety of each child individually, as well as keeping the children safe from each other. Because the children were unable to feel their own pain, they had no sensitivity to the pain of others. Although a pain-sensitive person could stay safe with such a child, the two siblings could not be left alone with each other, because they were both unable to tell when their actions had caused injury.

This story has haunted me since I first read it. I don't know what happened to that family. I do know that their tragedy illustrates the fact that people can't be sensitive to the pain of others unless they are able to feel their own pain. As much as people complain about pain, it's very helpful. Neurologically, the ability to feel pain allows you to keep your own body safe, and it enables you to understand (by extension) that others feel pain, too. Whether pain is physical or emotional, your capacity to feel it allows you to be considerate of your own needs, as well as the needs of others.

When I encourage you to confront the pain of past wounding, I'm not advocating revenge on your parents or on anyone else who may have hurt you. Of course, the *desire* for revenge might be present in your rage about past abuse, so it's important to find safe ways to express this rage (see "The Anger Primer" for help). However, *hurting back* simply repeats the cycle of abuse. In other words, the cycle of abuse will continue until you take responsibility for *healing* your pain, instead of *inflicting* more pain on yourself or others.

Accountability is better than revenge. The beauty of accountability is that it places responsibility for hurtful behavior squarely on the shoulders of the person who is being hurtful. In addition, accountability allows those who have been hurt to process their feelings without the added burden of thinking they somehow caused their own pain. For more about how accountability can help both sides of an abusive situation, please refer to the chapter "Four Principles of Effective Apology."

People who hurt others can also hold their own abusers accountable. Generally speaking, people who have a pattern of hurting others were often themselves abused. The point is, accountability says *the buck stops here*: I'm responsible for my actions and you're responsible for yours, regardless of the past.

In addition to holding people accountable for their actions, accountability means that people are responsible for confronting and healing their own pain. For instance, if a person has sustained abuse from parents or other people, it's still up to that individual to do his or her own emotional work, whether or not the abuser ever does any work.

The promise of accountability is that it takes only one person to stop the cycle of abuse. As a survivor of abuse, I can't necessarily do anything about my abusers' past or present behavior, but I can

Blaming mother is just a negative way of clinging to her still.

NANCY FRIDAY

What I'm trying to say is that, if a kid is having trouble or is discouraged, the problem is not just inside the kid; it's also in the system, the society.

JAMES HILLMAN

refuse to be treated disrespectfully now. In addition, I can work on my own patterns, so that I don't act hurtfully toward myself or others now. This work often depends on my ability to seek out the roots of my pain, even if this means questioning my own upbringing.

For a few minutes now, take some time to consider the level of respect in your family of origin. For example, were you allowed to speak up when you didn't like the way your parents treated you? Were you encouraged to have personal boundaries in relation to your parents? Is the very thought of you having boundaries (in relation to your parents) a ridiculous idea to you? If so, why? Were you allowed to *talk back?* Did your parents say they were doing things *for your own good,* as a justification for forcing you to do things against your will? Were you allowed to question them about this?

Were you taught how to express anger—even toward your parents—in ways that were appropriate to your age level of responsibility? Does the idea of showing anger toward your parents bring up feelings of terror, guilt, or disgust? When you were hurt by your parents' actions, did they respond compassionately, or did they say you *had it coming?* Did your parents take responsibility for their part in your hurt? Did they ever apologize? Most importantly, *were you treated in ways your parents would never allow you to treat them?*

I don't ask these questions so you can berate your parents, or so you can feel guilty about how you are raising children, if you are a parent yourself. Instead, I ask these questions to stimulate memories of your own childhood, and to introduce a framework for healing that gets the focus off forgiveness and onto your feelings.

If you were not beaten, raped, molested, or maimed, it doesn't mean you weren't mistreated. The bottom line is this: Abuse happened every time you were discounted or disrespected. If you doubt the profound and cumulative effects of such discounting, I encourage you to read more about the idea of *soul murder* in the books of Alice Miller (see bibliography).

Disrespect breeds disrespect. Even if you seem to treat others well, you may still be perpetuating the cycle of abuse if you treat *yourself* disrespectfully. Whether you turn the abuse inward or outward, however, the solution is the same: Face, feel, and heal your own pain. There are a million ways to do this, including shortcuts and quick-fix approaches. Though shortcuts have never helped me in the long run, everyone's needs are different. Find what works for you.

If there is anything that we wish to change in the child, we should first examine it and see whether it is not something that could better be changed in ourselves.

CARL JUNG

With all this talk of abuse, I want to make it clear that I'm not being radical with the word *abuse* so that people can bitch and moan about their pain all the time. Neither am I talking about abuse in these broad terms so you can track down everyone who has ever slighted you and demand restitution. Not hardly. Instead, I'm asking pointed questions about abuse for the simple reason I've stated many times before. That is, I'm encouraging you to face and feel your own pain. This is not about wallowing and it's not about masochism. It's about the fact that those who are compassionate about pain are less likely to inflict it.

At this point, I want to share another idea that shaped my concept of forgiveness. In 1985, a fellow counselor made the following statement to a support group: "Forgiveness is the natural result of feeling all your feelings." This means that if you reach a point where there is no more emotional charge about a previously painful situation, you might call that state *forgiveness*. However, your job is to stay focused on your feelings and let the end result take care of itself.

Feelings and forgiveness are like sex-play and orgasm. If you focus on achieving orgasm, you won't have nearly as much fun in bed. On the other hand, if you focus on your experience in the moment, feeling every sensation and emotion as they arise and move and dissipate, you'll not only have more pleasure, but you'll probably forget about the orgasm altogether. Ironically, this is one of the best ways to ensure good orgasms: by not focusing on them. If you make love like this, orgasms will arise as a natural result of feeling all your feelings. Doesn't that sound exactly like what that counselor said about forgiveness?

Granted, it's not as much fun to work through painful feelings as it is to have sex. However, the principle is the same: Feel all your feelings and let the end results take care of themselves. Frankly, I doubt if you can actually *cease to feel resentment against an offender* (as the definition of forgiveness says) unless you *feel* that resentment first. Paying lip-service to forgiveness is not the same as doing the hard work that allows forgiveness to arise naturally from the ashes of your pain.

Around the same time that counselor made her statement about feelings and forgiveness, I spoke about these subjects with a minister friend of mine, whom I will call Richard. One day while we were walking in Seattle's Ravenna Park, I posed my dilemma to him: "Everybody talks about forgiveness and says I have to do it, but nobody tells me how!"

Loving parents in particular should want to find out what they are unconsciously doing to their children. If they simply avoid the subject and instead point to their parental love, then they are not really concerned about their children's well-being but rather are painstakingly trying to keep a clear conscience.

ALICE MILLER

Without sex there would be no history.

PETER COYOTE

If an author's best source is an unhappy childhood, perhaps a future best seller will come out of the pain, thus helping others and providing financial success. We can only decide what to do with our pain. That is our only option.

BERNIE SIEGEL

Richard laughed, then he gently explained that forgiveness was not mine to do. He said that forgiveness lies in the realm of miracle, and all I can do is identify the issues in my life that need forgiveness. After that, Richard said I would have to turn the matter over to something bigger than myself.

Richard's words struck a note of resonance in me. I knew I could identify the situations in my life that needed forgiveness, and I liked the idea of surrendering the actual act of forgiveness. This released a lot of my guilt about not being able to do forgiveness *good enough* or *fast enough*. Overall, it was liberating for me to realize that forgiveness comes through prayer and grace, not from an imposition of will.

All these ideas about forgiveness were put to the test in my own life when I started having memories of childhood sexual abuse. Beginning in 1989, when I was 35, these memories began to surface gradually in all kinds of different situations, over many years' time. The fact that these memories came up uninvited, after more than two decades of work on myself, only added to my shock. Prior to this, I thought I knew everything there was to know about my past. I was wrong.

Before I say more about my own story, I'd like to briefly address the controversy that surrounds the subject of repressed memory. This includes the issues of whether or not people can forget and then retrieve memories of past trauma, whether such memories can be manipulated or manufactured, and whether unscrupulous or deluded therapists *plant* these memories in the minds of their unsuspecting clients.

Obviously, the intricacies of this controversy are beyond the scope of this chapter. However, I want to at least mention the issue of repressed memory, because it complicates the already confusing issue of forgiveness. If you don't know what's true, if you unexpectedly retrieve "new" information about your past, or if you discover that your therapist is messing with your mind, the scope of your forgiveness work may turn out to be much bigger than anticipated. Also, if you falsely accuse someone, or conversely, if you deny the truth of your own body, you may struggle with forgiving *yourself*. Thus, the question of repressed memory does indeed complicate matters.

After witnessing and participating in various aspects of this controversy for years, including honest consideration of all positions and their ramifications, I've come to the conclusion that the truth resides somewhere in the middle. I don't believe it's a black or white matter, with one side right and the other wrong. Everyone holds a piece of the truth.

There is no question that people can repress memories of trauma. For example, most American men who suffered the cruelty of infant circumcision without anesthesia don't remember this surgery later in life. However, I'd argue passionately—with plenty of backup research—that involuntary genital cutting has a deleterious effect on the male psyche, not to mention its harm to the body and to normal sexual functioning. If you doubt my words, I encourage you to openheartedly seek out reliable medical information and documented research (see bibliography for Billy R. Boyd's *Circumcision Exposed: Rethinking a Medical Cultural Tradition*).

Eventually, people in America will come to abhor involuntary male circumcision as much as they abhor involuntary female circumcision. At that point, in the name of equal rights for both sexes, *all* involuntary circumcision will be forever banned. Personally, I have no idea how our country can justify such brutal treatment of baby boys, given our penchant for human rights. As it is, the healing work of grief, rage, fear, and forgiveness must continue at personal, familial, societal, and spiritual levels for those who understand the profound and far-reaching effects of involuntary circumcision.

If you want an example of repressed memory beyond infant abuse, consider Post Traumatic Stress Disorder, which can happen to people of any age who experience war horrors or other extremely traumatic situations. PTSD has many forms and symptoms, some of which can be completely debilitating. Memory loss is common, though it is sometimes followed (perhaps even years later) by a reexperiencing of the traumatic events.

The point is, human brains are geared for survival. Sometimes survival requires temporary or permanent loss of memory, especially in cases where people experience more physical or emotional pain than they can bear. In *Vital Lies, Simple Truths*, Daniel Goleman writes eloquently about the biological value of this powerful phenomenon, which may be called denial or amnesia, depending on the context.

On the flip side of the repressed memory controversy are those who say it's all a bunch of bunk. In this camp are the people who believe recovered memories are the work of manipulative therapists or drama-addicted offspring who are hell-bent on blaming innocent parents. As you can tell from the tone of that last sentence, my biases tend toward the other direction. However, I do believe there

Fear, pain, crippling, disfigurement and humiliation are the classic ways to break the human spirit. Circumcision includes them all.

A CIRCUMCISION VICTIM
THE JOY OF UNCIRCUMCISING
BY JIM BIGELOW

Denial doesn't work. It can never lead to forgiveness and reconciliation. Amnesia is no solution.

DESMOND TUTU

I think one should forgive and remember....If you forgive and forget in the usual sense, you're just driving what you remember into the subconscious; it stays there and festers. But to look, even regularly, upon what you remember and know you've forgiven is achievement.

FAITH BALDWIN

are unethical therapists who wreak havoc with the lives of their clients, and I believe there are people who *make up* their memories, however consciously or unconsciously. Truly, I deplore the actions of such therapists, and I grieve for the families that have been ripped apart by false accusations.

Since I started counseling people in 1981, I have witnessed the unexpected recovery of childhood abuse memories in many clients. In all honesty, I would say that in each case, these people neither sought nor welcomed the intrusion of traumatic memories from the past. In other words, no one I know wants to be a survivor of abuse. In fact, most of these people (including me) resorted at one time or another to drugs, alcohol, eating disorders, insanity, or other forms of addiction or illness, in order to retreat from the reemergence of traumatic memories.

Eventually, if healing is to occur, the addictions and illnesses must begin to shift. In my own case, thirty years of denial gave way once I had enough tools, safety, and support to work with the memories in a gentle and compassionate way. For example, certain people came into my life who were knowledgeable about sexual abuse, so they were able to extend wisdom and encouragement and to help me in my recovery work.

In addition, I think my memories waited to reemerge until I had ceased to require forgiveness as a prerequisite for healing. More specifically, I'd finally gathered enough courage to disobey the family rule that admonished me to always *forgive and forget*, with the emphasis on *forget*. As long as I was afraid to challenge this injunction, I needed to stay in denial. My denial was effective, too. After all, if I couldn't remember anything, what was there to forgive?

Eventually, my body led me to the knowledge of childhood sexual abuse. When I trusted these body memories, they kept coming and were gradually joined by visual and auditory memories. On the other hand, when I doubted these memories or tried to deny that anything happened, the auditory and visual memories stopped coming. Of course, some people might take this as proof that I was manufacturing these memories.

However, when I tried to suppress the memories, my body symptoms would increase, resulting in more pain, physical distress, and illness. Gradually, I realized that the only way to keep going forward in my healing work was to go deeper into the fear, and deeper into the memories as they arose. Sometimes these memories would come for no apparent reason, while I was meditating or just sitting quietly. At other times, the smallest touch, a particular sexual act, or someone's tone of voice would trigger flashbacks.

Though this process was awkward and often crazy-making, each step into the pain led to greater awareness, stronger self-confidence, more creativity, and increased physical and emotional well-being. Clearly, the way for me to heal was to face and feel my own wounding. It was as if my body simply wanted to be *witnessed*. Through these efforts more than anything, I discovered firsthand that forgiveness is not a prerequisite for healing.

In the final analysis, I had to make a choice: I was either going to trust my body—or not. Because I spent most of my childhood and much of my adult life denying my body, it was no easy task for me to trust my body a little bit, much less completely. To this day, I struggle with the question of *what really happened*. I'm aware that memories can arise from many levels of existence, including collective (human) memory, cellular (body) memory, dream memory, and of course, memory of personal life events. Obviously, these multiple options make *knowing* a difficult challenge.

Those who wait vigilantly for the opportunity to pounce on yet another recovered memory adherent may relish my admissions of doubt as proof that I'm living a fantasy. If *pouncing* helps them feel safer in their position of total denial, then more power to them. All I know is that whenever I attempt to deny my body's experience, I get more debilitated. Thus, I choose to trust my body, so that I can move forward in my healing.

Returning to the subject of forgiveness, I have to say that during my years of sexual abuse recovery work, I had some profound experiences of forgiveness. However, these experiences were neither expected nor pursued. As my minister friend Richard had explained years before, I think my experiences of forgiveness happened through grace. For the most part, I was just busy feeling my feelings, and gradually my resentment toward my abusers faded. Sometimes, though, there were unexpected epiphanies of forgiveness, like the time I was in the middle of a tumultuous breath work session.

That time, I was breathing quietly when something unusual started happening. I began hyperventilating, and terror pulsed through my body as I suddenly reexperienced a past incident of sexual abuse. My helper sat supportively nearby as my body spasmed involuntarily and I cried out in fear. Since he knew that I was a veteran breath-coach myself, he didn't interfere.

At some point, I blacked out for a few moments. When I came back to consciousness, the room was flooded with bright light, and I *heard* new information that enabled me to understand why the abuse had happened. In that moment, I was overcome with compassion.

I know that
I know
Nothing,
And
In that unknowing,
The salvation of
Pure acceptance
Blossoms.
In ignorance
I find that
Which is empty.
I become the interior
Of the vessel—
Shatterless.

LINDA ROSS SWANSON

Forgiveness renders the relationship fluid again, allowing you to see other aspects of that person. And you, too, are freed to exist more fully, not frozen into one posture.

MARC IAN BARASCH

Only the brave know how to forgive. A coward never forgives. It is not his nature.

ABIGAIL VAN BUREN

Later, I asked my helper if there had been some sudden change in the light. He said *no*. The fact that this experience happened to me—someone who was not actively seeking forgiveness—made it all the more remarkable.

Although this and other gifts of forgiveness were beautiful and transformative, I must be fair to those who may never have—or even want—such experiences. The truth is, these situations did not bring an end to my healing work. Some people might say that my experiences of forgiveness weren't real if I felt any subsequent pain or anger about my abuse. I disagree.

Claudia Black's words, mentioned earlier in this chapter, provide a more enlightened way to look at the issues of forgiveness and abuse. Neither pain nor healing is a linear process. It's normal for people to go in and out of various emotions—and various stages of recovery—as their journey unfolds. In my own case, I used to focus on *getting done* with my emotional work. Every time I thought I was done, however, another layer would present itself. As long as I'm alive, I'll probably have more work to do. Perhaps this is true for everyone.

If forgiveness flows from the realm of grace, then the road to healing may simply lie in facing, feeling, and integrating your own wounding. If you can come to terms with your pain, it will deepen your compassion for the pain of others. This compassion, in turn, will naturally lead in the direction of forgiveness. You can trust your heart to lead the way.

THE RESOLUTION PRAYER

In the late 1980s, I was given a one-sentence prayer in my meditations. After watching it transform my life for several months, I began sharing it with friends and clients to see if it had value for them. The reports were consistently impressive, ranging from amazement to overwhelm. This simple prayer seems to stimulate clearing at many levels. Before I say more, let me give you the prayer:

> *Anything unresolved in my life now resolves itself gently, easily, and completely, for the good of all.*

The purpose of this prayer is to get your conscious mind out of the way. In other words, it's not your job to figure out what needs to be resolved. Leave that up to Big Mind, or whatever you call the unifying force of the universe. Whatever you call this force, the Resolution Prayer presupposes that it exists, and that you can take advantage of this larger source of knowing by invoking it through the power of prayer.

By the way, the idea of Big Mind doesn't necessarily have anything to do with the concept of God. It's quite possible to be an atheist and still take advantage of Big Mind. One of my favorite shamans is an atheist, and he's one of the most spiritual people I know. Also, if you object to the word *prayer*, you can still use the Resolution Prayer or any other prayer. Just substitute another word for prayer. For instance, certain cultures believe that prayers are simply your thoughts.

Incidentally, if you don't understand how prayer works, you can still use it. You don't need to understand electricity in order to turn on a light, and you don't have to understand physics to drive a car. Likewise, you can harness the power of focused thought even if you don't understand the mysterious forces behind it. Personally, I don't have a clue how prayer works, but that doesn't stop me from using it.

I think that the human mind is not necessarily the biggest thing in the universe.
MICHAEL HARNER

If you are sure you understand everything that is going on, you are hopelessly confused.
WALTER MONDALE

One way to invoke Big Mind through prayer is simply to hold an intention in your heart. Specifically, in the first part of the Resolution Prayer, the point is to let Big Mind decide what your next layer of healing should be. That's what it means to request that *anything unresolved in your life now resolves itself.* This is a trick to get the little mind, or ego, out of the way. Essentially, you're asking that your unresolved issues clean themselves up, without any effort on your part.

Sometimes this will actually happen through a process called grace. That is, some of your old patterns may dissipate merely because you've expressed a willingness for them to do so. More often, however, resolution work stimulates old patterns to replay themselves in present time. This gives you an opportunity to make new—and hopefully more conscious—choices about how to act. Rest assured that if one of your old patterns shows up again, it's because the issue is not yet resolved.

The next portion of the prayer is the *gently and easily* clause. This is a request that the resolution process be as undisruptive as possible. Believe me, it's not a good idea to do the Resolution Prayer without this kind of clause. If you skip the *gently and easily* request, your unresolved issues might rush into your life all at once. There's a lot to be said for taking the bull by the horns, but I recommend that you err on the side of sanity.

In the old days, I believed in the *no pain, no gain* theory, so I did metaphysical work without concern for gentleness. As a result, I spent a lot of time learning to duck and cover! At some point, I realized that my tendency to accelerate spiritual work was just another attempt to *control* my healing by speeding it up. It took me years to realize that if I went too fast, I'd only have to come back later and pick up the pieces.

One word of caution: Your idea of gentle and easy might not be the same as Big Mind's concept of it. If you don't think your results are gentle and easy, take a moment to consider how much more intense your situation could be. In other words, if you use this prayer, assume that whatever happens is as gentle and easy as possible, given everything and everyone involved.

The next part of the Resolution Prayer is the *completely* modifier. This word was added after months of regular use of the prayer, because I noticed that certain patterns were indeed *resolving* themselves, but they weren't *completing.* Adding this word to the request lets Big Mind know you want your unresolved issues to get finished, rather than remain in a perpetual state of resolving themselves. This was another lesson in being careful about what I ask for!

The final clause of the prayer, *for the good of all*, is in keeping with the standard metaphysical practice of aligning your personal benefit with the greater good. If you want to survive, much less prosper, it's wise to work with the flow of the universe instead of against it. You might be able to swim upstream for a while, but ultimately, your personal allotment of energy is no match for the great river of life.

Overall, the purpose of the Resolution Prayer is to ask Big Mind to do as much of the work as possible. Therefore, it's important to let Big Mind do the work. Avoid any tendency to get compulsive about the prayer. Don't write it a million times. Don't recite it endlessly like a mantra. Don't post it on little notecards and stick it up all over your house. Just say it out loud once a day. That's it.

Each small task of everyday life is part of the total harmony of the universe.

ST. THERESA OF LISIEUX

Saying the prayer out loud does two things. First, it makes a distinction between your clearly stated intention and all the other random thoughts running around in your head. Also, when you speak out loud, it sets up the vibration of sound, which adds power to your prayer. Sound is a form of energy, and its vibration can be used to break up old patterns. For example, many different languages utilize the transformative power of sound to alter thought patterns, alleviate physical distress, or induce higher states of consciousness.

After you say the Resolution Prayer out loud once a day, let it go. Turn over the work to something bigger than you, and see what happens. Pay attention to everything that comes into your life. Notice similarities between different situations. See if you can spot any themes. Do your best to stay aware, avoiding reactive and automatic responses. This may take some practice, because unresolved issues can stimulate physical or emotional pain. As a result, addictive habits may also intensify if you use the Resolution Prayer regularly. Try to ride the crest of your patterns, instead of letting yourself be pulled down by them.

When you see an old pattern manifesting, a simple approach is to *identify it, thank it*, and then *do something different*. This approach is more helpful than exclaiming hopelessly, "Oh, no! It's happening again!" Self-talk like that only reinforces the pattern in present time. By the way, if you think it's silly to thank a pattern that has wreaked havoc in your life, don't forget that it also helped you survive (see "Addictions as Teachers").

Whenever you encounter absurd rationalizations coupled with intense resistance, in yourself or in others, the next move may be a letting go of the position once held so intensely. The noise, the death rattle, is the last effort to maintain a failing point of view.

JENNIFER JAMES

Patterns often put on a big show before they die. It's like a death rattle. If you regard this death rattle as an indication that your patterns are returning with greater force, you'll be lost. On the other hand, if you keep your wits about you and remember that the intensity is just for dramatic effect, you can simply give your pattern a hearty round of applause as it goes by. Enjoy the parade!

The more unresolved issues you have, the less subtle your lessons are likely to be. I don't say this to scare you, but to warn you. Even still, it's important to realize that you have a choice about how to respond to your emotional patterns as they arise. If you approach situations with curiosity and humor, rather than judgment and blame, old patterns can resolve themselves more easily. Your own perceptions will play a big part in how gentle and easy your resolution work will feel to you.

A former breath coach of mine used to say that if you have a *charge* (intense emotional response) over three on a scale of ten, then your feelings are not *only* related to the present situation, but to a past event as well. Therefore, if the Resolution Prayer triggers a lot of powerful feelings for you, please be as responsible as possible. Remember that the people in your life now may have very little to do with your restimulated emotions. Find ways to honor and express your feelings, of course, but do it wisely, or you'll create more problems than you resolve.

At some point, your work with this prayer may take off, and the quantity or intensity of old patterns may leave you feeling overwhelmed, despite your request for gentleness. If this happens, you can always stop doing the prayer and take a rest. If you prefer to rise to the challenge by going deeper, don't forget that there's no prize for doing it alone. If you get stuck, an outside perspective can work wonders for morale. Don't be afraid to ask for help. As one of my mentors says, "You don't have to go into the deep, dark forest alone. Take a buddy!"

Thus, if the reappearance of old patterns begins to overwhelm your life, you might want to enlist the aid of a trusted friend or counselor. An objective observer can help you identify blind spots in your thinking that may be contributing to your overwhelm. On the other hand, if the general intensity of your healing lessons seems to be gradually decreasing, assume you're on the right track, and stay the course.

Ironically, there may be times when your lessons are becoming increasingly subtle, and you know you're on the right track, but then a real BLASTER knocks you for a loop. This doesn't necessarily mean you're regressing. Instead, it may simply mean that you're getting bigger challenges, if you've successfully resolved less difficult issues. Welcome to graduate school! Consider the occasional blaster as an invitation to test your skills. Plow into it with the same curiosity, humor, and mindfulness that you developed while working on smaller issues—and don't forget to give yourself a pat on the back for making good progress.

If you're wondering how you can tell when a particular pattern is done, here's the answer: It's over when it stops showing up in your life. Don't worry if a pattern takes many years to dissipate. After all, who knows how many years it's been building? Try not to judge yourself for your rate of healing. Whatever is presented to you is what needs your attention. That's all.

Healing is like housecleaning. If you want to clean house, every room will require your attention at one point or another. You can't very well keep all the closet doors closed, in hopes that the proverbial skeletons will never fall out. Besides, once you get the closets and everything else up to snuff, it will still take work to keep your house maintained. In my experience, small doses of regular housecleaning are usually easier than major overhauls. By analogy, when you use the Resolution Prayer to *clean house*, I recommend that you continue using it to keep your life clutter-free.

We can do no great things; we can do small things with great love.
MOTHER TERESA

After I used this prayer for about a year, I noticed that everything was running pretty smoothly in my life. I got a little cocky, thinking my old issues had resolved once and for all. After a short time, however, I discovered subtle manifestations of old patterns showing up again. I realized that my cockiness was premature, and I decided to keep using the prayer every day, just for the sake of maintenance. The point is, no matter how up-to-date you get, new situations are always presenting themselves. Resolution is a constant task.

Fortunately, the universe is a very patient teacher. It will keep giving you the same lesson over and over, in every form imaginable, until you get it. You don't have to worry about missing the chance to resolve a particular issue. Quite the contrary. You may wish the opportunities to clear up old patterns were not quite so endless!

She felt again that small shiver that occurred to her when events hinted at a destiny being played out, of unseen forces intervening.
DOROTHY GILLMAN

If you use the Resolution Prayer regularly, be respectful of its power. If it triggers more wildness than you want to face, it's okay to back off. Perhaps you could say the prayer once a week, rather than every day. Experiment with it until you find a rate of resolution that fits your comfort level. Keep it at a level where you feel challenged, yet safe. If you feel continually overwhelmed, upset, or just plain scared, you may be going too fast. Learn your own warning signs that show when you're pushing too hard, and honor your limits. The goal is compassion and growth, not intensity and speed. Gentle and easy begins with you.

Creativity's Gift:

Writing from

the Core

SECTION

THREE

THE MAGIC OF WRITING

Writing has been my first love since I was a little girl, so it's only natural that writing became one of my primary tools for healing. Writing is an intensely physical act. Hands and eyes and paper and ink dance together, as neural pathways bulge with electrical impulses. It's all so *physical*, and yet this physical act triggers my deepest feelings and touches my soul. Ultimately, writing activates all levels of existence: physical, mental, emotional, and spiritual. Is it any wonder that writing functions so exquisitely as a mode for healing?

For me, writing is ecstasy. It's in a class all by itself. Give me a pen, a yellow legal pad, and a chunk of time, and I'll lose myself in the sensuality of ink rolling onto paper. All those curves and loops and lines and angles tumbling out like acrobats across the page! When it's time to turn handwritten pages into clean, crisp copy, I head to my trusty old IBM Selectric II for the next phase. My fingers fly across the shiny black plastic keys, as I listen to the familiar clack and hum of my vintage 1970s mechanical workhorse.

Lots of people say I should switch to a computer. They say it would save time, but I don't care about speed. Writing is like good sex for me. I want the juiciest experience possible! Computers (like vibrators) are fun, and they get the job done, but they pale in comparison to the slow-hand approach.

Computer fans say that all their fancy software programs decrease the drudgery of editing one's own writing. But rewriting isn't drudgery for me. It's my passion! I go into an altered state when I attack a stack of typewritten copy with my ruthless blue Bic. Then, back at my Selectric again, I relish the physical act of retyping each word, phrase, sentence, and page until the whole thing hangs together.

Every time the words pass from my heart, through my hands, into the keys, and onto the paper, something very different happens from when I've done editing on a computer. I can't describe it except to say that it's like *laying track*, to borrow the words of another

Everywhere I go, I find a poet has been there before me.
SIGMUND FREUD

I think there is a world market for maybe five computers.
THOMAS WATSON
CHAIRMAN OF IBM, 1948

typewriter lover. This book was written and rewritten countless times, one track at a time, end to end, in a continuous flow. Most computer fans don't understand, but I wouldn't let anyone deprive me of this process for anything!

My passion for manual rewriting reminds me of a story Rich Haag once told me. Rich was a favorite mentor from my undergraduate days at the University of Washington in Seattle. After doing a few years of school elsewhere, I attended the U of W from 1974 to 1976. I went halfway through their Landscape Architecture program before deciding to switch majors. Rich was one of the professors in the program, and he was a special friend as well. As a landscape architect, Rich was a wizard. As an artist, he knew how to transform the bleakest landscape into a 3-D symphony of delights.

Since his design work was much in demand, Rich didn't have a lot of free time. One day, a group of his students took pity on his relentless schedule, and they planned a surprise for him. While Rich was at work, they weeded all the gardens at his farm outside of town, where he retreated every night. When he arrived home and saw what they'd done, he was dismayed. "What? You've taken away my *recreation!*" That was Rich. Sticking his hands in the fertile earth to pull weeds was an exercise of love for him. It wasn't drudgery; it was pure pleasure.

My labor-intensive style of rewriting turns me on, and my "purring tiger" typewriter *juices* me. If someone would design a computer with the gutsy touch of an old IBM, I might consider switching. Actually, I doubt if I'd switch even then, because computers suck my soul out and leave me exhausted within minutes (even with the best shielding I can buy).

In contrast, I get increasingly energized the longer I *ride* my faithful mechanical workhorse. One of my worst fears is that I won't be able to keep getting parts for these magnificent machines! In any case, I agree with Andre Dubus, another die-hard typewriter fan, who said, "People say you can write faster on a computer, but I don't want to write fast; I want to write deep."

Writing needn't be your first love in order for you to use it in your self-explorations. Also, it's perfectly fine to use computers if they make you happy. However, when you experiment with the exercises in this section, I recommend that you *always* write by hand, for reasons that will become clear as you read further in these chapters about creativity and healing. Overall, when you play with the suggestions offered here, follow the line of least resistance and see where it leads you. Feel free to improvise, and feel doubly free to invent new techniques that are just for you.

If you'd rather sing or dance or sculpt or draw, perhaps you can translate the suggestions in this section into these other modes of expression. The Five-Minute Free Write, for example, could become a five-minute dance or doodle. In other chapters, you might try singing your pain, sculpting your dreams, or making music to express your joy. Give your imagination free rein and have a good time. Creativity and healing make wonderful bedfellows. Let your passions flow!

Poetry is what comes up behind us and whispers the singing name of home in our ears.

JOHN CIARDI

Author's note for second edition, June 2008: It finally happened—I surrendered to the digital age and made the switch to computers. This change took place gently and gradually over a few years, as I used my typewriter less and less. and fell more and more in love with various upgrades of my Apple computer (I've always been a "Mac girl" since the first time I used one in 1985).

Eventually, I noticed I was never using my faithful Selectrics anymore, so I donated them to a couple of elderly ladies at the local retirement home, who were thrilled to have them. I'd owned four of those magnificent workhorses over three decades, but two of them died in service to the 15-year process of writing this book.

Despite the fact that I wrote this chapter before I made the switch, I decided to leave the original chapter intact for the sake of history. I'm sure many readers now and in the future won't have a clue what an IBM Selectric is, and they'll probably think I wrote this book sometime in the Dark Ages!

THE FIVE-MINUTE
FREE WRITE

Before I went into private practice as a counselor, I worked for a mental health agency in Seattle. Along with my other duties there, I facilitated a writing group for the clients, who were considered "seriously emotionally disturbed" adults.

Because I have manic-depression in my background, and because I have experienced psychiatric wards as a patient, I felt a special bond with my clients at the agency. To me, the words *seriously emotionally wounded* would have been a more compassionate and accurate way to describe these people, instead of calling them "disturbed."

Labeling someone *disturbed* is at best a judgment call, based on an inability to comprehend and appreciate the perspective of the person being labeled. In contrast, when people's ideas and behaviors are seen as valid within the context of their own lives, it's usually easier to find ways to support them without resorting to arbitrary—and therefore limiting—labeling. Let me tell you a personal story to illustrate what I mean.

In 1975 and 1976, I went in and out of being *crazy*—which I define as being unable to keep my act together in consensus reality. During that time, there was one friend who never stopped seeing *me* underneath all the wildness of my manic behavior. That man was Joe Rahn, whom I first introduced to you in the chapter called "How to Be Seriously Silly."

When I was with Joe, I not only didn't *feel* crazy, I actually acted more sane. In retrospect, I think this was largely due to the fact that Joe never saw me as crazy. It's not that he was in denial; it's just that he saw me as *wounded* rather than insane. As a result, he felt protective of me, but he didn't try to control me in order to alleviate his own concerns about my unusual behavior.

Most importantly, Joe was not *afraid* of me, and he never judged or labeled me. He took my words at face value, and he tried to help me get whatever I said I needed. He continued to assume that I knew what was best for me, even though everyone else thought I was nuts. Because he treated me with respect, I was able to treat myself with more respect.

Through Joe's love, I came to understand that there are better ways to deal with "crazy people" than to shoot them up with Thorazine and strap them to beds, which also happened to me. I vividly remember waking up in restraints, alone in my room on the psychiatric ward. I was terrified that I had done something awful to be treated that way. When a staff member finally came to release me, I asked what I had done to deserve restraints. She said that I'd been walking the halls the night before, unable to sleep. That was it!

To be fair, I realize that love—and the time it requires—are both in short supply on psychiatric wards. There is no question that the love of a true friend is not easily duplicated in a hospital setting. However, I still believe that it's possible to bring more respect and more *kindness* to the treatment of people, especially to those people who get caught under the wheels of a speed-addicted culture that runs roughshod over sensitive souls.

Ultimately, Joe's gift to me became my gift to others when I began working as a counselor several years later. It was as if I carried Joe around with me in my back pocket. Whenever I met a client who was walking a path similar to the one I'd walked long ago, Joe's fearless compassion welled up in my heart and joined my own growing capacity to be fearless in the face of other people's pain. I may never attain the effortless ease with which Joe extended this compassion to me, but nonetheless, his love remains a powerful beacon that lights my way.

With the clients at that agency in Seattle, Joe's kind understanding brightened the room every time I did a writing class, even though I never told anyone about him. The thing is, writing is an act of creativity, which means that it is an act of *love*. In addition, writing takes *time*. As I mentioned before, time and love often get the short end of the stick in our overamped world. Yet people—especially those who have been seriously wounded—need time and love in order to live and grow.

During my twice-a-week writing class at the clinic, I tried to give people a sense of *temporal* as well as *psychological* spaciousness. Labels fell away as I encouraged everyone to join me in another world—the world of creativity. With awe and delight, I watched quietly as so-called dysfunctional people came alive with the spirit of passion.

People who never uttered a word elsewhere would read long stories out loud, as if they'd been master storytellers all their lives. Adults who were considered "uncontrollable" wrote silently for long

Everyone has a talent. What is rare is the courage to follow the talent to the dark place where it leads.

ERICA JONG

You can't eat language but it eases thirst.

BERNARD MALAMUD

To live a creative life, we must lose our fear of being wrong.

JOSEPH CHILTON PEARCE

If you want to write the truth, you must write about yourself. I am the only real truth I know.

JEAN RHYS

We do not write in order to be understood; we write in order to understand.

C. DAY LEWIS

periods by themselves, then they listened with rapt attention while others shared their work. Clients who rarely cracked a smile or showed any enthusiasm would suddenly be transformed during group brainstorming sessions. They would grab pieces of colored chalk and take charge of the blackboard, laughing and cajoling others to contribute their ideas.

Through the vehicle of simple writing exercises, these exceptional people revealed the nature of their true selves. In between the lines of their anecdotes, they unwittingly disclosed their own stories under the guise of fictional characters. I learned more about my clients during our writing groups than I did in all the other therapeutic activities offered at the clinic.

Each of our writing classes began with a Five-Minute Free Write. This became so popular that people would complain if I forgot to include it. The Five-Minute Free Write is so easy that everyone could join in, knowing that whatever they wrote would always be good enough. Criticism was verboten, and people had permission to share their stories or to be private with them. Because of these ground rules, everyone felt safe to give their thoughts free rein.

Aside from the above guidelines for working in the context of a group, there is really only one rule for the Five-Minute Free Write. That is, once you start writing (by hand), you don't stop until the time is up. When my clients and I wrote together at the agency, I played the role of timekeeper so they could concentrate on writing. If you're working alone, you can set a timer or use a clock. Personally, I prefer a timer when I'm alone, since it allows me to write without stopping to check the time.

When you start a free write, don't worry about punctuation, capitalization, spelling, dangling participles, or any other rules of grammar. In fact, you can even turn your writing into one big run-on sentence. To do this, start with a capital letter at the beginning, write without punctuation, and then complete your five-minute "brain purge" with a period at the end, when the buzzer goes off.

If no words come when you sit down to begin, you can simply write "nothing nothing nothing" or "bongo bongo bongo" until you think of something else. If nothing coherent occurs to you, don't be coherent! Write down whatever weird or wonderful thoughts pass through your mind. Don't censor anything. Remember, your free write is for *you*, and you don't have to let anyone else see it. If you must promise yourself that you will destroy your work immediately after you're done, then make yourself that promise, if it will help you tell the truth.

Do whatever it takes to create safety for yourself. If you want to write for ten minutes instead of five, go ahead and write for ten minutes. If you want unlimited time for your free write, then give yourself all the time in the world. This exercise is designed to satisfy the little kid inside of you. Some kids need lots of encouragement to come out and play. Let your free write be playful!

My friend Peg Price taught me to take care of my inner child *first*, before trying to do anything on an adult level. She said that even if I'm on a tight schedule, it's still good to give my inner kid some *playtime* before I start the work.

You know how impossible it is to get anything done if you have a two-year-old on your hands who is hungry and needs to eat *right now?* Children are much more likely to cooperate with adults if their kid-needs have been met. In the same way, your inner kid shouldn't always be expected to defer to grown-up rules about delayed gratification. Sometimes, perhaps. But always? No.

Many of us grew up with the Puritan ethic that says: *No play until the work is done.* Have you ever noticed how there's always more work to do, so playtime never comes? If you keep this up for years, it's likely that your inner kid might get a little ornery, rebellious, or downright depressed. Free writing is one way to satisfy the child part of you *first,* before you attend to other tasks.

For those of you who can't relate to an inner-kid analogy, here's another way to look at the Five-Minute Free Write. I love to swim, not only because it makes my body feel great, but because it puts me into a meditative state. When I swim 40 or 50 laps in a big pool, the first few laps are always the hardest. I often feel inept or out of synch at the beginning, as if I don't even know how to swim. Once I hit my stride, though, I feel as if I could swim forever.

Five-Minute Free Writes are like the first few laps of a long swim. Your writing might feel jerky or smooth initially, but the only way to *go the distance* with your writing is to get through those first few awkward minutes of warm-up. It doesn't matter if you're doing a free write for its own sake or as a prelude to bigger things. The first few words, sentences, or paragraphs of any writing task will often feel the hardest. This is typical. Don't let it throw you.

When I'm faced with a blank piece of paper, it's the same as when I'm faced with a cold swimming pool (and pools are *always* colder than my body). I know I'll feel good once I get going, but how do I shift from my comfy place of inactivity to a flow of water— or words? Here's the best way I've found to get through that moment of resistance: *Dive in!*

Writing is like taking off your clothes in a crowded room and turning around slowly—twice.

JANICE LEVY

A writer is someone for whom writing is more difficult than it is for most people.

THOMAS MANN

LISTENING TO PAIN

Very frankly, I hope there is a special place in hell for people who tell little children that if they would only be good enough, their sickness would be cured.

HAROLD KUSHNER

Your health issues are not an "F" on your spiritual report card.

STEVEN M. HALL

Most people would prefer to run from pain rather than listen to it. If you've found your way to this chapter, I bet you're one of the few who would rather listen than run. Perhaps you've learned the hard way that avoidance doesn't always work. Maybe you've tried everything possible to numb the pain, only to discover that this diminished your capacity to feel anything at all.

On the flip side, you may have been so bombarded by pain that it overwhelmed you to the point of despair. Even if you wanted to shut it off, you couldn't, so now you're highly motivated to find a new approach. Whatever your situation, I commend you for your courage, because it takes great courage to explore pain.

Before I go any further, let me acknowledge the value of painkillers, herbal analgesics, and other forms of palliative medicine. Don't be too hard on yourself if you need help with pain. Everyone has their breaking point—and you don't have to be anywhere near yours before you seek external assistance.

This chapter is about *listening* to pain, not making yourself a hostage to it. There's no need to turn your explorations into an either/or dilemma. Give yourself permission to feel your painful symptoms as much as you can, and to alternate this work with breaks from the pain. You can go back and forth between *feeling* and *numbing*, learning more about each part of the process as you go. Both sides of the dance have value. Discover for yourself what each side has to offer, and learn your own signals about when you need a break from pain.

The first step in listening to pain is to realize that pain does *not* mean that you've been bad, nor does it mean that you're being punished. This kind of punitive thinking will get you nowhere fast. If you blame yourself for having pain, you'll only heap emotional pain on top of your other pain. This is not only redundant, it's counterproductive, like fighting fire with fire.

As an alternative, consider the idea that your pain wants to teach you something. The message could be as mundane as "Don't stick your finger in the socket!" Or it could be something more esoteric and complex. Whatever the case, would you relate to pain differently if you imagined it as a teacher, an ally, or a guide?

Since I've worked with various forms of chronic pain since I was a teenager, I know from personal experience how difficult it is to treat pain as a teacher, especially when it feels more like a torturer. I'm not going to ask you to *deny* the torturous aspects of pain. Instead, I suggest that you *include* the harshness and horrors of pain in your work with it. In addition, I encourage you to have all your feelings about it. Just because pain is your teacher doesn't mean you can't get pissed at it! The point is, you can use every part of your experience with pain to help you grow. That, in a nutshell, is why pain is such a powerful teacher.

I would say that chronic disease especially requires us to exhibit a deep kindness toward ourselves.
MARC IAN BARASCH

Turning Fear into Curiosity

I notice that when I relate to pain as a teacher, this helps me *open* to it. Sometimes the simple act of opening to pain is enough to change it. Many of us contract with fear when physical sensations feel painful. While this is an understandable and often automatic response, contraction usually exacerbates pain.

The unending paradox is that we do learn through pain.
MADELEINE L'ENGLE

Next time you experience sensations in your body that distress you, see if you can let go of your preconceived notions of pain. Can you find a way to approach the sensations with curiosity instead of fear? This may be difficult at first, because your window of curiosity may only stay open for a few seconds if your pain is intense. Again, it's okay to take breaks. Practice being curious about the sensations as long as you can, then do whatever you would otherwise do to deal with the pain.

Of course, you can always open your window of curiosity again later, if you feel up to it. Either way—whether you're dancing with the pain or parrying it—stay in touch with your commitment to self-care. Don't let your explorations of pain deteriorate into masochism. That's not what this is about.

...there's a difference between being responsible for my disease, in terms of causing it, and being responsible to it, meaning being capable of responding to my body's distress.
DERRICK JENSEN

Now, are you ready to roll up your sleeves and dig in? At this point, don't worry about writing anything down. That will come later. First, it's time to gather data. Pain will be the topic of research, and you will be the scientist who is studying...*you!*

To begin, set aside a chunk of time and choose a space where you'll feel comfortable and free from the possibility of interruption. Unplug the phone, turn off the radio/television/computer, and hang a "DO NOT DISTURB" sign on the door. Also, put some paper and a pen nearby, so they'll be easy to retrieve when you're ready to jot down a few notes later.

The art of medicine consists of amusing the patient while nature cures the disease.

VOLTAIRE

Let's start with an experiment in *physical position.* You have the option to stand, sit, lie down, or move around in any way. Find the positions that *ease* your pain—and then find the positions that *exaggerate* it. For a few moments, play with going back and forth between easing and exaggerating your pain. Allow the pain to intensify for a moment or two, then move back into a position that eases it again. Don't worry if you can't feel any difference in the pain by changing your position. Just tuck this technique into your memory, so you can use it again another time. Work with this experiment for as long as you like, and then proceed with the next step.

While you are tuned in to your physical experience, gradually enlarge the scope of your awareness, remembering that you are a scientist who is observing a natural phenomenon—the phenomenon of pain. See if you can ascertain *where* the sensations of pain are located in your body. Does the pain radiate out from a tiny pinpoint of space in one particular area, or does it wash over you like a wave? Does the pain disappear elusively as soon as you get close to it, only to reappear in another part of your body when you least expect it?

After you take some time to observe the pain's location and its patterns of movement, gather a little more information about it. Do you notice any images arising from the pain? Perhaps you can see an old conflict flickering in the fires of your pain. Can you make out the shadowy figures of anyone from your past? Maybe the mouth of a ferocious animal appears suddenly, baring its fangs at you. Or perhaps a blood-covered knife forces its way into your consciousness as you go deeper into the pain.

Paradoxically, the images that arise from pain are not always distressing. One time, when I was exploring a form of chronic pain that I call "the monsters in my gut," I discovered the image of a kitten who was sitting quietly, doing nothing. Sometimes pain speaks to me by showing its antidote. In other words, that kitten only *feels* like a monster when I ignore its need—my need—to sit quietly, doing nothing at all.

Whatever you see when you peer into your pain, don't forget that your only task is to *witness your experience.* If you get too scared, turn to the chapter called "Death as an Adviser." Once you're there, look for the subheading called "Safe Channels and Surfing the Waves." It will give you more tips about working with fear. For now, simply *be with* the images that arise from your pain, and play with them as long as they interest you.

If you like, you can *become* one of the images in order to learn more about it. To do this, abandon your observer position and adopt

One often learns more from ten days of agony than from ten years of contentment.

MERLE SHAIN

the perspective of the image itself. For example, what would you say if you were one of those shadowy figures from the past, arguing up a storm inside your brain? If you saw a ferocious animal, can you switch now from human to animal, and find out how it would feel to be a menacing creature staring you down, preparing to make a meal of you? And what about that bloody knife? Can you move like a switchblade, carving out a crimson path of destruction in your wake?

When you inhabit an image, don't worry about looking silly. Stay focused on the *essential nature* of the images conjured up by your pain, whether that essential nature is expressed through a relationship conflict, an animal, an archetypal figure, an object, a sound, a particular movement, a holy utterance, a mysterious scent, or anything else.

The Language of Pain: Traveling to a Foreign Country

The language of pain and body symptoms is the language of imagination and dreams. Although this may include verbal language, it also extends far beyond it. If you don't understand the nature of the messages presented to you through your body, please be patient. Respect that the messages are valid despite your bewilderment.

As an analogy, imagine that you've just landed in a foreign country with no translating dictionary and with nothing to guide you except your best intentions and a willingness to learn. The local people are well-meaning, of course, but they can only speak to you in their native tongue. Under these circumstances, I doubt if you'd discount their words simply because you don't understand what they're saying. Also, I bet you wouldn't berate them for not speaking *your* language. After all, you're in *their* country.

It's the same with physical sensations, symptoms, illness, and pain. If you make an expedition into the land of your body, don't expect it to speak to you in the verbal language to which you are accustomed. Your pain and your symptoms will speak to you in the language of the body. This language is infinitely complex and richly layered with nuance. Eventually, if you listen carefully, you'll catch on to the basics of your body's native tongue. Then, with luck and continued practice, you can unravel more and more subtlety in each whisper of sensation and each sigh of pain.

After you've worked a bit with some of the images that arise from your pain, take some time to write about your experiences. Begin by jotting down the first words or phrases that pop into your head as you reflect on what you've just witnessed. Don't worry if it

A writer's injuries are his strengths, and from his wounds will flow his sweetest, most startling dreams.
SALMAN RUSHDIE

There is a healthy way to be ill.
GEORGE SHEEHAN

Out of pain grow the violets of patience and sweetness.
HELEN KELLER

Understanding is the ultimate seduction of the mind. Go to the truth beyond the mind. Love is the bridge.

STEPHEN LEVINE

The most beautiful experience we can have is the mysterious.

ALBERT EINSTEIN

The deeper that sorrow carves into your being, the more joy you can contain.

KAHLIL GIBRAN

doesn't make sense. Sometimes the most important body messages are those which don't seem to make any sense. At least, the rational mind may not understand them right away.

If you want to add some drawings or doodles to remind you of the images, that's great. Once you have a few notes or visual representations that honor the highlights of your dance with pain, tune in to your heart for a moment. Find out if there are any strong feelings that occur to you as you review your notes. Sometimes an image is so blatant that it reveals a clear message to you. Other times, you may need to contemplate your notes, put them away, and come back to them later before you can make any sense of the meaning. Even then, if the pain is chronic or extreme, there may be multiple messages embedded in the images you see. Sometimes it can take years of diligent work to understand what your body is trying to say.

Occasionally, despite your best efforts, you may never gain access to the inner chambers of your pain. If this happens for you, don't blame yourself. Such a scenario may have more to do with the mysterious nature of pain than with any inadequacy on your part. Not every riddle is meant to be solved. In fact, I think some of my chronic pain exists simply to wreak havoc with my desire for control, to enlarge my capacity for acceptance, and to help me surrender to the ultimate mystery of illness. These are incredible gifts.

I wonder if, like me, you have pain that teaches you about *grace* by bringing you to your knees. I wouldn't wish such pain on anyone, but if you've had this experience, you have my respect. I know it's not an easy path, and it's often made more difficult by well-meaning but invasive people who think *they* know better than *you* what your pain or illness requires of you. Don't be fooled!

You are the first, last, and best authority in relation to your own body. While it may be helpful to consult trusted friends or professionals about your situation, their helpfulness ends when their arrogance begins. If people act as if they know better than you what your body needs, I hope you know what it took me decades to learn: how to tell them, politely but firmly, to *buzz off*.

I don't know what you will discover when you go exploring in the land of your body. Neither do I know what your pain will teach you. However, I do know that the adventure will never end as long as you're alive. The tips I've given you in this chapter are just enough to get you started. You can approach your pain in a million different ways—from the sublime to the ridiculous, and everything in between.

If you prefer sounds to images, you can go back over my directions for working in the visual mode, and substitute the word *sound* every time I say *image*. If you're kinesthetic, do the same thing with *movement*. If you've got a highly developed olfactory sense, you might discern *scents* in your pain. In turn, these scents may bear messages or they might stimulate memories for you.

Believe it or not, some pain even has flavor and you can *taste* it. Who knows? Maybe you could scramble your pain like a couple of eggs, make an omelet, and then imagine yourself chewing, swallowing, digesting, and even excreting it.

Last of all, pain may have meaning that goes beyond the personal to the global. Sometimes when I sit with certain kinds of pain in my body, I discover a hundred women wailing with grief, as they cling to the mutilated bodies of their children. Sometimes I can see a gaping hole in the earth, with putrid, slimy pollutants oozing out of it.

Now and then, when I listen closely to my pain, I can hear the spirits of my Cherokee ancestors whispering in dismay, and if I pay close attention, I can make out their words of longing for more awareness among those who live now. Occasionally, if I hold tight to the tendrils of pain and follow them all the way down to their core, I see nothing but an explosion of light and a portal to another way of being.

Needless to say, it can be confusing to sit with all these levels of pain, wondering which messages belong to me, which belong to the community, which require action, and which require simple acknowledgment. If you experience this kind of uncertainty about your pain, be patient. Hang out with the sensations and the symptoms. Keep listening. Notice how you feel. Write or draw or dance or sing the messages you get. Take good notes, and give your understanding time to ripen.

If you are moved to action, whether it's in your own life or in the world, you'll act. If you want to simply *be with* the pain, you can do exactly that. The less you think about it, the better. Let your body show the way.

Suffering is the greatest spiritual teacher. It is through suffering that one learns whether God exists.

AESCHYLUS

ELEMENTAL HEALING

F ew people treat nature as an essential part of their lives, even
though it is obviously *the* most important part of everyone's
life. No matter how many technological advances we make,
and no matter how many conveniences modern life affords us, we'd
all be up the proverbial creek without a paddle if nature didn't
provide air, water, food, fire, and all the other elements necessary
for our survival.

Apart from basic physical sustenance, contact with nature buoys
the human spirit and fosters a sense of connection: self to self, self
to other, self to planet, self to cosmos. No doubt you know what I
mean if you've spent a lot of time outdoors.

If you don't know what I'm talking about, I have a few ideas
for you. Take a long walk alone on an ocean beach. Build a fire
under the stars and talk late into the night with a friend. Gather a
few members of your true spiritual family, pitch some tents near a
deep-running river, and spend a week with sleeping bags, Coleman
stoves, and unpredictable weather.

If you try these adventures and none of them convinces you
that you need nature, you may have grown up without the smell of
salt-water mists, the feel of hot wood smoke on your shivering hands,
or the taste of fresh huckleberries picked from a bush that the bears
missed an hour before you.

Maybe there's been too much plastic in your life—and not
enough raw wood. Perhaps you've had too many interfaces with
computers—and not enough dances with the night sky. Maybe there
have been too many cars on the freeway of your life—and not enough
footsteps in the sand.

The good news is, it's never too late to fall in love with the
earth that gives you life. You can begin with a piece of paper right
now, this paper that brings my words to you. For example, I give
thanks for the wood that gave birth to this page; I mourn the loss of
forests that died to feed our insatiable human appetites; and I work
to reverse this depletion through personal and community action.

All these thoughts and feelings came simply from considering the wood that produced these pages!

Look around you now, wherever you are. If you're in a room at home, find a piece of paper and a pen, and begin to write down everything *natural* that you see. A quick gaze around my own studio reveals an abundance of wood (and lots of paper made from it), steel made from multiple raw materials tempered by fire, glass from a mixture of silicates, fabrics from sheep and silkworms and wood and petroleum and plants, rubber backing on the carpet under my feet, and water (along with peppermint) in my cup of tea.

As you write about your room's gifts of nature, keep one ear tuned to your heart and the other tuned to your wonder. Give thanks in whatever way feels right to you. Take a few steps back from any tendencies to take all these gifts for granted.

Whenever I fall prey to the delusion that I'm not getting enough support from the world, I like to do a *nature inventory* like the one I just described. Once I start writing, it doesn't take long before I come to my senses and remember that I am *constantly* receiving massive support from the world.

A nature inventory can also be a useful tool if you ever feel shy or scared to ask for help (from your friend, your lover, your boss, your dog, God, or whomever). The truth is, you're already receiving so much help from the universe that you may as well ask for more. Anything you could possibly ask for would be insignificant in comparison to the Herculean help you're already receiving. Drop your hesitation and go for it! Ask for whatever you need, and see what happens.

To this end, take your relationship with nature a bit further now. Imagine what you would ask for if you could have anything you want for a home environment. Write about your favorite *natural fantasy*. Do you dream of a grass hut in Bali, where you walk around naked and pick fruit off the trees outside your open-air window? Would you like to live in a hacienda in the desert, with cactus flowers, flash floods, and lightning storms in the afternoon? Have you ever wondered what it would be like to have a cabin at the edge of a rainbow-kissed waterfall, or a beach house high above the ocean on a rocky outcropping?

Write specific details about your sacred setting. For instance, how does the temperature of the air change as the day progresses from dawn to dusk? What does the water taste like in your favorite place? What scents fill the air? Can you walk around barefoot, or do you need boots to go outside? Is it pitch-black at night, or do the lights from a nearby city obscure the brightness of the stars?

The land is a mother that never dies.
MAORI SAYING

The nation that destroys its soil destroys itself.
FRANKLIN D. ROOSEVELT

We need the tonic of wildness. We can never have enough of nature.
HENRY DAVID THOREAU

The body repeats the landscape. They are the source of each other and create each other.

MERIDEL LE SUEUR

If you like, you can take another direction with your nature fantasies. That is, you can imagine what it would be like to *be* a particular aspect of nature. For instance, have you ever wondered what it would feel like to be the core of a volcano in the midst of an eruption? Can you *dance* all that violent, out-of-control firepower, spewing boulders high into the air as molten lava rushes down in every direction? Wow!

If you're the quiet type, maybe you'd rather imagine yourself as a seed buried just beneath the surface of a carefully tended garden. It's spring. Can you feel the sun's warmth penetrating the soil, awakening the life within you? The faint outline of a twin-leaf shoot begins to appear from within the slowly dissolving skin of your seed casing. At the perfect moment, it will burst forth—*you* will burst forth—into the world, where you will experience wind and rain and an explosion of life in your fast-growing cells.

Whether you write about *being* a particular part of nature, or simply about living in a particular place, I urge you to keep writing until you have a complete vignette. By *complete*, I don't mean that you can't add to it later. You can add more details whenever you like. What I mean is, make your nature fantasy so richly layered that you can come back to it again and again, the way you'd come back to a favorite story, reading and savoring it until you have every detail memorized.

...when we are true to our own nature we become more deeply connected to all of nature.

JENNIFER JAMES

Use your nature fantasy whenever you need a *hit* of elemental healing. Let it take you on an imaginary excursion into the depths of your primal connection to nature. If your fantasy comes true, what a bonus! If not, you can always visit your heart-home in the privacy of your own daydreams. Either way, return to the images, sounds, smells, and textures of nature whenever you get stressed by the intensity of high-speed living.

Whether you connect with the natural world in your fantasies or in reality, find a way to bring *elemental healing* into your life every day. It's all around you. It's even inside you! All you have to do is notice and celebrate the wonder.

THE ADDICTION PRAYER

One night in 1989, I got a hankering to do a little experiment with my addictions. By that time, I barely even used the word *addiction,* because it has so many confusing and judgmental connotations. I couldn't find any space within its boundaries to explore my own knowing about addiction, so I took a few years off from using the word at all. This gave me a chance to find out what addiction means to *me,* apart from everyone else's ideas about it.

Eventually, I homed in on the definition that you read in "The Five-Minute Switch System": **An addiction is anything that stands in the way of total awareness and acceptance of yourself, others, and the world.** Because this definition is so all-inclusive, some people might complain that you'd have to be some kind of ascended master before you could consider yourself addiction-free. However, if the definition didn't make room for every possible addiction, it wouldn't allow for the fact that the more you grow, the more subtlety you will discover in the habits and attachments that cloud your capacity for awareness and acceptance.

With this in mind, I came to peace with the value of calling a spade a spade. I began to use the word *addiction* again, keeping my own definition foremost in mind. Of course, you can create your own definition of addiction if mine doesn't work for you. However you define it, though, this chapter presupposes your willingness to *name* your addictions for the purpose of getting a handle on them. If you can't acknowledge your addictions as addictions, how will you be able to do anything about them?

Thunderstorms and the Power of Naming

According to some ancient teachings, you gain power over something if you can name it. When you name all your possible addictions, you gain power over them, not in the sense of *overpowering* them but in the sense of acknowledging *their power over you.* This may seem paradoxical, but you can't get free from

If you begin to understand what you are without trying to change it, then what you are undergoes a transformation.

KRISHNAMURTI

the prison of your addictions unless you admit that you are *in* their prison. This takes humility.

I got a good dose of humility when I set out to name all my own addictions that night in the late 1980s. With a yellow legal pad and a blue Bic in hand, I was determined to list everything I could think of that might be interfering with my clarity and my compassion. I decided to do this list in the form of the following prayer:

I want help healing my addiction to _____.

Five pages and forty-two items later, I was finished. Some of the items on my list related to food or substances or relationships, but most of the entries were statements such as, "I want help healing my addiction to perfectionism," or "I want help healing my addiction to overextending."

After all the years of healing work I'd done, the sheer volume of possible addictions in my life was truly humbling. I was impressed! I also had a sneaking suspicion that if I worked with those forty-two habits for a while and then did the Addiction Prayer again, I'd probably have an equal or greater number of items on my list. This doesn't mean I wouldn't make any progress. It's just that the more I open my eyes, the more I see—and the more I see about myself, the easier it is for me to admit how much farther I have to go. Ad infinitum.

I got to test this theory—about the expanding list of addictions—when I was rewriting this chapter again in early 1999, ten years after I first did the Addiction Prayer. I remember the night I did my ten-year anniversary list. Actually, it was early morning. I'd stayed up late the night before, working on the chapter. At 4:30 a.m., I was awakened by a HUGE crash that shook the house.

At first I thought it was an earthquake, but then I saw a flash of light across the sky, and I realized it was a thunderstorm of El Niño proportions. In the next few moments, I was flooded with new information about two of my most pervasive addictions: the addiction to *control* and the addiction to *pride* (and its flip side, *shame*). At the same time, I was shown how these addictions were intertwined in two situations I was grappling with at the time. I was also given specific information about how to do another piece of healing work in relation to them.

The pre-dawn darkness, the thunder, and the punctuating flashes of light were so powerful that I decided to seize the moment to do another round of the Addiction Prayer. Since I hadn't done a list for ten years, I was curious to see what I would write this time. I was also curious to see if anything would change as a result of doing the prayer.

I turned on a light, grabbed a yellow legal pad and my trusty blue Bic, and started writing. Pages later, I was still writing. I had to stop when I got to one hundred entries, because I got a cramp in my hand. Otherwise, I'm sure I would have kept going.

The same thing was true for me in 1999 as was true in 1989. My substance addictions are virtually nonexistent, but I make up for it with a seemingly limitless array of attachments to certain ways of thinking, being, or acting. To inspire you to create your own personal exposé, here are twenty-one randomly selected items from my 1999 list:

It is preoccupation with possessions, or things, more than anything else, that prevents us from living freely and nobly.

BERTRAND RUSSELL

I want help healing my addiction to overgiving.

I want help healing my addiction to self-neglect.

I want help healing my addiction to appearances.

I want help healing my addiction to being *one down.*

I want help healing my addiction to one-upmanship.

I want help healing my addiction to blame.

I want help healing my addiction to praise.

I want help healing my addiction to comfort.

I want help healing my addiction to discomfort.

I want help healing my addiction to achievement.

I want help healing my addiction to health.

I want help healing my addiction to illness.

I want help healing my addiction to "loving too much."

I want help healing my addiction to change.

I want help healing my addiction to familiarity.

I want help healing my addiction to being special.

I want help healing my addiction to being shy.

I want help healing my addiction to improvement.

I want help healing my addiction to *knowing.*

I want help healing my addiction to being liked.

I want help healing my addiction to helping.

People who have not been in Narnia sometimes think that a thing cannot be good and terrible at the same time.

C. S. LEWIS

As you read those excerpts, were you surprised to see me list so-called positive activities or qualities such as comfort, health, or helping? I like to include these kinds of things on my list of addictions, not because I think they're *bad* or because I want them to stop, but because I recognize my high level of attachment to them.

I don't mind if I love comfort or health or helping, but I'm on dangerous ground if I feel as if I can't live without them. That's a signal of addiction for me. This doesn't mean I won't continue to cultivate these qualities or activities, only that I want to remember that they can be taken from me in the blink of an eye. Therefore, I want to love the blessings in my life the way I love butterflies: with an open hand, knowing they may fly away at any moment.

Important Tips and the Slow-Hand Approach

Before I say more about the process of working with the Addiction Prayer, let me call your attention to a few important tips about the way you write it. Although the items from my 1999 list were typeset from my handwritten pages so you can read them more easily here, please be sure that you *don't* use a typewriter or a computer to do your list. As with all the writing exercises in this book, it is essential to do your work by hand unless you are physically incapable of doing so, in which case I encourage you to do it any way you can.

There is no substitute for the slow-hand approach to written healing work. Therefore, when you begin your Addiction Prayer, *don't* just write the opening sentence one time, following it with a long list of single-word entries. Instead, write the prayer sentence in its entirety each time, filling in the blank with whatever addiction comes up next. No shortcuts!

I'm not making a bunch of rules to be punitive or to cramp your style. Rather, I'm asking you to go slow for specific reasons. First, going slow gives you time to *feel*. For example, when I asked for help to heal my addiction to health, I got scared that I'd suddenly be plagued by horrible illnesses that are even worse than anything I've ever known. Such fears are no fun, but they're important information and they require attention. It's okay to wait until later to explore any fears that arise for you, but at least give them a chance to come up. If you want more help with fear, refer to "The Anger Primer" or "Death as an Adviser" for tips.

Aside from providing space for you to feel, there's another reason I ask you to go slow by writing out the whole prayer every time. That is, it gives you a chance to focus on *asking for help* and

Self-knowledge and self-improvement are very difficult for most people. It usually needs great courage and long struggle.

ABRAHAM MASLOW

asking for healing. This is as important as focusing on the addiction itself. After all, the purpose of the list is not simply to regurgitate all your stuck points. While it's certainly powerful to name your addictions, it's even more powerful to use the prayer to help you transform them. The repetition of the sentence allows the prayer to become a mantra that deepens your intention.

S.O.S. Signals: Asking for Help

Don't be fooled by the simplicity of the Addiction Prayer. The truth is, it takes guts to ask for help in healing your addictions, since you can never know in advance what kind of help you will get. For instance, the help might come in the form of all hell breaking loose in your life, which might stimulate increased reliance on a particular addiction. In turn, this increase in compulsion could make you so painfully aware of your addiction's black-hole *energy suck* that you finally dump it once and for all.

By the way, when you use this prayer, you don't have to address anyone or anything. If you enjoy praying *to* someone or something, go right ahead. However, if you don't have a personal prayer connection, it's perfectly fine to say your prayer without addressing an outside or inside source. I do spiritual work both ways, and both ways are effective.

To understand what I mean about not having to address anyone when you pray for help, imagine that you're out in the middle of a stormy sea in a sinking boat. In such a situation, I'd bet your only concern would be to signal wildly for help. You might use the radio, wave your arms, scream loudly, or attract attention in other ways. I doubt if you'll be very picky about *who* answers your distress call, as long as *someone* does. Obviously, you can't expect anyone to know you need help unless you make it quite apparent that you're open to it, if not downright desperate for it. Thus, your job is to keep sending S.O.S. signals until help arrives.

If you're shy about asking for help, consider the fact that you are already receiving help in countless ways. Think about everyone and everything in your life. Did you bring all this into existence by yourself? Think about your body, your food, your shelter, your family and friends, your work environment, the earth, and the entire cosmos. The help you receive just to stay alive is *massive.* You may as well surrender to the notion that you do almost nothing, if anything, by yourself. As one of my shamans says, "There is no self-help." So don't worry about asking for help. You're going to get it anyway! Personally, I think the entire universe conspires to

Anyone who has ever "gotten it" by following some so-called method, has gotten it in spite of the method, not because of it.

LEE LOZOWICK

you can believe something
quietly for a long time
then one day you believe it
out loud
and everything changes

MARTHA VALLELY

FROM THE POEM "CALLING"

help you. The question is: Do you want to work *with* that help or do you want to work *against* it?

When you ask for help in healing your addictions, think about it as a statement of your intention. It's more like a mission statement than a plan of attack. This doesn't mean that you won't have to follow through with effort on the material plane, only that the Addiction Prayer's purpose is to activate the mysterious powers of healing that surround and support you.

In the same way that I asked you not to obsess on the Resolution Prayer, I'll make the same suggestion here. Complete your list of addictions, read it aloud once, and then put it aside in a private place. Let this be an experiment in magic. See what happens through the simple act of admitting and naming your addictions.

Food Addiction and the Universal Support Squad

Something unexpected happened for me the first time I did the Addiction Prayer: a major food habit stopped overnight, just like that. It was a habit involving bread, which had been my favorite food and main staple for more than ten years. Before doing the prayer, I hadn't even considered my bread habit to be an addiction, because I didn't think it was hurting me. In fact, I actually believed it was some kind of miracle food for me, because I ate a lot of it (six to eight thick slices every day) without gaining weight. What's more, I seemed to be slowly *losing* weight, which seemed like a bonus for a former anorexic who was still overly concerned about being thin.

A few months after I did the Addiction Prayer and stopped eating bread, I found out from a naturopath that I was "hideously allergic" to wheat. The huge amounts of bread that I'd eaten all those years had severely compromised my intestines' ability to absorb nutrients. That was why I was losing weight. Food was going right through me.

I have always known that at
last I would take this road,
but yesterday I did not know
that it would be today.

NARIHARA

The point is, I didn't know any of this when I did the Addiction Prayer. All I knew was that I couldn't imagine life without bread, so I had to admit that it was probably an addiction. Even still, I had no idea that I would wake up the next morning and stop eating bread without even thinking about it. For someone with my history of eating disorders, a diet change of this caliber—overnight—was a remarkable occurrence, to say the least. Even more amazing is the fact that I never went back to the habit.

Of course, there are no guarantees that the Addiction Prayer will affect any of the items on your list. Some of your addictions may stay with you for life, some may shift and change form, others may dissipate completely, and still others may only soften in their intensity.

In the latter category are those addictions that are like lifelong myths you can merely unravel a bit at a time. These kinds of major addictions may never disappear entirely, but you can learn many lessons from them as you glean their useful components and discard the rest. For example, I'm still working on my addiction to perfectionism and my addiction to overextending myself. If I didn't have these addictions, I probably wouldn't have spent decades in the self-help business, and I probably wouldn't have written this book. On the other hand, perfectionism and overextending can be my undoing, so I keep chipping away at them.

Since I'm such an overdoer, I like the Addiction Prayer because it is nonstriving. I state my intention, call in the Universal Support Squad, and then go about my business with as much awareness as possible. In the case of my wheat addiction, I wasn't even thinking about ending my love affair with bread when I sat down to write my list. However, my overall intention for change was strong. If it was time for my favorite food to disappear from my diet, so be it.

Another nice thing about the Addiction Prayer is that you don't have to figure out if, when, or how your habits might change. Although there are many chapters in this book that require your active participation as a change agent, this one is devoted to magic. Point your finger at an addiction and see if it disappears. Poof! Put a name on another one, and notice whether or not it changes form. Zap! Pull yet another addiction out of the closet, and find out if it falls flat on its face. Wham!

Feel free to be playful with your list of addictions. If you can't manage that, at least refrain from using your list to beat yourself up. Self-criticism will only bind you more tightly to whatever you want to release. If you end up with a list as long as mine, don't despair. Maybe it just means that you are deeply aware of your vulnerabilities and willing to be honest about them. In the final analysis, you might even compliment yourself for the length of your list. After all, every addiction you name is one less addiction you deny.

Advanced Version of the Addiction Prayer

After you complete your list, read it aloud to a trusted friend, mentor, or coach. Before you do, though, ask the other person to witness your list without comment, criticism, or strange exclamations. Your witness can simply thank you for sharing such intimate information, and then he or she can ask if you need anything.

There are some faults so nearly allied to excellence that we can scarce weed out the vice without eradicating the virtue.
OLIVER GOLDSMITH

A man does not quit playing because he grows old. He grows old because he quits playing.
PLATO

I do not take drugs—I am drugs.
SALVADOR DALI

If you feel shy or ashamed after you read your Addiction Prayer, acknowledge this to your witness, and take care of yourself around it. When I counsel people, I will sometimes turn around and look the other way (literally) when shy clients want to tell me something intensely personal. They don't want to *see me seeing them.* I can understand this kind of fear and shame, so I'm happy to oblige. In the same vein, give yourself permission to ask for whatever you need to feel comfortable before, during, and after your self-disclosures.

If you want your friend or helper to hold your disclosures in strict confidence, ask for that. If you want to hear that your witness still likes you despite—or perhaps because of—your addictions, ask for that. Whatever you need, be sure that you make a *container of compassion* around your truth-telling.

Choose your witness carefully, get heard in a way that feels good to you, and honor all the feelings that come up for you in the process. Just because you choose to expose your soft underbelly doesn't mean that you relinquish the right—or the responsibility—to protect it. Quite the contrary.

Veteran's Version of the Addiction Prayer

You can be successful in life in anything you do. All you have to do is stick around and watch yourself.
JOE RAHN

Once you've done the regular and advanced versions of the Addiction Prayer, take a giant step further by making a long-term commitment to it. First, choose a time of the month when you're likely to have an hour or so of uninterrupted time. Then, at the appointed hour, draw up your list, taking care to write down every possible candidate for addiction. Remember to write the entire prayer sentence with each new entry. When you're done, put your list in an envelope, seal it, and tuck it away in a safe place. Finally, get out your calendar and make an appointment with yourself to do the same thing in a month.

When it's time for round two, start fresh and do the Addiction Prayer again. Don't look back at your first list. Just do another one straight from the heart. When you're done, seal it and put it aside with the other one. Follow this procedure all year until you get to the twelfth month.

At the end of the year, complete your final Addiction Prayer, then find some time as soon as you can to do some reflecting. You'll need at least an hour. An open-ended chunk of time would be even better, in case you make some unexpected discoveries that merit on-the-spot exploration.

Although it's fine to read through all your Addiction Prayers, I recommend that you concentrate on your first and last ones. Open them up and read the two lists from start to finish, beginning with your original one. Consider the similarities and the differences. Pay attention to what has changed, and notice what hasn't changed. In particular, find out which addictions are still present, which have disappeared, and which new ones have appeared. If you do spot any new addictions on your list, ask yourself if they're new to your life or if they're only new to your awareness.

Take a few moments to write down your observations. If you feel celebratory or if you feel sad, find a way to express these feelings. If you feel angry or afraid, move with the emotion until it shifts. If some course of action occurs to you, take notes on this information so you can follow through later.

When you're done reviewing and contemplating your year-long dance with the Addiction Prayer, ask yourself the following three questions and record your answers.

1. What have I learned about myself from doing this year of work?

2. What have I learned about addiction?

3. What simple message can I hold in my heart as I carry this work forward into the coming year?

You will suddenly realize that the reason you never changed before was because you didn't want to.

ROBERT SCHULLER

DEATH AS
AN ADVISER

Earth and our own bodies are the ultimate recycling triumph: Our atoms are the product of the exploding fires of old stars.

BILL DIETRICH

I hope this chapter gives you safe harbor to contemplate your own death. If your beliefs about death are already set in concrete, or if you're too frightened to think about death, that's okay. You can always skip this chapter. However, unless you're some kind of ascended master, you can't skip death. No matter what you do or don't do, you're still going to die. What kind of a deal is that?

Personally, I think it's a good deal. Consider the alternative. Do you really want to live forever in the same body, while everyone and everything else evolves and changes form? I sure don't. As far as I'm concerned, death is one of nature's most brilliant inventions. You know that slogan, *renew/recycle/reuse*? Well, death is nature's ultimate recycler. Death recycles life! If it wasn't for death, you wouldn't be here, and neither would I.

In the physical world, there is no growth without death. Every moment of every day, your cells are in a constant cycle of death and rebirth. Deepak Chopra, renowned author and Ayurvedic physician, speaks eloquently about the human body's continual process of cellular destruction and regeneration. Quite literally, you are living in a different body from the one you had a few years ago—or even a few moments ago.

Approximately 98 percent of the atoms in your body are replaced each year.

MIKE MAILWAY

Death is all around. Your cells die. Animals die. Trees die. Stars die. Why would humans be any different? Everything that comes into physical existence eventually goes out of physical existence. If this wasn't true, things would get pretty crowded! Death is one of nature's ways of creating space. This is one of death's most valuable contributions to life.

Aside from these practical considerations, death is also a blessing in the metaphysical realms. It provides us humans with endless fodder for contemplation. Death is a doorway to *infinity*. It's literally the trip of a lifetime. Yet most people don't know when they're leaving, they don't know where they're going, and they have no idea if they're coming back. How about you? What do you think will happen when you die?

A Walk Down Memory Lane

Take some time now to sit with your thoughts about death. Begin by reminiscing about your past experiences with it. What events have shaped your beliefs about death? Perhaps you could write a personal account of death, tracing its effects through the twists and turns of your life. Include details about the deaths of friends, relatives, and animals you've loved. Notice all the nuances of emotion you feel as you remember your experiences with death.

Pay close attention to emotions that are so strong they carry you back to the time of your loss. Find a way to honor and express these feelings, without trying to fix or change them. Death has a special way of carving more space in the contours of your heart. From the depths of pain, compassion arises like a rainbow after rain. Be gentle with your grief; it's a precious source of understanding and empathy.

When you're ready, slowly shift your focus and consider your family tree. Do you know anything about the deaths of relatives in past or present generations? Did your relatives live a long time or did they drop dead at an early age? Do you believe that your own death is partly, fully, or not at all determined by family patterns, whether behavioral or genetic?

If the longevity of relatives doesn't factor into your thinking about death, then what do you believe does determine your lifespan? Is there a particular age at which you expect to die? If so, what age, and how did you come to have this expectation?

Do you believe that you can control the length of your life by making certain choices or exerting your will? Do you think fate plays a role in your death? Whether your worldview is monotheistic, polytheistic, pantheistic, agnostic, or atheist, how does the matter of death timing fit into your belief system?

Safe Channels and Surfing the Waves

Check in with your heart at this point. How are you doing with all these questions about death? Do you feel intrigued, inspired, excited, overwhelmed, bored? If you feel bored, the boredom may be hiding a feeling you'd rather push away. Go deeper. Find out what you *really* feel about death, way down in your core.

If this work is scary for you, take some time to be with your fear. Find a safe *channel*, as Arny Mindell would say, to explore your experience. Do you feel most comfortable in the realms of vision and images? Then perhaps you can write or draw your fear. Do you feel more grounded when you focus on your body? Then

Millions of persons long for immortality who do not know what to do with themselves on a rainy afternoon.

SUSAN ERTZ

The future is unconsciously prepared long in advance, and therefore can be guessed by clairvoyants.

CARL JUNG

maybe you could dance your fear, or maybe you could go for a walk while you think about it. Is sound or music your favorite way *in* to your soul? Then take your fear for a ride on the wings of song.

No matter what channel or mode you choose, remember to *keep breathing* while you feel the fear. Continuous breathing is one of your body's best tools for integrating emotion. Another tip is to imagine that you're surfing. Pretend that your fear is a wave in the ocean. Waves form, crest, break, and dissipate naturally, as long as nothing interferes with their movement. Fear is the same way. Let it *move* through your body like a wave through the ocean. Tremble, shake, scream, cry. Anything goes!

If you want to learn more about fear, find a way to *catch* one of the waves as it crests inside you. Use your safe channel like a surfboard to keep you afloat. Breathe deeply and feel free to whoop and holler! Practice riding your waves of fear whenever they arise. Eventually, you may discover that fear becomes *excitement* if you can find a creative way to play with it.

Horrible Images and the Flip Side of Fear

In the language of waves, everyday fears are like ripples, and the fear of death is like a *tsunami*. If you can hang ten on a tsunami, you're probably a world-class surfer. That's great! Before you get too cocky, though, let me raise the stakes. Here's a zinger for you. *How* are you going to die?

This question may cause quite a stir in your guts. I recommend that you take this one in small doses. Tune in to your safest channel or mode of expression, as if you are tuning into your favorite radio station. Get as comfortable as you can, and consider the possibilities. There are countless ways to die. Some people say that your style of dying reflects your style of living. If this is true, what would that mean for you?

Invite your biggest fears to come out into the open. Regard them with great tenderness. If you see horrible images of death in your mind's eye, remember that these images seek your *attention*, not necessarily your *enactment*. Many people know their worst fear about dying. What's yours? What kind of death do you want to avoid at all costs?

However you answer that question, sit with the image, sound, or feeling that represents that fearsome kind of death. *Keep breathing* and stay in your safe channel. What is it about that way of dying that frightens you? Let the image or sound or feeling instruct you about your fear. This is not about death per se. It's about *you*. Let death teach you about you.

What is life? It is the flash of a firefly in the night. It is the breath of a buffalo in the wintertime. It is the little shadow which runs across the grass and loses itself in the sunset.

CROWFOOT

How you die will speak volumes about how you lived.

TIMOTHY LEARY

Violent death is violent only to those who remain behind to view it.

EMMANUEL

When you're ready to take a break from working with *how* you might die, switch to the flip side of your fear by exploring your preferences about death. What kind of death would you like to have? Don't worry, it's okay to fantasize about death. Lots of people do. If death is *all* you think about, you might be wise to seek professional counsel. In general, however, death fantasies don't necessarily indicate neurosis or mental illness. They may simply indicate a healthy curiosity and an active imagination.

In the moment of death, do you want to be awake and aware? Would you rather be oblivious to what's happening? Would you like to die in your sleep? Do you want to die alone or do you want friends and family around you? Would you like to die at home or in a hospital, in a meadow or in a forest, on a mountaintop or in the desert, on a boat or in a rocket ship? What time of day or night would you like to die? Where in the world would you like to die? Would you prefer to die in outer space?

Some yogic teachings say the best way to die is alone, because there is less distraction and fewer people projecting their fears and trying to hold on to you and making a big circus out of the whole thing. So go off by yourself and die like a deer in the forest. That has a certain attraction. But if it happens some other way, then it happens some other way.

RICK FIELDS

Details, Details, Details

After you die, how would you like your body to be cared for, and by whom? Do you know your legal rights in regard to the disposition of your body after death? Once you're dead, would you like a funeral, a memorial service, or some kind of celebration in your honor? Would you prefer people to acknowledge your death privately? If you do want a gathering, what would it be like? Have you informed family and friends about your plans?

Have you done all the necessary paperwork for your death? Do you have a will? Have you formulated a Durable Power of Attorney, so someone can act in your behalf in case of incapacitation *before* you die? Do you have a Living Will in place, so your loved ones don't have to guess what you want, if you're physically or mentally unable to state your preferences in regard to resuscitation or life support?

Dying is not a medical event.

IRA BYOCK

If you haven't made these preparations, what's stopping you? Do you think there will always be time for that *later*? Do you think it's your family's job to deal with those responsibilities? What if your family dies with you? Do you prefer to avoid thinking about death altogether? Do you believe that preparing for death will make it come sooner?

Life becomes immense when we start recognizing that there is no assurance that we will live out this day.

STEPHEN LEVINE

Imminent Death

To complete this chapter, I want to suggest one more exercise for working with death. To do it, I'll ask you to consider imminent death as a way to get clearer about your life. I encourage you to

*Life gets mighty precious
when there's less of it to waste.*

BONNIE RAITT

*The poet reminds us that a
civilization that denies death
ends by denying life.*

OCTAVIO PAZ

*You wanted me to tell you
about death. All right! Then
don't be afraid of hearing
about your own death.*

DON JUAN

Have a blast while you last.

HOLLIS STACY

write down your ideas or speak them into a tape recorder. Witness your thoughts now, then notice how they change over time.

To begin, imagine that you're going to die in five years. Would you change anything in your life? Would you do anything differently in your relationships? Would you let go of any relationships? Would you spend more time with certain people? Would you spend more time alone?

How would you treat your present livelihood? Would you stop working? Would you change careers or start your own business? Would you push harder, slow down, or maintain the status quo?

Think about your personal habits. Would you do something about those pesky addictions? Would you go deeper into them, since you're going to die anyway? Would you jettison your vices, so you'd have more energy for the time you have left? Would you eat more, eat less, eat differently? Would you be more sexual or less sexual? Would you find a way to live out your secret fantasies?

If you had five years until death, would you live more outrageously? Would you take more risks? Would you dress more wildly, be more outspoken, show off your talents? Would you make more time for creative pursuits? Would you change your politics, become an activist, or fight for some cause? Would you drop out, hide out, or succumb to despair?

Would your interest in the material world intensify or fall away? Would you accumulate more possessions or let go of more stuff? Would you become more hedonistic or more ascetic? Would your passions take you deeper into the pleasures of the flesh, the contemplations of the mind, the ecstasies of the spirit, or all three?

As you explore your answers to these questions, notice any other questions that arise. Get them all out on the table. Go for it! Milk your death for all it's worth. It may be the best adviser you'll ever have. Death always tells the truth, calls you on your bullshit, and forces you to pay attention to what's truly important.

If you're ready to up the ante once again, go back to the beginning of this subsection, which is titled "Imminent Death." This time, answer the same questions as if you have *one year* to live. When you're done with that, take a break and then start again, imagining that you have only *six months* to live.

Finally, ask yourself the big question. If you were going to die *tomorrow*, how would you live today? How would it feel to have only one day left? If you're going to die tomorrow, is there any unfinished business you need to complete? If so, how about doing it right now? *Right now* may be all you have. Who knows? Death is always around, waiting. Will you be ready when it comes to tap you on the shoulder?

Joy: A Warrior's Path

How's the joy level in your life? Many of us didn't grow up in environments that encouraged pleasure. In fact, some of us were taught *not* to trust pleasure, as if it would inevitably get us in trouble or at least lead us astray. I don't know about you, but I'm still learning to *follow my bliss*, to use the words of Joseph Campbell.

Occasionally I have to remind myself that if I do what brings me joy, it really will be the best gift I can give to everyone and everything. I was taught to believe the opposite: that joy comes from trying to figure out what others want—and then providing it. The only problem is, when I go in that direction, it feels like all the blood drains out of my body. This is not a good sign, obviously.

By the way, when I talk about joy, I'm not necessarily talking about the kind of wild ecstasy that makes your eyes roll back in your head as you lose touch with reality. That kind of joy is great fun, but if you expect fireworks and sirens to herald the presence of supreme pleasure, you'll miss out on all the sweet subtleties of joy's other manifestations. Therefore, this chapter focuses more intently on the kind of joy that lets you know your actions are in synch with your heart. This is true bliss, and it may show up in feelings of quiet delight, fervent enthusiasm, or anything in between.

If one is lucky, a solitary fantasy can transform one million realities.
MAYA ANGELOU

After ecstasy, the laundry.
ZEN SAYING

Brainstorming for Joy

The first step toward experiencing more joy in your life is to *notice* what brings you joy. This may sound obvious, but have you actually taken the time to do it? Either way, take five minutes now to pull out a pad of paper and a pen. Jot down some things that give you pleasure. See if you can come up with at least ten or fifteen activities, sights, sounds, tastes, smells, states of being, or other experiences that make you feel *passionately alive*.

Those last two words are good guideposts to help you identify joy. Remember, though, that your kind of passionate aliveness may

A joyful heart is the inevitable result of a heart burning with love.
MOTHER TERESA

Being happy is a virtue too.
LUDWIG BORNE

look different from anyone else's. Some people look like lightning bolts when they're impassioned, while others look like beatific Buddhas. Pay attention to how you feel *inside*, not how you look on the outside.

When you're finished with your list of ten or fifteen joys, put your pen in your other (nondominant) hand, and do the same exercise. If you're not familiar with nondominant handwriting, suspend any judgments you might have, and just play with it.

Don't worry about how your nondominant handwriting looks. If you think you can't write with your other hand, do it anyway. It doesn't matter if it takes you ten minutes to draw one big, scrawly letter. Scrawl away!

Even though I've been experimenting with nondominant handwriting and drawing since the early 1970s, my left hand never ceases to amaze me with its ability to reveal new information. It acts as if it's plugged into a different source of knowledge than the one I usually access.

As it turns out, that's exactly what's happening, as I learned when I began studying Lucia Capacchione's work several years after I started doing left-handed creations on my own. Capacchione is famous for her books about nondominant handwork (see bibliography). She helped me understand why these expressions feel so powerful.

Basically, the dominant hand has more direct access to one hemisphere of the brain, and the nondominant hand has more direct access to the other hemisphere. Since the two hemispheres rule different aspects of function, feeling, and thought, it follows that each hand can convey these different aspects according to the hemisphere they most easily express.

Since the dominant hand tends to express the style of the dominant hemisphere, you can learn more about the *nondominant* parts of yourself by using your other hand to write or draw. These nondominant parts might include repressed thoughts or emotions, certain aspects of your personality that never get any attention, or qualities of your soul that haven't yet come to full flower.

For example, you might use your nondominant hand to access the voice of physical or emotional pain, symptoms of illness, scary feelings, forbidden thoughts, or various parts of your body. You could also use it to dialogue with images of your parents, authority figures, fantasy lovers, or your inner celebrity. Capacchione's books also offer creative techniques to help you connect with your inner child, the part that often gets pushed aside in deference to adult priorities.

Even a happy life cannot be without a measure of darkness, and the word "happiness" would lose its meaning if it were not balanced by sadness.

CARL JUNG

When I did my own two joy lists, it was clear that my left (nondominant) hand expressed more of my playfulness. In addition, I noticed that my nondominant hand came up with more ideas about joy. Since I grew up in a rather repressed family, it's not surprising that the lion's share of my bliss associations got relegated to the nondominant part of my brain—not to mention the nondominant part of my life. Bit by bit, I have coaxed my joy out of the closet by encouraging it to take a more dominant role.

Shoot for the moon. Even if you miss it you will land among the stars.

LES BROWN

Here are the two lists I drew up while writing this chapter:

Dominant Hand	Nondominant Hand
Writing	Praying
Drawing	Dancing
Drumming	Writing
Dancing	Drawing
Singing	Blowing bubbles
Listening to music	Flying in my dreams
Praying	Singing
Dreaming	Drumming
Breathing	Swimming
Swimming	Walking ocean beaches
Making love	Sitting on big rocks in the desert
Meditating	Cuddling
Working with death	Hanging out with a close friend
	Watching fire
	Listening to water
	Riding five-gaited horses
	Smelling fresh bread
	Growing flowers
	Landscape gardening
	Reading comics and children's books
	Playing with cats
	Watching the Rolling Stones perform
	Riding Harleys *real slow*
	Stargazing

Joy and Fear: Obstacles to Bliss

When you make your lists, don't censor ideas based on what you believe is possible, financially or otherwise. If you know what makes you happy, but you won't even let yourself *want* it, how are you ever going to *have* it? It makes no difference if you think you deserve what you want. Go ahead and want it anyway. Find out what happens when you step into your fear of being happy.

If you believe that you'll be struck dead by lightning for pursuing your passion, then by all means, pursue it. If your fear comes true, at least you'll go out with a bang! On the other hand, if you sacrifice your pleasure on the altar of fear, you'll never get one step closer to your bliss.

If the saints among us are any indication, it would appear that the most evolved state is a state of joy. Obviously, it's not only children who understand this. However, somewhere between childhood and sainthood, joy often gets derailed. The stresses of everyday life pile up, putting a lid on joy's natural effervescence. Family responsibilities, social expectations, religious rules, work pressures, and planetary strife all impinge on each of us in different ways. To make matters worse, the dominant cultural paradigm is *not* based on the idea that you should follow your heart. In a world run by money, bliss is generally considered to be irrelevant, because it can't be factored into the bottom line.

In the midst of this unsupportive if not downright hostile environment, how can you possibly cultivate a sense of joy? First of all, I've noticed that it helps to have a *radical attitude*. Feel free to rebel against the dominant paradigm! If you're going to ride into battle for bliss, you'll need a fanatical belief in your cause, as well as a thick hide to withstand cutting remarks and blistering looks of disdain. What? You don't believe me? Then you've probably never mentioned the word *bliss* in a roomful of folks who believe that life is about working hard until you die.

If you're not the rebellious type, a *quiet* approach to joy can be equally effective. If you like, you can be completely private about your efforts to recover bliss. That way, you won't run the risk of exposing your tender experiments to the crushing blows of ignorant criticism or other discouraging words.

Whether you choose privacy or outright rebellion, your approach isn't nearly as important as your *desire*. In other words, you must *want* your sense of joy. People often skip this step, because many of us have been admonished not to want anything at all. However, joy isn't about self-centered indulgence. It's about honoring your heart. If you don't honor your heart, what's the point of having one?

Enchantment is our natural state.

DEEPAK CHOPRA

To know what you prefer instead of humbly saying Amen to what the world tells you you ought to prefer, is to have kept your soul alive.

ROBERT LOUIS STEVENSON

If you're scared to want joy, I can probably guess some of the reasons for your fear. Before I do, though, take some time now to write down some of your own ideas about why you might fear happiness or pleasure. When you're done, keep reading and see if your thoughts resonate with anything I mention in the next few paragraphs.

What can you lose if you have your own heart? And what can you win if you do not?

EMMANUEL

One common reason that people fear joy is that it's a *feeling*. By nature, feelings are unpredictable and resistant to control. This is usually enough to make people fear emotions and therefore suppress them. Although it's easy to understand why people would repress feelings such as anger, terror, and grief, why would they want to keep a lid on their joy?

For one thing, a feeling of joy is especially scary to people who are accustomed to struggling. If you've struggled all your life to survive, you might be afraid that if you stop struggling, you'll die. This may sound ridiculous, but check it out. You can test to see if you have this pattern by asking yourself, "Have I ever been afraid that something *bad* might happen if I get *too happy*?"

If you get nervous about being truly happy, be kind to yourself about it. Perhaps you were shamed as a child for your joyful exuberance. Maybe you were punished for masturbating or for doing something else that put a big smile on your face. If you feel anxious about pleasure or happiness, stop reading and hang out with your memories for a while.

When you feel like criticizing your children, remember who raised them.

DALE TURNER

Imagine that the child you once were is sitting next to you right now. Get a crayon or a colored felt-tip pen for your nondominant hand, so your inner tyke can use it to talk with your adult self. On the flip side, let your adult self speak through your dominant hand now by giving it a pen or other favorite writing utensil. To help you begin this dialogue between the adult and child parts of yourself, I'll throw out a few ideas for you to consider.

As you sit with the following questions, find a way to paraphrase them so a child would understand what you're asking. Then write down your paraphrased questions with your dominant (adult) hand, and let your kid respond through your other hand. Hopefully, this dialogue will help you access some of your early experiences with pleasure and joy.

Did your parents, caregivers, or other adults warn you (as a child) not to be *too* happy, *too* rich, *too* successful, *too* beautiful, *too* smart, *too* giving, *too* trusting, or *too* anything? Did the adults in your life tell you that it's selfish to want anything for yourself, as if *selfish* is a dirty word? Did they tell you to "hide your light under a bushel," because others who are less fortunate might see you and feel bad? Did anyone come right out and tell you that the pursuit of pleasure would lead to eternal damnation?

After you ask your kid-self about unpleasant or scary memories related to joy, find out if you have any positive associations with it. Were there any people in your childhood who encouraged you to follow your bliss? Did you have any special animal friends who helped you experience joy? How about imaginary friends? Did you have any of those, and if you did, what role did they play in your delight? Were there any secret places you visited in order to stay close to your heart?

Keep this kind of dialogue going, using your best skills as a conversationalist. Remember that you're talking to a kid, so let your questions be simple. If you don't get a response from your nondominant hand, be sure to ask the question in another way. If the silence persists no matter how you phrase your questions, switch to another subject for a while, or ask your kid-self how he or she feels right now. Follow that feeling, and find a way to express it through writing, play-acting, or drawing. Then ask your kid (via your nondominant hand) what he or she wants to do next. Follow that for as long as it feels right, and then come back to this exercise.

After you complete your dialogue, pull out your joy lists, and see if there's anything you'd like to add to either list. Perhaps your dip into childlike awareness triggered some new ideas about pleasure. Make whatever additions occur to you, and then get ready to take your lists in a new direction.

Healing the Work-Play Split

Consider how your joy lists relate to your work life. How many items on your lists are included in the way you make a living? All of them? None of them? A high percentage or a pitiful percentage? Do you notice a pronounced split between work and play? If not, congratulate yourself for your impressive integration of these two aspects of life. On the other hand, if your career isn't a big source of pleasure for you, ask yourself why. Is work supposed to be serious? Did someone tell you it's not okay to have a good time on the job? Are you afraid you might get in trouble if your boss sees you having fun? If you're self-employed, are you scared that if you lighten up, nothing will get done?

Assuming that you notice a gap between your work duties and your joy activities, would you like to change that? Again, the first step in changing something is to *want* to change it. If you want to get more pleasure from your work life, take out several pieces of paper and get ready to brainstorm.

There are only two lasting bequests we can give our children; one is roots, the other wings.

MOTTO OF MERCY HOME
FOR BOYS AND GIRLS

It does not matter what *you do in life. The only thing that matters is that you do what you do with love.*

ELISABETH KÜBLER-ROSS

For each entry on your joy lists, see if you can come up with three or four ways that you could make money doing that activity. If you don't need money, see if your joy lists are represented in the way you do volunteer work, the way you relate to others, and the way you spend your time in general. Believe it or not, it's possible to discover ways to honor your joy lists 100% in your life—including your work life. This isn't necessarily easy. For those of us who have had a severe work/play split, it may take years to bridge the gap.

I'll give you an example from my own life. I remember a conversation I had with my father a few days before I left for college out of state, when I was seventeen. He said that he had never discovered what made him truly happy, in terms of a vocation. He said that he figured out what he could do well, and he settled for that as a career. I suspect that he was trying to discourage me from setting my hopes too high, since he was well aware of my youthful idealism. However, it broke my heart to know that such a talented, intelligent, and deeply compassionate man had never found his true calling. His story only made me all the more determined to follow my heart.

During that same conversation, my father also told me that I shouldn't bother to take singing lessons in college (I really wanted to), because I obviously had no talent for it (according to him). Since he had abandoned his own joy, it's understandable that he advised me to do the same. Even still, I was crushed. To this day, I've never taken singing lessons. However, fifteen years after that long talk with my father, I reconnected with my singing voice in a special way.

It happened because of a wonderful year that I spent living with Leslie Heizer. A mutual friend had introduced us, and within a short time we were sharing a house together in Seattle. I remember one particular afternoon when Leslie came home while I was singing. She greeted me in the threshold of my room, and in a spontaneous burst of joy, she joined me in song. It was exhilarating!

Leslie, who is a gifted musician, told me afterward that I have a beautiful voice. I was stunned. Her compliment made me realize how much I had hidden my voice from others because of criticism that was ancient history. With Leslie's gentle encouragement, I began to come out with my singing a little bit at a time. Ultimately, it doesn't matter if anyone else likes my voice. I *need* to sing simply because it makes me happy.

The punch line to this story is that singing later became part of my work. I'm not a performer, of course, but when I facilitate certain kinds of workshops, I sometimes sing during opening or

Nothing has a stronger influence psychologically on their environment, and especially on their children, than the unlived life of the parents.

Carl Jung

Use what talents you possess—the woods would be very silent if no birds sang except those that sang best.

Henry Jackson Van Dyke

For most people, the activity portion of life is overemphasized at the expense of the rest phase. Don't suffer from picnic deficiency!

DEEPAK CHOPRA

Those who say it cannot be done should not interrupt the person doing it.

CHINESE PROVERB

I feel sad for a person who says, "I'll just take care of myself." I think that's a hungry ghost realm.

RAM DASS

closing rituals. Also, when I do shamanic healing work, I usually begin by singing my *power song*.

At seventeen, if someone had suggested that I might make money singing, I probably would have laughed. Fortunately, I've had a lot of bliss-mentors since then. Playmates of all styles and persuasions have taught me that doing what I love is not only permissible, but also essential to health.

I hope my story inspires you to be expansive and creative when you begin generating ideas about how to bridge work and play. Don't forget to use both hands to write during your brainstorming sessions. Ask your friends for their perspectives. Keep your pages of ideas and hone them over time. Feed your desire to integrate work and pleasure, because your desire will spur you to action.

As you go about implementing your ideas, be irrepressible in your passion and realistic in your expectations. Don't let anyone tell you that you *can't* do something. On the other hand, be compassionate about the *timing* of your dream's manifestation. While it's true that thoughts can manifest in a flash, most of us aren't that spiritually adept. Besides, the *process* of ordinary physical manifestation is one of the most interesting shows in town. Nursing your creative ideas to fruition over time can be as satisfying—and as miraculous—as watching a seedling grow into a tree.

If you focus on the end result instead of on the process, you might not know how to savor the end result once it comes. If joy is the watchword, then do what you can to en*JOY* the journey, not just the destination. If you believe that you must sacrifice present joy for the sake of future joy, question that belief. Can you find another way?

A Warrior's Path

It's possible to keep a tender thread of connection to your joy despite everyday challenges, setbacks, and drudgery. However, this takes patience, courage, and a continual willingness to drop old attitudes. It's not always easy to stay in touch with your heart, listen to your body, and honor your needs while still respecting the needs of others. True joy requires *all* these levels of awareness. It's a lot to juggle. This is why the path of joy is a warrior's path.

Knowing this, consider one more step in your efforts to bring more joy to your daily work. Let's say that you'd like to experience more pleasure at work, but it's just not happening. Now morning has arrived, and it's time to get up and get going. What do you do? Would you rather stay in bed? I understand.

When I feel like that, I take a few moments to have a chat with all the different perspectives mulling around inside me. I try to listen to each aspect of my awareness, including the one which demands that I *take that job and stuff it!* In the end, it often comes down to the fact that no part of me is going to survive if I don't get up and do what needs to be done, since I'm responsible for my own bills.

There are days, however, when my body, mind, and spirit say *no* despite the pressure of financial responsibilities. Usually, I have to be pretty sick for this to happen, though I secretly love the idea of "calling in well." In any case, if my objections to work become the norm rather than the exception, then I know something needs to change. Occasionally, this means that I need to consider another career option. Most of the time, however, it merely indicates a need to change my approach to work.

Again and again, I find that my joy level takes a dive when I forget to *pay attention* to whatever brings me joy. This happens because I lose my *focus*. In other words, it's my job to perceive the joy that already exists within and around me. It's not the world's job to deliver bliss on a silver platter, with flashing neon signs and ringing bells.

I notice that if I hold certain questions in my heart, it's easier for me to cultivate pleasurable experiences throughout the day. I'll give you some of the questions I use to keep my *joy meter* ticking, and then you can write down similar questions for yourself, in your own words. Here are a few to get you started.

How can I find more pleasure in this situation? How can I do what I need to do, and have a good time doing it? How can I do what I need to do, and have a *better* time doing it? How can I *amp up* my enthusiasm right now? How would I do this activity if I felt passionate about it?

Notice that each of my questions begins with the word *how*. I like *how* questions because they presuppose that you can find an answer. These kinds of questions stimulate your brain to come up with answers, because they assume that an answer is possible. An answer *is* possible, and an attitude of *expectancy* for joy will open more doors to it.

Spend an hour with a healthy baby, and you'll see that joy can be natural and effortless. You shouldn't have to work at it, and you shouldn't have to earn it. Unfortunately, joy has gotten a bad rap in the world of most adults. In part, this is because joy is associated with passion, aliveness, empowerment, creativity, and freedom—all of which are qualities that contribute to individuality, rather than conformity. This scares people who believe that if everyone follows

What a strange machine man is! You fill him with bread, wine, fish, and radishes, and out come sighs, laughter, and dreams.

NIKOS KAZANTZAKIS

Being, not doing, is my first joy.

THEODORE ROETHKE

Hold fast to dreams for if dreams die, life is a broken-winged bird that cannot fly.

LANGSTON HUGHES

their bliss, we'll have total anarchy and nothing will get done. I believe the opposite is true.

The most joyful people I know are the ones who follow their passion. Not coincidentally, these are often the same people who encourage others to do the same. The human heart will never be satisfied with caring only for itself. If you give wings to your joy, it will be the best gift you can give to humanity because it will *include* humanity, starting with you and spreading outward.

THE GRATITUDE CLEANUP LIST

Lots of people talk about getting up to date in regard to unfinished business, in terms of resolving outstanding conflicts. Yet few people talk about the importance of cleaning up unfinished *gratitude*. How's your relationship with gratitude? Is the experience of thankfulness a regular occurrence for you, or do you forget to acknowledge all the support that is constantly coming your way?

Although this chapter will focus primarily on cleaning up unfinished gratitude toward other people, you can extrapolate the following suggestions to include other creatures and other aspects of reality. I'll offer a few tips for these variations toward the end of the chapter. For now, let's start with people.

The first step in gratitude cleanup work is to make a list of everyone toward whom you feel grateful. I know this sounds obvious, but have you done it? If not, take out some paper and a pen, and start reminiscing. Write down people's names as their faces pop up in your memory. Perhaps you felt appreciation recently for a friend's favor. Maybe someone in your family has always *been there* for you when times got tough. Perhaps a total stranger saved your life once. Or maybe an acquaintance helped you to renew your faith in living when your heart was in despair.

If you want to be thorough, begin at birth (or as far back as you can remember). Consider your entire life in terms of all the people who have helped you along the way. Don't forget to include *shadow teachers*, those people who catalyzed unexpected growth for you, although that growth may have been painful. Such people deserve gratitude as well.

As you write your list, make a notation by the names of people toward whom you feel gratitude, yet you resist telling them. In such cases, it's possible that you may have other feelings that need your attention first. It's not unusual to have more than one kind of emotion in relation to others. For instance, you might feel both gratitude and anger toward people in your family.

Look at everything as though you were seeing it for the first or last time. Then your time on earth will be filled with glory.

BETTY SMITH

I have learned silence from the talkative, toleration from the intolerant, and kindness from the unkind; yet strange, I am ungrateful to these teachers.

KAHLIL GIBRAN

If the only prayer you say in your whole life is "thank you," that would suffice.

MEISTER ECKHART

If some of the people on your list trigger multiple feelings for you, it doesn't mean that you can't express gratitude to them. You can. First, however, you might want to take a few moments to acknowledge your other feelings. This could be as simple as noticing them and saying *yes* as you experience them in your body.

Here's a quick exercise to take this a step further. As you sit with a particular emotion, imagine yourself wrapping your arms around it as you breathe in. Then, when you exhale, imagine your arms opening to set the feeling free. Breathe in, and surround the feeling with compassion. Breathe out, and let it go. As you exhale, experiment with various vowel sounds, such as *ahhhhhhh*. Choose a sound that makes your belly soften and relax.

You can do this simple breathing technique as many times as you like, until the intensity of the feeling diminishes or until another feeling appears in its wake. Repeat this exercise with each emotion as it arises until you feel peaceful enough to continue.

When you return to your list, look again at the names that you marked because you resist expressing gratitude to them. If your resistance has dissipated for any of these people, draw a heart, a star, or some other new notation to cancel the old mark. If any names still trigger an onslaught of conflicting emotions, that's okay. Proceed with gratitude cleanup work for the others, and let the hard ones go for now. Don't turn gratitude into a *should*. That would be as silly as covering a diamond with mud. Gratitude can only sparkle when it is given freely, without obligation or expectation.

A thankful person is thankful under all circumstances. A complaining soul complains even if he lives in paradise.

BAHA'U'LLAH

When you're ready, you can move on to the next step. Those of you who are chronologically oriented might choose to number the people on your list, so you can systematically handle your gratitude cleanup work in numerical order. My own style is more casual. I choose the first name that jumps out at me, and I start there. Then I work my way through the list over time, selecting names based on my whims. Occasionally, I sprinkle in one of the tough ones—someone who has challenged me as well as blessed me.

Whether you follow my organic style or adopt a more systematic approach, be sure to find a method that makes it easy for you to keep moving through your list of gratitude recipients. Once you have a plan, the next step is to choose the forms of communication you want to use to express your thanks. You can write letters, make phone calls, arrange face-to-face meetings, or send e-mail messages. Decide for yourself which form is best for you in regard to each of the people on your list.

If you hate to write letters, for example, it doesn't make sense to force yourself to write them, even if you know the other person likes letters. On the other hand, if you're too shy to call or to talk in person, or if you want to send permanent reminders of your appreciation, letters might be a great choice for you.

Of course, it's nice to be considerate of other people's preferences. However, the first step is to express yourself in ways that work for *you*. After you know what you want to say and how you want to say it, then consider the personal tastes of your gratitude recipient. The bottom line is, if you don't feel good about what you're doing, the other person will notice your discomfort. In the best-case scenario, your style of delivery should enhance your message, not detract from it.

As you work through your list, keep this in mind: If you call or write only one person a week, that will add up to fifty-two people a year. Pretty impressive, huh? If that feels like too much effort, though, perhaps you could aim for one or two thank-you's a month.

For those of you who can't stand goals or deadlines, forget about a schedule, and approach someone on your list whenever the spirit moves you. What counts is your intention to share your appreciation more often and more directly with the people involved. Strike a balance in your gratitude cleanup work. Don't force the issue, but don't fall asleep on the job.

Remember that when you express appreciation, you're doing it for your own sake first of all. If your thank-you makes the other person feel good, that's a nice bonus, but it's not the main focus. In fact, some people may ignore your gratitude, throw it back in your face, or ask what took you so long, and what about all the things you forgot to mention?

Thus, it's important to let go of any expectations you might have about how the other person will respond to your words of thanks. If you're trying to win brownie points, make yourself look good, or show your moral superiority, then you'd better watch out. You may be in for a surprise, and it probably won't be pleasant!

Ultimately, there is only one valid reason to express gratitude, and that is to honor your own heart. If you withhold appreciation, it's like putting a lid on a fountain. Free expression of gratitude keeps the waters of your heart flowing.

It's great if you can appreciate your mentors, friends, and family while they are still alive. However, there may be people on your Gratitude Cleanup List who are dead. What then? You can still acknowledge their contributions to your life; you'll just have to be a little more inventive.

One technique is to write a letter to the person, and then read it at his or her gravesite. If you don't know where the gravesite is, if

From too much love of living,
From hope and fear set free,
I thank with brief thanksgiving
Whatever gods may be
That no life lives forever,
That dead men rise up never,
That even the lowliest river
Winds somewhere safe to sea.

SWINBURNE

There are never enough
"I love you's."

LENNY BRUCE

you don't want to go there, or if the person was cremated and scattered to the wind, you can simply read the letter out loud to yourself. As an alternative, you could read the letter to a trusted friend. Sometimes the presence of a witness can stimulate more layers of healing.

If you have unfinished business or unexpressed pain in relation to the dead person, be sure to write about those things, too. Don't worry about hurting your friend's (or relative's) feelings. If there is no life after death, then how can you hurt them? On the other hand, if the soul lives on, the person's spirit may already know how you feel, now that there are no human veils and pretenses between you. In that case, why hide?

When you're done writing and reading your letter, you could take it a step further by actually sending it. The trick is to put the letter in an envelope using only the person's first name, with no address and no return address. Be sure to put a stamp on the letter, since the postal carriers will still have to deal with it. I've heard that post offices have a "Dead File" for letters that can't be delivered. Perhaps you—and the spirit of the deceased—would enjoy the humor of that!

The only problem with mailing your letter to the Dead File is that it keeps your words hanging around somewhere, which may feel counterproductive to the intention of release. If this bothers you, another option would be to tear up the letter and burn it (see "The Fire Ceremony" for additional tips).

If writing is not your preferred method of expression, you can say thanks to a dead person by spending time with his or her photograph. Say everything you want to say silently or out loud, while gazing at the picture. If emotions come up, take a few moments to *move* the feelings in safe ways. Keep talking to the person's photograph until you get tired or until you run dry, whichever comes first. You can always do another round with the picture later, even months or years later.

As I mentioned early in the chapter, people aren't the only ones toward whom you may feel gratitude. You can express appreciation for animals, plants, objects, your body, ideas, experiences, the earth, the sky, and the entire cosmos. If you include more than people on your Gratitude Cleanup List, feel free to get wildly creative, in addition to using the techniques already suggested for people.

For example, you could pick up beach litter to honor the oceans. You could donate food to acknowledge the earth's bounty, which has kept you alive all these years. Perhaps you could volunteer to clean up a stream or a park, at the same time you clean up unfinished

As the cultivation of wisdom proceeds in life, I think most people end up praying more prayers of thanksgiving and gratitude rather than prayers of demanding and asking.

LARRY DOSSEY

If you wish to make an apple pie from scratch, you must first create the universe.

CARL SAGAN

gratitude for the water, the fish, the wind, and the trees. In a quiet moment, you could sit with a grove of bamboo and *listen to it grow,* while you give thanks for nature's beauty.

One of my favorite ways to clean up unfinished gratitude is to dance. I dance to the stars, to the cycle of life and death, to the interplay of joy and pain, and to the unfathomable mystery that swirls around me and sustains my soul. Even though I know that I dance to honor my own heart, that's not how it *feels.* It feels like my dance of gratitude blesses everyone and everything as much as it blesses me. In fact, how could it be otherwise?

The story is told of a British anthropologist who undertook a field trip to India. One evening he crept through the jungle and caught sight of an old holy man dancing ecstatically in the forest. The anthropologist watched this delirious, joyful display in fascination until he couldn't contain himself.

"Pardon me," he said, "but what makes you dance out here, alone in the jungle?"

The holy man looked bewildered and replied, "Pardon me, but what makes you think I'm alone?"

DEEPAK CHOPRA

MY FAVORITE FORGIVENESS PROCESS

My Favorite Forgiveness Process combines ideas from two of my most important mentors in regard to forgiveness, Sondra Ray and Morrnah Simeona. In the mid-1980s, I did extensive work with Sondra Ray, who is a rebirther, teacher, author, and founder of the Loving Relationships Training. Sondra, in turn, introduced me to the late Morrnah Nalamaku Simeona, a native Hawaiian *kahuna*, which means "keeper of the secret."

Morrnah taught a forgiveness process called *Ho'oponopono*, which is designed to cut and clear karmic ties back to the beginning of time. Together with her colleague, Ihaleakalā Hew Len, Morrnah traveled all over the world to teach Ho'oponopono to thousands of individuals and organizations, including the United Nations.

Although it's not right for me to teach the Ho'oponopono prayer, I'd like to share a principle of healing that I've learned from regular use of this prayer since 1985, when Morrnah first imparted it to me. I call this principle the *intention of two-way healing*. That is, when I do Ho'oponopono, I affirm (in very specific ways, according to the prayer) that forgiveness is happening in both directions, in terms of the people who are involved.

For example, if I'm doing Ho'oponopono in relation to my mother, I speak the prayer in its entirety in terms of forgiving my mother, and then I do it a second time in terms of her forgiving me. Obviously, this is a gross oversimplification of a long and eloquent prayer. However, I trust that you can get a sense of my intention that healing will happen both ways.

Some people might object to me affirming that my mother forgives me. After all, isn't she the only one who can do that? The truth is, I don't know the answer to that question, but I believe something mystical happens when either person expresses a desire for healing to happen both ways. I won't digress into lengthy metaphysical explanations for this belief. Instead, I'll simply encourage you to experiment with this idea to see what you discover.

In addition to the principle of two-way healing that I learned from Morrnah, I learned another powerful forgiveness tool from Sondra Ray. Sondra said that there's a line in the Bible that states (very roughly paraphrased): If you really want to forgive, you must do it seventy times seven. Sondra decided to incorporate this 70 x 7 concept into her use of affirmations.

For her 70 x 7 process, she suggested that you write the following sentence seventy times a day for seven days in a row. You fill in the first blank with your name, and then fill in the second blank with the name of the person, place, or thing you'd like to forgive:

I, _____, forgive _____ for everything.

If you prefer, you can substitute a description of some incident that bothered you, instead of using the word *everything* at the end of the sentence. However, if you're going to write something seventy times a day for seven days, you may as well cover all the bases and keep it simple.

Putting Sondra's 70 x 7 affirmations together with Morrnah's principle of two-way healing brought me to this, the sentence I use for My Favorite Forgiveness Process:

I forgive _____ and_____ forgives me.

You can add your name at the beginning, as Sondra recommends, or do the abbreviated version, as shown above. I use the shorter version for the sake of brevity. The short version is long enough when you're writing it seventy times a day for a week!

Once you've completed your seventy sentences, you can save the pages until the end of the week if you like, but then be sure to destroy them. Tear them up and recycle the papers, or burn them in a ritual of release (see "The Fire Ceremony" for more help). Another option is to recycle or destroy the pages each day. Either way, don't save them. *Let go!* That's the whole point.

It's essential to do the forgiveness process seven days in a row, without skipping a day. If you miss a day, you have to start over. This isn't meant to be punitive. Rather, the purpose of doing something seventy times a day for seven days is to keep your focus clear, and your follow-through strong. If you space out, don't beat yourself up about it. Just start again. Whenever I've forgotten a day and had to begin again, it invariably happens in situations where I need to spend the extra time working with that particular person or thing. I must also confess that this only happens with the people or things I most resist forgiving. *Busted again!*

Forgive your enemies, but never forget their names.
JOHN F. KENNEDY

Be observant if you would have a pure heart, for something is born to you in consequence of every action.
RUMI

There's another important tip about doing My Favorite Forgiveness Process. That is, the affirmations must be written by hand: no typewriters, computers, tape recorders, or dictaphones. Something very different happens when you write by hand, as opposed to working on a machine. I'm not enough of a scientist to explain it, but I know from experience that this is true.

Apart from any scientific explanations, writing by hand takes more *time*, which allows more *space* for thoughts and feelings to arise. This process isn't about writing for the sake of writing. It's about writing for the sake of healing. Sure, there are shortcuts. There are also lobotomies! I don't recommend either one as a substitute for the hard work of forgiving.

As an aside, I encourage you to read the chapter called "The Dilemma of Forgiveness." It's fine if you want to experiment with My Favorite Forgiveness Process without reviewing the other, more in-depth chapter beforehand. Whatever order you choose, though, I recommend reading both chapters, because they provide mutually supportive pieces of the forgiveness puzzle.

As I mentioned in "The Dilemma of Forgiveness," you don't have to *feel* forgiveness toward your chosen subject in order to show your *intention* for forgiveness. This is a good first step: to notice your unfinished business and demonstrate your intention for healing. Then, over time, you can work with your feelings and your behavior in regard to the unfinished issues.

Emotional and behavioral work are like the mortar that holds the bricks of your intention together. Mortar can be plenty messy, but when it's handled carefully, it makes a wall beautiful as well as strong. It's the same with feelings and actions. If you're sloppy with them, or if you neglect details in cleaning them up, all your good intentions will be for naught. The structure of healing that you build will reflect the quality of your care for every aspect of the work. Let the quality of your *mortar* match the strength of your *bricks*. In other words, your emotional and behavioral work should support and solidify the power of your intention for forgiveness.

When you're doing the 70 x 7 sentences, pay attention to the rest of your life as the week progresses. Whenever I do a round of My Favorite Forgiveness Process, I notice that it usually stimulates all my *stuff* to rise to the surface, like scum on a pond. Whatever stands in the way of forgiveness makes itself painfully apparent. There's nothing like a little intensity to test my resolve!

See if the same thing happens for you when you do a week of 70 x 7. Do you notice any synchronicities that might be related to your forgiveness writing? Do you feel the desire to act differently?

It matters immensely. The slightest sound matters. The most momentary rhythm matters. You can do as you please, yet everything matters.

WALLACE STEVENS

Do you find yourself wishing the other person (or situation) would change, so you wouldn't have to do so much work?

What kinds of feelings come up for you: anger, grief, fear, joy? Do you feel more accepting or, conversely, less tolerant? Do you notice anything unusual happening in your dreams? Do you feel more tired than usual or more energized? Do you perceive any difference in your attitude toward the person or thing that you're forgiving?

It's perfectly okay if you don't notice anything related to any of these questions. Maybe I'm asking the wrong questions for you, or maybe you're a strong skeptic, and you're determined not to let some silly exercise make a difference in your life. Whatever the case, I congratulate you for giving it a shot. Consider taking this leap of faith: Assume that you're planting seeds by doing the forgiveness sentences. Perhaps you'll discover the fruits of your labors later, when you're least expecting it.

Sondra said that whenever she did her forgiveness process, she received an abundance of flowers from people. This intrigued me, so I decided to test it, without telling anyone in advance about my little experiment. The same thing happened for me. I got lots of flowers! It didn't just happen the first time, either. The same thing happened whenever I did a week of 70 x 7 sentences.

One time I vowed that I would do My Favorite Forgiveness Process for as long as it felt right, choosing a different subject each week. I didn't stop for seventeen weeks. The first week I forgave *everyone*, and the last week I forgave *everything*. In between, I worked with forgiving my body, food, womanhood, family, men, God (that was scary), Cat, pain, sex, money, and a number of other people and things. It was very liberating—and you'd never believe how many flowers I got!

During the four-plus months that I was doing my forgiveness marathon, all kinds of people brought me flowers. Clients gave me flowers "for no reason." Friends showed up with bouquets. People I'd just met left me flowers on the doorstep. Those months of floral abundance gave me a chance to test my theory that you can never have too many flowers. In that span of 17 weeks, the only week I didn't get any flowers was the time I was forgiving Cat. When that week was over, I realized that I should have given myself flowers. So I bought myself a stem of stargazer lillies, my favorite flower.

During those seventeen weeks that I repeatedly cycled through my forgiveness process, I figure that I wrote the word *forgive* 16,660 times. I wrote it twice in each sentence, seventy times a day (2 x 70 = 140), for seven days in a row (140 x 7 = 980), for seventeen weeks

We live in a sweep-under-the-rug culture: We make messes, and then we ignore them. Or we hope no one finds out about them. Or we bury the mess in the Nevada desert— and then hope the bucket doesn't leak.

Louise Rafkin

Any idea seriously entertained tends to bring about the realization of itself.

JOSEPH CHILTON PEARCE

(980 x 17 = 16,660). That's a lot of focus on forgiveness. Needless to say, it was also a very rich time, psychologically and soulfully. There were plenty of butt-kicking lessons to show me where I was stuck. On the flip side, there were equally plentiful gifts of healing and grace.

I don't believe it's fair—or even accurate—to say that everyone must forgive in order to heal. How can anyone judge another person's path of healing? For all I know, some people may need to learn what happens when they hold a grudge for an entire lifetime. Who can say? Still, I must acknowledge the power of forgiveness in my own life.

For me, forgiveness is not necessarily about forgiving an act; it's about forgiving another human being. For me, forgiveness brings a softening, a yielding to a larger perspective, an accepting of my commonality with everyone and everything. Forgiveness deepens my humility.

Ultimately, I believe I am simply one cell in the body of humanity. This means that at some level, I am capable of—and perhaps even liable for—every possible human act, no matter how devious or destructive. This also means that when I forgive others, I forgive myself, and vice versa. Taking responsibility for my *shadow* may be difficult, but it's a necessary step toward forgiveness.

Whatever your perspective on this loaded subject, I hope My Favorite Forgiveness Process supports you in a way that fosters more compassion for the human experience. It seems that we are all victims and perpetrators, exchanging roles in blatant and subtle ways, not always realizing the ripple effects of our actions.

Forgiveness provides one way to embrace the duality of these roles by surrounding them in a sea of understanding. It provides a way to *interrupt the pattern:* to get off the wheel of harm and retribution. Someone has to take responsibility and make the first move. Perhaps that someone can be you.

THE FIRE CEREMONY

Fire is the ultimate symbol of transformation. Poets, mystics, and scientists alike have written about the awesome power of fire. Indigenous cultures from around the world and across time have used fire not only to support survival, but also to provide a basis for their ritual and magic. In contrast, most industrialized societies have turned to electricity for cooking, light, and heat. In the process of sacrificing fire in favor of more complicated sources of energy, people have lost regular and direct contact with a basic element of nature. In addition, fire's central importance as a vehicle of spiritual renewal has been all but abandoned.

What is to give light must endure burning.

VIKTOR FRANKL

While it's probably unrealistic to expect everyone to reinstate fire as the primary source of light and heat, fire can still be honored in daily life. This can be as simple as lighting candles for meals or using fire in ritual work. The Fire Ceremony described here will offer one basic form for this kind of work. The ceremony has many applications, limited only by your capacity to improvise according to your changing needs.

Because fire can be dangerous, I request that you read this entire chapter before you try the ceremony. Please make special note of *all* the details of the instructions, especially those that relate to safety precautions. My intention here is to teach you how to do *very small* fire ceremonies—whether in an outdoor firepit (best option), in an indoor fireplace (second best option), or in a carefully prepared, nonflammable space within your home (least desirable option). Not everyone is lucky enough to have a firepit or a fireplace, which is why I will provide you with information about option number three (see below).

If a writer is so cautious that he never writes anything that cannot be criticized, he will never write anything that can be read; if you want to help other people you have got to make up your mind to write things that some men will condemn.

THOMAS MERTON

Now, before I incur the wrath of every fire department in the country by suggesting that you can do a fire ceremony anywhere other than in a fireplace, let me assure you that my intention here is NOT to encourage random acts of conflagration. Instead, I want to teach the Fire Ceremony despite the inherent risks in doing so, because my goal is actually the same as every fire department's, namely, FIRE SAFETY.

You need to claim the events of your life to make yourself yours.

ANNE WILSON SCHAEF

If a man gives way to all his desires, or panders to them, there will be no inner struggle in him, no friction, no fire. But if, for the sake of attaining a definite aim, he struggles with desires that hinder him, he will then create a fire which will gradually transform his inner world into a single whole.

P. D. OUSPENSKY

Thus, for my sake as well as yours, I implore you to remember this as you consider the Fire Ceremony: *You are legally responsible for your actions, no matter how well or how badly you follow my instructions, so please take this ritual very seriously, or don't do it at all.*

To do this ritual of transformation, you'll need some paper and a pen, fire (a candle or even a match will do), a ceramic bowl, and a safe place to burn a small amount of torn paper. If you live in a single-family dwelling, as opposed to living in a wide expanse of barren sand, you'll have to be particularly careful about safety precautions. By the way, if you live in an apartment building, it's *not* a good idea to do the Fire Ceremony unless you have a fireplace, because the risks are too great. In such case, I recommend that you wait until you can use a friend's fireplace or until you can find a safe place outdoors to do the ceremony.

Thus, the best indoor place to do this ritual is in a fireplace. When you use a fireplace, be sure the vent is open (forgive me for stating the obvious, but you'd be amazed what people forget). Also, make sure the room itself is adequately ventilated. Finally, the Chimney Safety Institute of America recommends that you keep a five-pound, ABC-rated fire extinguisher at home.

If you don't have a fireplace, then take some time—before you begin the writing part of the ceremony—to prepare the space where you will burn small pieces of your torn pages (at the end of the ritual). If you take this time at the beginning, everything will be in place for you when you're ready to use the fire. This, in turn, will free you to follow the flow of your ritual awareness more fully during each successive step.

If you don't have a fireplace in your home, the best indoor option for doing this ritual is to do it in the bathroom, taking your ceramic dish with you into the bathtub or the shower stall. Showers and tubs are good places for mini-sized fire rituals because there is plenty of water available, just in case. Even still, please remember that I'm talking about burning a few torn pieces of paper in a fireproof dish, which you would place on the bottom (porcelain) surface of the tub or the shower. I'm not talking about building a campfire in your bathroom!

Despite the fact that you'd have water available, I discourage you from proceeding unless you have a working smoke alarm in your home, as well as a functional ceiling fan in your bathroom. The smoke alarm will keep your ceremony in line: If you set off the alarm, you're burning too much paper at one time. In regard to the fan, I include this recommendation not only for safety's sake, but also for the sake of aesthetics. I'm always amazed by how little smoke it takes to leave a dirty residue, whether on the walls or in the air. Therefore, keep the fan going during your ritual, and if you have windows in your bathroom, keep them open, too.

If you are going to do your ceremonial burning in a small bowl in the tub or in the shower, first remove the shower curtain or any towels or other flammable materials nearby. Take the time to be safe. If you are in a hurry, or if you deny the importance of *preparing the ground*, you will risk disaster and you'll sacrifice much of the ritual's power. Ritual is about form and detail, attention and thoroughness, intention and follow-through. It's about quality, not quantity, and speed is irrelevant.

By the way, when I suggest that you do the final act of your Fire Ceremony in the bathtub or in the shower stall, I'm not saying that you have to do the whole thing in there. You'll be doing your contemplations and writing in a chosen sacred space, then circling back to your carefully prepared *indoor safety center,* when it's time to release your material to the fire.

Bear with me while I offer a few more precautions. By now you know the bottom line, which is this: *be extremely careful* when you do fire rituals, even if you do it naked in the middle of the desert. I have singed hair, altar cloths, clothes, and carpets in moments of carelessness. Some of my friends have confessed to close calls with house fires while doing these kinds of rituals. It only takes a second for the wrong thing to go up in flames. **Respect fire always!** Never turn your back on it. Never leave candles burning unattended, even for a moment.

If you plan to do the ritual outdoors, be sure to burn small amounts at a time in your ceramic bowl, in a place protected from wind, vegetation, and flammable objects (or flammable creatures, for that matter). The purpose of the Fire Ceremony is to release and transform, but it's important to be in control of what you release and transform!

Once you've chosen and prepared a place to do safe burning, you can begin the more esoteric aspects of the ritual. First, take as much time as you need to center yourself. Unplug the phone and turn off the radio, the television, and the computer (if any). If you like, you can put on some sacred music. Then find a quiet space to sit and write. Some people like to do their ceremonial work in front of an altar or within some other specially designated space. If you don't already have a place like this, simply choose a quiet spot that appeals to you.

Loss makes artists of us all as we weave new patterns in the fabric of our lifes.
GRETA W. CROSBY

When the visitor arrived he found the holy man in prayer. He sat so still that not even a hair on his head moved. When the holy man had finished his prayer, the visitor asked where he had learned such stillness. He replied, "From my cat."
EDWARD HAYS

The heart that breaks open can contain the whole universe.

JOANNA ROGERS MACY

Now it's time to write, so get out your paper and a pen. Write down whatever you'd like to release, transform, or heal. Here are some examples to help you get started:

- An illness, pain, or condition in your body.

- Hatred or ill-will toward yourself or another person.

- Confusion about your direction or your life purpose.

- Fears about anything and everything.

- Unfulfilled desires, fantasies, or dreams.

- Unresolved conflicts with a person, place, or thing.

- Any addiction or compulsive habit.

- Attachment to a person, place, or thing that prevents you from moving forward in life.

As you write, describe the situations and your feelings as fully as possible. Be specific and thorough. If you're angry, write about every aspect of your frustration, no matter how petty you think it is. If you have physical or mental pain, or if you are experiencing illness, describe it in detail, including any feelings of fear, grief, anger, confusion, or shame.

Take some time to open your heart to this experience of *inventory*. If you become so emotional that you can't write, stop and *be with* your feelings as best you can, without trying to fix or change them. When you're ready to return to your writing, do so. Continue this process until you've written down everything you want to say for now. Don't worry about forgetting something, because you can always do the ceremony again later. If you want, you can add the following statement to the bottom of your list, just to cover all the bases: "Anything I knowingly or unknowingly have omitted is automatically included in this ritual."

When you're finished, stay in your sacred space while you savor the act of tearing up the pages of your writing. As you make a little pile of torn paper, imagine that your fears, angers, griefs, blocks, and attachments are now beginning the journey of transformation. In a moment, gather all the scraps of paper and put them in your fireproof dish. With reverence for yourself and your truth-telling, carry your bowlful of challenges to the safe space you have already prepared for the final act of burning.

Life is like an onion. You peel it off one layer at a time, and sometimes you weep.

CARL SANDBURG

If you've written many pages of material, it will be necessary to burn the pieces of paper in several stages, a little at a time. Always err on the side of safety. Also, remember that attention and thoroughness are essential aspects of ritual, so if it takes you an hour or more to burn all the pieces, that's okay. More time means more opportunity to tune in to the nuances of letting go. It will also give you a chance to *thank* whatever you're releasing. After all, your problems and challenges haven't only hindered you; they've also helped you grow.

I like to burn a little sage along with the pieces of paper. Sage, which is also called the *cleansing smoke*, is a valuable aid in clearing harmful energies (see "The Talking Circle"). If you don't like sage, or if it's not available, there are many other herbs and incenses that can be used to cleanse your ritual space. By the way, ceremonial sage is different from the sage that is used for cooking. If you're not familiar with plants used for ritual, consult an herbal directory, ask a knowledgeable friend, or check out the resources at your local metaphysical bookstore.

As you burn what you've written, state out loud (or silently, if you prefer) that you are now releasing these matters to their *right place*—or to the cosmos, the spirits, God/dess, your higher self, nature, the earth, or whatever suits your style. Ask that all the beneficent forces help you transform whatever experiences you've detailed in your words. In addition, ask that any harmful energies be safely dissipated. Finally, ask that the best resolution to your situation manifest now, *for the good of all.*

That last phrase is especially important, because it expresses your desire to merge what is best for you with what is best for everyone. Of course, you could probably impose your will in aggressive ways and disregard the needs of those around you. However, I doubt if this approach will work in the long run. It's hard to swim upstream against the River of Life without getting tired—or going under.

Frankly, I think it's just plain smart to align your intention with the well-being of the whole. If you don't believe me, you can delete the *good of all* phrase from your healing work, and see for yourself what happens when you ignore the greater good. I always encourage people to do their own scientific experimenting with metaphysical principles. There's nothing like a little universal butt-kicking to bring the point home.

When you've completed your ritual, give thanks for the fire, the space, the paper, your feelings, the spirits, and everything else involved. As a final step, you can scatter the ashes over the earth somewhere (be sure all embers are fully extinguished). As an alternative, I sometimes flush the ashes down the toilet, just for the sake of humor. Ritual doesn't have to be deadly serious!

I shall tell you a great secret, my friend. Do not wait for the last judgment. It takes place every day.
ALBERT CAMUS

Blessed is the flame that burns in the secret places of the heart.
JANET BIEBER

We who lived in concentration camps can remember the men who walked through the huts comforting others, giving away their last piece of bread. They may have been few in number, but they offer sufficient proof that everything can be taken away from a man but one thing: the last of the human freedoms— to choose one's attitude in any given set of circumstances, to choose one's own way.

VIKTOR FRANKL

Your resistance to change is likely to reach its peak when significant change is imminent.

GEORGE LEONARD

After you've taken a few moments to reflect, return to your other activities. As you go about your life, pay attention to your experiences while remembering your intention for healing. In the process of effecting change, your job is to identify your problem areas, do your inner and outer emotional work, ask for help (spiritually as well as practically), be willing to receive that help, and then *follow through with your intention in your actions.*

Obviously, you can't simply do a ritual and expect everything to be different, without any other effort on your part. Sometimes miracles happen: You go to bed a caterpillar and wake up a butterfly. More often than not, however, it takes effort to grow wings, and it takes effort to fight your way out of the cocoon. Someone once said that invention is 1% inspiration and 99% perspiration. Spiritual work is the same way. Follow-through may be difficult, but it's as essential as your intention.

As life continues to unfold, you might have thoughts about the problems you released in your Fire Ceremony. If so, remember your intention. Use the memory of your ritual to center yourself by reminding yourself of the *feeling* you had while doing it. *Imprint* this feeling in your cells by remembering your experience with appreciation for your efforts.

Focus your thoughts on releasing old patterns and embracing the new, even though you don't know how this will look. You might even imagine an *image* of the new, or you could choose a particular color of light to represent it. As an alternative, you could dream up a beautiful musical sound, or you could select a special song to symbolize the spirit of change. In this way, you can make it easier for yourself to embrace change, as opposed to fearing it.

If your commitment to change begins to falter, try doing the Fire Ceremony again. Also, if you're working with deep-seated issues in your life, it might help to do the ritual every day for a week, or perhaps once a week for several months. Longstanding habits take time to release, because they have many layers. Be patient. Above all, don't beat yourself up about anything. That only serves to bind you to whatever you want to release.

To conclude, let me offer a few more general tips about the ceremony in relation to change. One thing to remember is that a problematic situation may remain the same, but your *perception* of it may shift, so that you no longer consider it a problem. This kind of change is often overlooked, yet it can be as powerful as if the circumstances themselves had changed.

Another tip is to consider the fact that we puny humans are definitely *not* in charge of the overall timing of events. As a recovering control freak, it took me years (more like decades) to realize that I can't control much of anything. I'm in charge of my perceptions, my intentions, and my actions—but not the results. Sometimes I still want what I want when I want it, but the truth is, I feel relieved when I remember that I'm not in control of the universe. After all, the entire universe is involved in the outcome of any situation, no matter how small.

Once I asked Ram Dass if he ever prays for anything. He said, "When I pray, I never ask for anything, because I don't even know why things are the way they are. The only thing I ask is, 'Help me understand better what's happening, so my actions will come out of more wisdom.' "

Thus, when you do the Fire Ceremony, it's best to focus on what you would like to change *within yourself*. If you review the list offered earlier in this chapter, you'll see that everything relates to *internal* feelings, attitudes, habits, or conditions. Even if you're confused about a relationship, for example, it's still *your* confusion.

The bottom line is that you can only change yourself. Fortunately, systems theory maintains that if you change one part of a system, the whole system must change. This means that if you change your part in any situation, the entire situation must change. However, the changes that occur may or may not match your expectations. It's a razor's edge walk to let yourself want what you want, while letting go of whether or not you ever get it. This is easier said than done, yes?

It's certainly possible to cultivate an attitude of childlike anticipation and curiosity toward change, but this usually takes practice. The Fire Ceremony can help you increase your comfort with change by helping you focus on its transformative qualities. As you scatter the charred remains of your written problems, trust that new life will rise up from the ashes of old pain, bringing new opportunities for growth.

For peace of mind, resign as general manager of the universe.
LARRY EISENBERG

The true wonder of the world is available everywhere, in the minutest parts of our bodies, in the vast expanses of the cosmos, and in the interconnectedness of these and all things.
MICHAEL STARK

Person to Person:

Relating with

Respect

SECTION

FOUR

The Basics
of Listening

Wouldn't it be great if everyone learned the art of listening from healthy role models at home? It would also be wonderful if basic listening skills were included in the core curriculum of primary and secondary schools. I believe that many of the world's ills arise from people's inability to truly hear, understand, and respect one another. The truth is, it's not necessary to agree in order to validate each other.

Consider your own relationships. Do you feel *heard* by your family and friends, and do you honestly *hear* them? Can you respect other people's thoughts and feelings when they differ from yours? Do you know how to fully receive other people's communications as *gifts*, or do you wait with bated breath for your chance to speak?

The exercises in this section offer structured techniques for practicing good listening skills. Like all formal exercises, they may feel stiff and awkward at first. For people who resist structure, these techniques may trigger resistance—or downright rebellion. If this is true for you, congratulate yourself for your spirited independence and then try the exercises anyway. Perhaps you could tell your rebellious part that these techniques are actually a rebellion against old ways. That might help you relax.

The first time I tried methods similar to those included here, all kinds of feelings came up for me. The exercises felt phony, at best, or terrifying, at worst. Over the years, however, these skills have become an integral part of my communication style. At this point, what used to feel formal simply feels respectful.

The ideas and exercises in this section are designed to stimulate deeper levels of intimacy between you and other people, and between you and various aspects of yourself. As you'll probably discover, even the simplest of these processes can trigger feelings, not only because of the subject matter, but because you'll be communicating in new ways. If feelings do come up for you, complete the exercise as best you can, and then take a moment to be with your experience. If your emotions overwhelm your practice sessions, let your intuition

Listening is a form of accepting.

STELLA TERRILL MANN

When our children were growing up, if they came to me with their troubles, I usually suggested solutions for them— join a group, see a therapist, take vitamins. They said, "You're no help." But when I sat and listened, they thanked me for what I did and told me how much I had helped them.

BERNIE SIEGEL

guide you to other chapters in this book that can help you sort out your feelings.

When you're ready to try some creative listening techniques, the first thing you'll need is a partner. Ask someone with an open mind and a good heart—someone you trust. You and your friend can sit and face each other while you talk, or you can go for a walk. Face-to-face interactions usually intensify the feeling of intimacy, which can feel exciting or suffocating, depending on any number of factors. Walking with someone typically involves less eye contact, and it has the advantage of physical movement. Metaphorically, walking is nice because you're both moving forward in the same direction while you talk with each other.

In any case, you can experiment with sitting or walking. Notice how they are different for you. Do whatever feels safer first, and then up the ante by trying the style that feels more difficult for you. With practice, you'll develop more comfort with each approach, so you can choose the best one for any given situation.

The next step is to decide who will be the first speaker and who will be the first listener. Then choose a topic. If you need ideas, there's a list of options provided toward the end of this chapter. To illustrate the basic principles of listening, I'll have you begin by sharing things about *yourself*. After all, it's the subject you know best! Proceed by using the following sentence with your partner, filling in the blank with anything that comes to mind.

Something I'd like you to know about me is _____.

Each time you say something about yourself, your partner can respond with a quiet nod or with a simple statement of *thanks*. After you've had a few minutes in the speaker position, change roles, and let your friend talk while you listen.

When you're the speaker, the important thing is to remember *not* to ramble. Make simple statements, as opposed to weaving tall tales embellished with details. Keep it short and sweet, even if you feel a little silly. When you're on the listening side of the equation, remember that it's your job to respond *only* with a brief acknowledgment.

In regard to the listener nodding or saying *thanks*, it's not my intention to block longer conversations just for the sake of blocking longer conversations. Rather, the idea is to encourage the art of good listening by reducing your response to a bare-bones minimum. The focus of attention should remain solely on the speaker. This is an integral part of good listening. It's also the part that people resist the most.

Listen to your child enough and you will come to realize that he or she is quite an extraordinary individual.

M. SCOTT PECK

It may take practice to receive other people's words without interrupting, finishing their sentences, commenting, or waiting impatiently for them to stop talking, so that you can speak. For instance, one of the obstacles to good listening occurs when someone's words remind you of an experience from your past. At that point, you may suddenly lose your attention for the other person as your mind fills with details about your own story. Before you realize what's happening, you might start talking about yourself before you take the time to acknowledge the other person's words. I call this *swiping the focus*. It's one of my pet peeves. I hate it when I do it, and I hate it when others do it to me.

If you have trouble listening to other people without swiping the focus or adding commentary, try this: Pretend you're a tape recorder. I'm not kidding! A tape recorder is the ultimate good listener because it never interrupts, it never offers unsolicited opinions, and it never misses a word of what was said. Can you listen so attentively that you can repeat back what the other person said? Good conversationalists are actually those who are the best *listeners*. I'm not suggesting that you never speak, only that you give as much consideration to how you listen as to what you say.

When you say *thanks* after people say something to you, it communicates to them that you have truly listened and that you value their thoughts. Believe it or not, you can use this technique in real life. If people ask why you say thanks, tell them you're learning to treat other people's words as gifts, and that you honestly appreciate what they have to say. Most people will be honored by your efforts to give them your full attention.

Another reason I suggest that you respond to people's sharing by saying *thanks* is that it allows you, as the listener, to acknowledge the speaker without commenting on what was said. Invariably, comments are statements about *you*, not the speaker. Even if you are complimentary, praise basically conveys the message, "I like that," which again is about you. On the flip side, criticism makes another statement about you, namely, "I don't like that." Either way, notice that such comments shift the focus from what is being said to *your opinion* about what is being said.

While there is nothing inherently wrong with commenting on other people's thoughts, the point of these skill-building exercises is to minimize dialogue in order to clarify the roles of listener and speaker. The danger is that my cautionary tips will make you so self-conscious that you'll never speak again! That's not my intention. I'm emphasizing the role of listening simply because I think it is sorely neglected.

It is better to sit still and be thought ignorant than to speak and remove all doubt.

ABRAHAM LINCOLN

In everyday conversations, people often become overfocused on speaking (or wanting to speak), even when they're supposed to be listening. As a result, no one ever really gets heard. In business terms, the *transaction* of a communication doesn't get completed. Therefore, the basic listening techniques provided here have a two-fold purpose: to help you learn to *give* nonjudgmental, undivided attention as a listener and to help you learn to *receive* this kind of attention as a speaker.

The Zen of listening is to keep your focus entirely on the speaker. Granted, this is all but impossible for those of us with active brains, but it's still a worthwhile intention. Treat this intention like a mantra. When you catch your mind running off in a million directions, simply bring your focus back to the speaker. Don't beat yourself up about this. Just bring your wandering mind back to its single-pointed focus on the speaker.

Over time, you may discover that you can apply your capacity for multiple foci to all the nuances of verbal and nonverbal information coming from the speaker. As a bonus, I'll bet that if you listen really well, you'll get better attention from the other person when it's your turn to talk.

Obviously, you may have feelings about what's being said, and you might think of something you want to say while the other person is still speaking. What then? The answer is simple. File your thoughts away in that wonderful brain of yours. Wait until the other person has finished, and be sure to acknowledge his or her words. Then you can offer your perspective—one transaction at a time.

When you're working with the skill-building exercises included in this section, your acknowledgment can be a simple statement of thanks or a quiet nod, as mentioned earlier. In everyday life, you can also use a broader range of nonjudgmental statements, such as *I understand*, *I see*, *that's interesting*, or a thoughtful *hmmmm*. Although you'll purposely limit your response during practice sessions, don't be afraid to mix and match in ordinary conversations. Otherwise you might end up sounding like a robot!

Once you've mastered the art of simple acknowledgment, you might experiment with paraphrasing other people's words as a way to let them know you've heard them correctly. As with all good listening skills, your paraphrasing efforts should keep the focus on the speaker, not on you. This is not the time to make comments or to offer your opinions; it's time to feed back what you've heard as accurately as possible.

After the other person indicates that you've gotten it right, you can even ask if there's anything else he or she wants to say. This

To know someone here or there with whom you feel there is understanding in spite of differences or thoughts expressed—that can make of this earth a garden.

GOETHE

kind of graciousness may seem overly formal, but it's not about manners for the sake of manners. It's about respect for the sake of respect. If you think this level of undivided attention sounds excessive, just remember how good it feels when someone gives it to you.

Here's another pointer for good communication. Ask others if they want to hear what you have to say before you start talking. For example, you could say, "Can I tell you something?" or "Want to hear a story?" The point is, listening is a gift. *No one is required to listen to you!* To bring home this point, a dear friend of mine, Cindy Seymour, borrows a phrase from the Bible when she cautions against throwing your pearls before swine. In other words, if you speak to someone who doesn't want to hear what you have to say, you're wasting your words, and therefore, *you're* disrespecting *yourself.* That's the bottom line.

When you ask other people if they want to listen to you, it may feel contrived at first. However, the more I use this technique in everyday interactions, the more I realize that *permission is the cornerstone of respect*—both for myself and for the other person. You can develop your own style of wording to ask permission, just as you develop your own style of simple acknowledgment. In this way, you'll integrate new skills into your personal communications.

By the way, many experts in the field of behavior modification say that it takes at least three weeks for new habits to take hold. My own experience shows that while this may be true, I think longstanding habits may take much longer to dissipate. If you can suspend your expectations about how much time it takes you to change, so much the better. Give the exercises a chance to work for you bit by bit, in their own way.

To complete this chapter, I'd like to offer you that list of topics I promised earlier. You can practice with the following examples when you meet someone new, or you can use them to deepen intimacy with old friends. Either way, let me give a brief review of the process.

First, you and your partner will decide who will take the role of speaker and who will take the role of listener. Whoever speaks first will choose a particular sentence and work with it for a few minutes, repeating the sentence several times, and filling in the blank with something different each time. In response, the listener will simply say *thanks,* or something equally kind and succinct. After the first speaker does a few rounds, be sure to switch roles, so each person has a chance to play with both sides of the exchange.

It is not fair to ask of others what you are not willing to do yourself.

ELEANOR ROOSEVELT

You cannot truly listen to anyone and do anything else at the same time.

M. SCOTT PECK

Something I like about you is _____.

Something I like about myself is _____.

Something I'd love to do with you is _____.

Something I love to do alone is _____.

One of my favorite memories is _____.

One of my most embarrassing moments was _____.

Something I'm scared to tell you is _____.

One of my dreams in life is _____.

One of my favorite sexual experiences was _____.

One of my most disastrous sexual experiences was _____.

One of the best things that ever happened to me was _____.

One of the worst things that ever happened to me was _____.

One of my favorite childhood experiences was _____.

One of the meanest things I ever did was _____.

One of the kindest things I ever did was _____.

My family always taught me _____.

One thing I love about my family is _____.

One thing I hate about my family is _____.

Something I was never allowed to do as a kid was _____.

Something outlandish I'd like to do is _____.

One of my favorite things about being alive is _____.

One of the hardest things about being alive is _____.

Something I imagine about death is _____.

Something I fear about death is _____.

One of my secret fantasies is _____.

One of the funniest things I ever heard was _____.

> *There is guidance for each of us, and by lowly listening, we shall hear the right word.*
>
> RALPH WALDO EMERSON

> *My goal in life is never to have a moment when I could not say, "This is how I want to die."*
>
> MARK DEBOLT

As you can see, some of these topics are relatively innocuous, while others are designed to stir things up. Even if you don't have a big charge about something when you think about it by yourself, you may experience a lot of feelings when you express it to someone else. A good listener can help you push old, dusty skeletons out of the closet by witnessing your words with nonjudgmental attention. Of course, a good listener can also magnify your pleasure, expand your delight, and share the tender burden of pain.

When you experiment with these exercises, speak your truth honestly and listen to your partner with active curiosity. Take each other seriously, but keep your sense of humor. A healthy balance of focused intent and kind receptivity can temper any fears you may have about going deeper into the mysterious land of intimacy.

...then the day came when the risk to remain tight in the bud was more painful than the risk it took to blossom.

ANAÏS NIN

APPRECIATE
YOURSELF

You beat 14,000 other sperm to get here.

LES BROWN

One good way to build self-esteem is to actively appreciate yourself. Don't worry, though. I'm not going to tell you to stare into a mirror while you feed yourself endless paeans of praise. That kind of exercise is great if you want to push out fears of self-love, give yourself a shot in the arm, or remind yourself that you deserve as much appreciation as anyone else. Unfortunately, though, some people use that technique to stroke their egos into complacency or to override their underlying fears of inadequacy.

Yikes! With an introduction like that, you might think I'm trying to scare you away from appreciating yourself. Well, I'm not. It's just that I'm painfully aware that many people have some degree of resistance to the idea of personal appreciation. I figure if I address some of this resistance up front, it might help the process.

The truth is, I actually agree with some people's objections to exercises that focus on self-appreciation. I've heard (and often enjoy) many of the jokes that poke fun at esteem-building techniques that I myself used for years. Frankly, I think these jokes provide valuable and well-founded criticism of self-help exercises gone awry.

Still, I don't want to throw out the baby with the bath water. I believe there's a way to wade through the psychobabble and still keep one's feet firmly planted on the ground of true self-care. Thus, I walk a fine line here. I want to encourage you to appreciate yourself, but at the same time, I want to encourage you to *be clear* about exactly what you're appreciating. I'll say more about the importance of specifics as the chapter progresses.

The thing is, you can grit your teeth and affirm yourself into oblivion, but that may not get you very far in the long run. I don't think it's helpful to feed yourself pat phrases as a steady diet, as if pretty words can somehow overcome all the vulnerabilities that tug at the foundations of your self-esteem. Pretty words mean nothing if they're not supported by substance.

Substance comes with *action*. When I talk about actively appreciating yourself, I'm talking about treating yourself with respect in every way possible. This means respecting yourself in every thought, word, and deed. When you find yourself slipping, catch what you're doing, and replace it with something more respectful. Don't beat yourself up when you don't appreciate yourself. That just compounds the problem. Simply catch your mistake and redo it.

When you catch a nuance of disrespect, stop it dead in its tracks. Then replace it with something that feels kinder, more tolerant, and more accepting. This is how you appreciate yourself: by deleting more and more of what hurts and hinders, and by adding more and more of what helps and heartens.

Most of us have no trouble criticizing ourselves. Self-judgment has a long history of social and religious sanction. There are countless proverbs that warn against the dangers of singing your own praises, as if the powers-that-be don't want you to notice that you, too, are part of creation's beauty.

If you're like me, you may have received such strong training in self-effacement that you can barely appreciate yourself in the privacy of your own home. In social spheres, many of us were taught that it's admirable to discount ourselves in relation to others, as if this is a gracious act of humility. I'm all for humility, but I don't think it comes from making yourself look bad in order to make others look good.

Ultimately, it's as important to appreciate yourself as it is to appreciate others. If you only appreciate others but not yourself, your well-meaning words will have a hollow ring. It's like a starving woman who spends all her time feeding others. At one level, her selfless generosity may seem laudable, but at a deeper level, she gives *death* with her gifts of life. Every morsel that she gives away takes with it a piece of her own hide, as long as she denies herself the food she so readily provides others. This is not true giving, and it helps no one.

Most of us dance along the continuum between sacrificial self-denial and healthy self-love. I don't know about you, but I'm always looking for ways to honor my own needs while still respecting the needs of others. It's not always easy to strike a balance. After a few decades of work on myself, I admit that I'm still finding my way along this continuum. Even the simple act of doing self-appreciation exercises can stir up the pot and stimulate old fears for me.

Every time I rewrote this chapter, it brought up another round of shadowy creatures—old warnings about being too self-centered, cultural and familial admonishments about denying myself for the sake of others, and my own pathologies about the dangers of noticing, much less appreciating, myself. At least I now realize that

If you think you are too small to be effective, you have never been in bed with a mosquito.

BETTE REESE

the only way through this morass of monsters is to remember my own words again and again. *This is how I appreciate myself: by deleting more and more of what hurts and hinders, and by adding more and more of what helps and heartens.*

Each of those shadowy creatures in my psyche offers a golden opportunity to go deeper into self-love. Each one needs my attention and care; that's all. If I can approach each of these apparent roadblocks as an invitation rather than an inconvenience, the path of self-acknowledgment can grow from a razor's-edge walk to a spacious boulevard of celebration.

Now there's a thought. Can you imagine appreciating yourself so much that you *celebrate* yourself? Perhaps if you give yourself permission to go all the way with this, it might help you take at least a few more steps in that direction. Do you really think you'll turn into a megalomaniac if you open the door to personal appreciation?

I doubt if you need to worry about megalomania, but if you are concerned about igniting a glut of conceit, consider this: Megalomaniacs are actually quite insecure. Perhaps more than anyone, they desperately need instruction in the art of honest self-acknowledgment.

The point is, if you can come to peace with your *inner megalomaniac* (I think everyone has one), then you may find it easier to give yourself more slack about personal appreciation in general. Here's a trick to play with that extreme. Imagine that you are the Supreme Ruler of the Cosmos. Next, take a few minutes to appreciate some of the things you've created.

Get specific. Don't just stroke your galactic gloriousness with nebulous compliments about beauty and grace and other ephemeral delights. That's all very nice, but I want you to concentrate on the details. Appreciate your creation of earth and water and stars and your favorite jeans and sweet jasmine and fireflies and sex and moonlit beaches and birds in flight. Keep going until you find and catch the cresting wave of *total appreciation*—until you discover that true acknowledgment is much more a celebration of *creation* than a celebration of self.

This is the paradox of self-love: When you go all the way into it, you end up loving everything along with yourself. The dichotomy between self and other disappears when you realize that everything you love about yourself is simply something that you love, period. This doesn't mean that you're not special, only that you're not alone in being special.

The shadow is 85% pure gold.
CARL JUNG

You are a child of the universe no less than the trees and the stars; you have a right to be here. And whether or not it is clear to you, no doubt the universe is unfolding as it should.

MAX EHRMANN

The qualities that you value in yourself are qualities that also belong to many others. When you appreciate yourself, you're simply acknowledging the presence of these qualities in *you*. What's wrong with being observant? In the final analysis, self-acknowledgment isn't about personal aggrandizement; it's about gratitude, it's about love, and it's about the feeling of spaciousness that arises in your heart when you remember your gifts.

With this in mind, let's get more personal. In a few moments, I'm going to ask you to take some time to actively appreciate yourself. First, though, I'd like to say a few more words about specifics. In the same way you went into detail when you appreciated your creations as the Supreme Ruler of the Cosmos, I'll encourage you to do the same thing when you acknowledge yourself as an individual.

Don't just stroke your ego with vague expressions of flattery about what a good person you are, or how worthwhile your existence is in the grand scheme of things. While there's nothing inherently wrong with this approach, I notice that for me, it seems to activate resistance from the part of me that disagrees with the idea that I'm completely wonderful. In fact, sometimes this feisty part has no desire to be anything but *bad* in the most radical, rebellious, delicious sense of that word. Thus, flowery proclamations of total goodness bother the part of me that will always be incorrigible. This is okay. I just need to find ways to appreciate *all* of me, including the feisty and rebellious parts.

One way to do this is to focus on specifics. If your goal is to cultivate an experience of appreciation, it won't help to blather on about generalities that activate hordes of contradictory feelings. Instead, I suggest that you name each of the qualities, skills, talents, styles, and beliefs that you value about yourself. Be sure to include the wild and mischievous aspects of your character. Give each quality plenty of room to stand on its own. This will not only help you validate all the details that make you unique; it will also help you focus on your feelings of gratitude, as opposed to focusing directly on yourself. That's the point: to keep your heart bathed in the *experience of appreciation*.

To inspire your excursion into detailed personal acknowledgment, I'll go first. How can I expect you to expose yourself if I don't do it? Granted, you can keep your accolades private, while I must publish mine in order for you to be able to see them. Nonetheless, I hope that if I hold my vulnerability out to you, it will encourage you to be vulnerable with yourself.

It is not the things we accomplish that are important, it is the very act of living that is truly important.

BILL JACKSON

I'm feeling mighty shy, but here goes:

- One thing I appreciate about myself is my ability to create in the midst of chaos.

- One thing I appreciate about myself is that I keep chipping away at my pathologies, trusting that there is always gold hidden in the pain.

- One thing I appreciate about myself is that I do my damnedest to take 100% responsibility for myself, my thoughts, and my actions, even when I'd rather take a vacation from it all.

- One thing I appreciate about myself is that I have learned to truly love my body, despite all odds.

- One thing I appreciate about myself is that I have overcome significant life-threatening illnesses.

- One thing I appreciate about myself is that I survived three psychiatric hospitalizations and used these experiences to grow.

- One thing I appreciate about myself is that I process collective pain as part of my spiritual work, as a way to *give back* for all I'm given.

- One thing I appreciate about myself is that I repeatedly take risks and defy conventional thinking in order to follow my heart.

Now it's your turn. As in my examples, you can use the following sentence.

One thing I appreciate about myself is _____.

Fill in the blank with something different each time. Sit quietly by yourself and speak your words out loud, letting your appreciation wash over you like a warm breeze. Take your time and enjoy it. Nobody's watching!

If you have trouble coming up with anything, don't despair. No doubt you have good reason to avoid what for you may be a scary act. Please be kind to yourself if you hesitate. If your mind goes blank when you approach the threshold of personal appreciation, sneak around the back and come in another door, so to speak. I'll give you some suggestions for doing this.

Learning to love our bodies is the fast road to high self-esteem.

JAMES JARVIS

If the mind should go blank, don't forget to turn off the sound.

DALE TURNER

One way I learned to feel safer with personal acknowledgment was to receive it from other people as I gradually learned how to give it to myself. Perhaps you can enlist the aid of a friend who treasures you. Ask him or her to brainstorm on the subject of appreciation—of *you!*

If you like to write, then jot down everything your friend appreciates about you. Feel free to chime in whenever the spirit moves you. If you don't like to write, turn on a tape recorder and make an auditory list. Be descriptive and specific, and be sure to include the things you both *secretly* admire about you. If you're shy, it might help to ask your friend for a promise of confidentiality.

Once your list or tape is complete for the moment, keep it in a safe place, and use it whenever you need a booster shot. If your self-esteem hits the pits regularly, you may want to assign yourself a daily or weekly appointment with your list or tape. When you use it, make certain that you give yourself enough time and space to let the appreciation sink in.

If your acknowledgments feel like psychobabble to you, stop and find out what you need in order to receive this simple gesture of self-care. Don't proceed until your door is truly open. If you think this exercise borders on gloating, then I encourage you to go ahead and gloat. The point is, how are you going to find out the difference between gloating and honest self-acknowledgment if you don't let yourself explore the edge between them?

Think about it this way. What's the worst that could happen if you go overboard and end up gloating? You might find out that you really are the Supreme Ruler of the Cosmos, and that you are an insufferable, self-centered fool. Well, if it comes to that, at least you can appreciate yourself for being centered in the self. What better place is there to be centered?

Seriously, though, I trust that you can see what I'm up to with my teasing. Each time you encounter a piece of resistance to self-appreciation, don't avoid it, and don't fight it. *Follow it!* Find out what your objections need from you, and then give them whatever they need to feel heard and *appreciated.*

This is how you appreciate yourself: by deleting more and more of what hurts and hinders, and by adding more and more of what helps and heartens. You can do it. I know you'll find a way.

You give to the world your greatest gift when you're being yourself.

DEEPAK CHOPRA

We're either killing ourselves or nurturing. There is no in-between.

IHALEAKALĀ HEW LEN

ADDICTIONS
AS TEACHERS

Many people think addictions are bad or wrong, but it's not true. In point of fact, your addictions have probably helped you survive, though of course they may also have harmed you. To show you what I mean about addictions being helpful, I'll tell you a story about a woman I knew many years ago named Suzanne (not her real name).

Suzanne was a passionate, artistic, intelligent, beautiful, and kind-hearted woman. To the outside world, she appeared to have it all together, yet she struggled with deep emotional pain that drove her to compulsive binge-vomiting. Because she managed to maintain a normal weight, no one knew about her bulimia.

Look for a long time at what pleases you, and longer still at what pains you.

COLETTE

People who have never had an eating disorder may find it hard to understand how anyone could eat and throw up. Most people are so repulsed by this behavior that bulimics may be too ashamed to tell anyone about it. I know about this kind of shame personally, because I was bulimic for eight years in the 1970s. Since Suzanne knew about my past, she felt safe to confide in me about her struggle.

One day, she came over to my house in tears. She had just returned from a very expensive in-treatment program for women with eating disorders. During the six weeks it took for her to complete the program, she had done well. Now that she was back in the midst of her regular life, however, she was throwing up again.

Contradiction is the criterion of reality.

SIMONE WEIL

Although I understood her grief and guilt about having spent thousands of dollars for treatment only to regress later, I assured her that the time and money had not been wasted. Every step counts, and every experience of acceptance counts, even if they happen in the sheltered environment of a treatment center.

At the clinic, Suzanne had discovered what she needed in order to exist without binge-vomiting. In part, her success there was due to the program's compassionate permission to engage in any behavior, without fear of disapproval or punishment. In addition, the staff provided 24-hour counseling support. Gradually, Suzanne was able to choose out of bulimia because her underlying emotional needs were deeply addressed. Although she and I both realized that it would be difficult to recreate that level of support in the real world, I offered to help in whatever way I could.

The first thing I told her was that I thought she was being much too hard on herself. After all, the stresses of everyday life far exceed those encountered in a treatment center. It was not realistic for her to expect herself to jump back into her normal routine without resorting to old coping mechanisms. She and I both realized that *unrealistic expectations* (trying to be perfect for the purpose of approval and control) are a contributing factor in eating disorders. I urged her to show herself as much compassion as she would show me. If she could alleviate some of the pressure to be perfect, she might feel less pressure to be compulsive.

In addition to this and the other emotional considerations we discussed, I suggested that Suzanne give special attention to her physical care, because bulimia can be extremely damaging to the body. I recommended that she replace fluid loss by drinking plenty of purified water. I also asked her to remember that repeated vomiting can seriously upset the body's delicate electrolyte balance, even to the point of causing death.

I didn't tell Suzanne these things in order to scare her into changing. Instead, my intention was to call a spade a spade. That is, both bulimia and anorexia can cause death, including sudden, traumatic death from heart failure. I think it's important to face this fact, and to *get real* about the seriousness of eating disorders.

With ruthless compassion, I told Suzanne that if she was going to play Russian roulette with death—just as I did during my years of anorexia and bulimia—then I recommended that she do it with her eyes open, and with awareness of all the possible consequences. Although this kind of direct truth-telling might seem harsh to some, Suzanne knew I was speaking from a place of love, not judgment. She also realized that I knew what I was talking about from many years of my own experience with anorexia and bulimia.

Along with my encouragement to monitor her fluid intake and electrolyte balance, I suggested that Suzanne provide her body with exceptionally good nutrition whenever she managed to keep a meal down. Last of all, I told her the story of my teeth and how they were permanently damaged by bulimia. Nine of my once-perfect molars had to be reduced to stubs and then reconstructed with gold crowns. Regurgitated stomach acid had destroyed the enamel. Not all bulimics lose their teeth, but just to be safe, I asked Suzanne to be honest with her dentist and to give her teeth special care.

We have so much fear of not being in control, of not being able to hold on to things. Yet the true nature of life is that we're never in control; we can never hold on to anything. That's how life is.

PEMA CHÖDRÖN

Death is the only wise adviser that we have.

DON JUAN

*What doesn't kill me makes
me stronger.*

ALBERT CAMUS

*The curious paradox is that
when I accept myself just as
I am, then I can change.*

CARL ROGERS

Most importantly, I asked Suzanne what would have happened to her if she had not become bulimic. Without hesitation, she said she would be dead by now. I said, "Yeah, Suzanne, get it! *Bulimia saved your life!*" She looked at me as if I was crazy. I said I was serious. Without the coping mechanism of binge-purging, she would probably be dead from suicide. In that light, she understood that her addiction was not wrong. It had helped her to stay alive when she knew no better way to deal with her tumultuous emotions.

The truth is, it's not wrong to avoid or anesthetize feelings with addictions, even though this approach only provides a temporary fix. No doubt we all do the best we can, given everything. If Suzanne needed to numb her pain through bulimia in order to survive, then that's what she needed to do. None of us can ever really know the depth of another person's pain. It makes no sense to judge Suzanne— or anyone—for trying to alleviate pain. Criticism only adds to people's pain by heaping shame on top of it.

With Suzanne's story in mind, perhaps you can look at your own addictions in a new way. Think about how they have helped you survive. Obviously, it's important to recognize how your addictions have hurt you (see "The Brutal Truth" and "The Three-Day Window" for more help with this). However, if you are already aware of the harmful side of your addictions, I encourage you to explore the helpful side more fully.

Ultimately, addictions are helpful because they can be used as tools to help you learn about yourself and your needs (see "The Five-Minute Switch System" for more details). Obviously, you must be willing to listen very carefully to your heart in order to hear the teachings of your addictions, since their destructive side can be so overpowering. Most people use their addictions to *go unconscious*. Therefore, it takes practice to use the habits that put you to sleep as tools to help you *wake up*.

To use your addictions to help you awaken, the first step is to regard them with acceptance, rather than criticism. Acceptance doesn't mean you'll never change your behavior; it simply acknowledges the fact that change comes only when you work *with* something instead of against it. This reminds me of a story told by Sy Safransky in the October 1996 issue of *The Sun*, a story which he attributes originally to Jack Kornfield:

> *The Master Ryokan never preached to or
> reprimanded anyone. Once Ryokan's brother asked
> the master to visit his house and speak to his
> delinquent son. Ryokan came but didn't say a word*

of admonition to the boy. When he prepared to leave the following morning, he asked his nephew to help him with his shoes. As the boy laced Ryokan's straw sandals, he felt a warm drop of water on his head. Glancing up, he saw Ryokan's eyes were full of tears. Ryokan returned home, and the wayward boy changed for the better.

Never underestimate the power of emotion. The simple act of acknowledging your feelings about your addictions may serve to increase your awareness of their detrimental effects. Like the Master Ryokan's tears, your feelings may lubricate the wheels of unexpected change. Can you show yourself as much love as the master showed his nephew? If you focus your attention on *total acceptance* of yourself, then anything that is *not* you must eventually fall away on its own. This isn't magical thinking; it's a basic principle of healing.

Let my hidden weeping arise and blossom.

RAINER MARIA RILKE

I realize that total self-acceptance isn't easy for most people. It's more like a sacred goal toward which you move with alternate speed and hesitation, depending on the challenges at hand. Perhaps you can take one small step toward acceptance by using a simple exercise now to explore the dual nature of your addictions. You can use the following two sentences as a written process. Better yet, speak the sentences out loud with a partner, following the general guidelines outlined in "The Basics of Listening" at the beginning of this section. If you work with a partner, remember to give each person a turn with the speaking role.

The test of a first-rate intelligence is the ability to hold two opposed ideas in the mind at the same time, and still retain the ability to function.

F. SCOTT FITZGERALD

One way my addictions have hurt me is _____.

One way my addictions have helped me is _____.

If you want to work with how your addictions have helped or hurt you in general, use the sentences as they are. If you'd rather consider the effects of a specific addiction, use the word *addiction* in its singular form. Either way, you don't actually have to name the addiction, unless you feel comfortable doing that. Naming your addiction will definitely up the ante in your truth-telling. However, the important thing is to write or talk about your habits in a way that allows you to be honest about your experience. To help you get started, I'll give you a few examples from my own life:

- One way my addictions have hurt me is that they kept a veil—and sometimes a wall—between me and other people.

- One way my addictions have helped me is that they deepened my compassion for others who struggle with addiction.

- One way my addiction to self-starvation hurt me is that it damaged my organs, glands, and bones.

- One way my addiction to self-starvation helped me is that it gave me a greater awareness of the daily possibility of death.

When you cycle through a few rounds of these sentences, pay particular attention to what you learn about the underlying reasons for your addictions. You may be surprised to find many paradoxes as you examine the pros and cons of your habits. If it's true that health is the ability to hold paradox, then this simple exercise may contribute to your health!

If you're unwilling to consider the positive side of your addictions, they will be more difficult to change. It's like the image of St. Peter wrestling with the devil, in which the devil says to St. Peter, "I will not release thee, lest thou bless me." If you can bless your addictions, you can use them to set yourself free.

Neurosis is the inability to deal with ambiguity.

SIGMUND FREUD

Dialogue
with the Body

It can be confusing to do healing work if different parts of your body seem to want different things. Many of us have experienced this kind of confusion during the simple act of deciding what to eat. Your mouth might crave something sweet and gooey, your brain might demand complex carbohydrates, and your digestive tract might beg for a big plate of vegetables. To complicate this, you may have emotional attachments to particular foods. In a fit of indecision, you might try to satisfy your conflicting desires by eating a little bit of everything, but your body as a whole might object to such a gastronomical onslaught.

You could take a different approach to this dilemma by paying attention to the inclinations of all your body parts, one by one, waiting until you can discern which food beckons most insistently. When you're hungry, you might not want to spend any time coming to a thoughtful decision. If you're willing to do the work, though, you could let yourself have some fun with it.

I get an image of you sitting around a round table with visual representations of your stomach, your brain, your taste buds, and whatever other body parts want to join the discussion. Each anatomical character speaks up in turn, and you consider their various viewpoints. What a riot! The point is, you can have a good time with your decision-making process, rather than treating it like an arduous chore that you merely tolerate in order to reach a desired end.

The same thing applies to healing work in general. For instance, I may have a dozen different sensations happening in my body at once. The prospect of sorting through all these sensations can be invigorating or a royal pain in the butt, depending on my mood. Even when I experience this work as a pain in the butt, however, I can use this to my advantage. Maybe that part of my body really is in pain, and if I tune in to it, I'll learn something valuable. Sometimes the most ignored parts of my body are precisely the ones that need more attention.

The Church says: The body is a sin.

Science says: The body is a machine.

Advertising says: The body is a business.

The body says: I am a fiesta.
EDUARDO GALEANO

Take care of your body and you take care of the earth.

JACOTA RAI

A terrifying symptom is usually your greatest dream trying to come true.

ARNOLD MINDELL

If you'd like to check out some of the messages your body has for you, ask one of your friends to join you for an hour or so. Decide who will be the first speaker, and who will be the first listener. When you're ready to begin, sit or stand facing each other. Next, take a few moments to focus on your breathing. Gently close your eyes and allow your attention to turn inward. As you breathe continuously, imagine that you are becoming the most sensitive *receiving* mechanism in the world. You are able to pick up the tiniest signals and sensations from all the *transmitters* that are stationed all over your body—in every capillary and corpuscle, in every neuron and tendon, in every follicle and gland.

With great care, and without trying to change anything, notice the first thing that catches your attention. Maybe your elbow itches or your feet ache. Perhaps your stomach is gurgling, or maybe you feel some kind of distress. Whatever feeling or sensation calls to you, give it your full attention. Keep breathing, and tune in to the part of your body that speaks to you through this feeling or sensation. With as much curiosity and openheartedness as possible, imagine that this body part has something to say to you. Your entire focus now is simply to discover its message.

As an example, let's say that you feel an unusual sensation in your feet. Let's also say that you've agreed to be the first speaker, so you'll take center stage. While you continue breathing, pay attention to the feelings in your feet, and imagine that your feet have now been given a voice. Your feet can talk! Since they can speak, what would they like to tell you? As you become aware of whatever message they have for you, tell your partner what you've heard. You might say something like this: "My feet say that they're tired of holding me up all the time, and they wish I'd stand on my head sometimes."

After you say the first message out loud to your friend, he or she can honor your words with a quiet nod, a soft *mmmmm*, or a simple acknowledgment of *yes* or *thanks*. If you prefer your witness to remain silent, that's okay, too. Just be sure to let your partner know what kind of response will help you keep your attention on your body.

Once you've shared what you heard from your feet, turn your focus inward again. Wait to see if your feet have any other messages for you. Maybe your left foot will start twitching, and you'll notice that you feel kind of antsy. When you tune in to your foot, it says, "I'd like to kick my mother for being so cruel to me."

In these examples, notice how your feet are speaking in first person *I* statements. If this happens for you, go with it. Let your feet speak as if they're the *whole* you. This will help you identify with your feet more fully, and thereby allow you to validate their perspective more completely.

By the way, if your foot says it wants to kick your mother, I'm not suggesting that you act on this message unless, of course, you want to do some work with a heavy bag or a pillow (see "The Anger Primer" for help). In other words, I'm simply encouraging you to listen deeply to your body, and to acknowledge what you hear by letting your partner witness the information you receive. I'm *not* encouraging you to be abusive or irresponsible.

Within the context of responsible expression, I definitely recommend that you *go for it* with your truth-telling. Don't censor the messages you get from your body, and don't worry about being socially, morally, or politically correct. If you're only willing to hear information that fits some preconceived notion of how you think you *should* feel, you'll miss out on the juiciest tidbits. Open your heart to all the mysterious sensations, the disowned fantasies, the shadowy wisdom, and the marvelous enchantments contained in your body. Every cell, every organ, every bone, every synapse, and every burst of energy has a story to tell you.

If something powerful comes up for you during this exercise, and if your partner is game, you might want to go beyond verbal expression of your body's messages. In regard to the previous example with your feet, you might find out what happens if you actually stand on your head. Is there something about standing on your head that offers new perspectives for you? Try it and find out where it leads you.

When you're done with that, you might want to go a little further with the message you got from your left foot, the one that wanted to kick your mother. Follow this inner image, and find a way to express it that *doesn't* involve kicking your mother. There are a hundred ways to "kick your mother" without actually doing it. For instance, you could draw it, dance it, or sculpt it. Just be sure that however you do it, you honor the *physical* level. Don't get cerebral with your passions!

When you give yourself permission to go beyond verbal expression into something more dynamic, you might experience some wild sensations, or perhaps even pain. On the other hand, if you have a lot of fear about physical experiences, the increased permission may cause a sudden *shutdown* in your body. If this happens for you, please be patient, and trust that your body has good reason for protecting its vulnerability. Begin with whatever you *do* feel, then expand this feeling until you can sense a way to verbalize or otherwise

Your health is bound to be affected if, day after day, you say the opposite of what you feel, if you grovel before what you dislike and rejoice at what brings you nothing but misfortune. Our nervous system isn't just a fiction; it's a part of our physical body, and our soul exists in space, and is inside us, like the teeth in our mouth. It can't be forever violated with impunity.

BORIS PASTERNAK

It does not do you good to leave a dragon out of your calculations, if you live near him.

J. R. R. TOLKIEN

We should take care not to make the intellect our god; it has, of course, powerful muscles, but no personality.

ALBERT EINSTEIN

express it. Take your time, and do whatever you're moved to do within a context of safety and respect for you and your partner.

If you've ignored the whisperings of your body for a long time, it may take some coaxing to get your body to reveal its messages to you. I like to ask my body outright to talk with me. At the same time, I hone my ability to be patient. Ultimately, I trust my body's knowing about when and how much it wants to share. If my mind thinks it knows better than my body, I tell my mind to back off and honor my body's wisdom. Frankly, I think my body is a million times smarter than my intellect.

When you tune in to your own body, remember to pay attention to the tiniest of sensations. It's possible that your little toe has some earth-shaking insight into a problem that has bothered you for years. How will you know unless you give it a chance to speak?

THE OPEN HEART
SAFETY CHECK

Some people say that your heart must always be open: that you must express everything you feel and be receptive to everyone else's feelings in return. While there is certainly a high side to this ideal in terms of emotional honesty, I think some people use it to make unrealistic demands about self-disclosure. Privacy deserves equal consideration. To me, emotional health includes the flexibility to be open or reserved, depending on the situation.

I've learned valuable lessons about healthy self-disclosure by contemplating the *physical* nature of my heart. My heart beats deep inside my body, housed in a casing of tissue and encircled by rib bones interwoven with strong muscles. In other words, my heart is well protected. I wouldn't want my vulnerable, life-supporting heart hanging out on my sleeve.

Therefore, even while I value the concept of openheartedness, I like to temper it with self-respect. My style of openheartedness begins first with a promise to protect my heart, no matter what. Protecting my heart is different from closing it. In *Webster's*, the word *protect* means "to cover or shield from injury or destruction." Thus, I want to shield my heart from injury or destruction. In terms of my emotional heart, this doesn't mean I go around being guarded in everything I say and do. Instead, it means that I move in the direction of greater openness, while also respecting that this brings increased vulnerability.

Vulnerability requires special consideration. Through painful trial and error, I've discovered that it's not loving to expect myself to be open with everyone at all times. My sense of emotional safety may fluctuate, depending on a thousand internal and external factors. The question is: How do I know when to share what, and with whom? How can I gauge—in advance—whether or not I have enough emotional safety to disclose something personal?

One way is to use what I call the Open Heart Safety Check, which uses the image of your real, beating heart to help you

Love that stammers, that stutters, is apt to be the love that loves best.

GABRIELA MISTRAL

Using another as a means of satisfaction and security is not love. Love is never security; love is a state in which there is no desire to be secure; it is a state of vulnerability.

KRISHNAMURTI

To determine the weight of a blue whale's heart, multiply your own weight by 9.5. If you're small, the whale with that heft of heart would be small. If you're big, the whale with such a heart would be big.

MIKE MAILWAY

Like an ability or a muscle, hearing your inner wisdom is strengthened by doing it.

ROBBIE GASS

Q: In a 70-year human lifetime, how long is the heart at rest?

A: About 40 years.

MIKE MAILWAY

experiment with healthy self-disclosure. Because your heart is so well protected inside your body, you might take its safety for granted. However, you can become more aware of your heart's vulnerability if you imagine yourself holding your heart in your hands. I realize this is quite graphic and viscerally intense, but it will give you an instant and sobering perception of your heart's true vulnerability—much more so than if you only think of it as being hidden deep within your body.

To practice working with the Open Heart Safety Check, you'll need a partner. Though this technique may take a bit of explaining initially, you'll be able to use the image quickly and easily once you get the hang of it. To begin, sit comfortably in chairs or on the floor, facing your friend. To make the directions simpler, I'll assume that you will be the first speaker (see "The Basics of Listening" for general guidelines and helpful tips).

First, take a few moments to focus inward. Let your mind drift randomly, and allow your thoughts to wander among the mental archives of your past experiences. In particular, spend some time perusing memories that have some kind of emotional charge. Perhaps you will remember an embarrassing situation, or maybe you'll think of an event that moved you to the heights of ecstasy or pushed you to the depths of despair.

Once you've retrieved a few of these personal memories from your data bank, the next step is to select a story that you might be willing to tell your friend. I recommend that you start with whatever anecdote feels safest for you to share. You can always up the ante with your intimate self-disclosures as you become more familiar with the exercise. Remember, you're in charge of protecting your heart. The goal is *not* to see how far you can push yourself. The goal is to see how well you can stay *within* your comfort level, while you gently expand your boundaries of openness.

As you consider the story you've chosen, imagine that you can somehow reach into your body to pull out your living, beating heart. Make the details as vivid as possible. Hold your cupped hands outstretched in front of you and imagine that your heart is actually resting there in your hands. Feel the weight of your heart there before you, as you feel the vulnerability of its exposed state.

While you hold this image foremost in your awareness, consider now whether or not it's right for you to share the personal story you've culled from your memories. To make a decision about this, ask your heart. Feel your heart pulsing in your outstretched hands, while you consider your sense of safety with that particular person in that particular moment. Does your heart feel enough trust to disclose the piece of information you've chosen? Or does your heart suddenly want to retreat back into your body?

If your heart says it's safe to tell your story, go ahead and tell it. If your heart says *no*, honor that boundary. Don't argue with your heart. No matter how much you *think* you might grow from risking past your point of safety, true intimacy doesn't come from overriding your fear. Instead of treating fear like a wall that must be destroyed, imagine that it is a child who needs to be comforted. Be patient and tender with your fear.

If your heart says it's not right for you to share that particular piece of information, this doesn't mean you can't say anything. It just means you shouldn't say that story in that moment with that person. Therefore, if you get a *red flag* from your heart, simply choose a different anecdote from your memory bank, and begin the exercise again.

Each time you consider a new tale, imagine that you're holding your heart in your hands as a symbol of your emotional vulnerability. Remember to return your heart to its safe place inside your body following each story it agrees to tell. Also, return your heart to safety again whenever it says *no* to sharing a particular memory.

Once you've had a chance to practice this technique a few times, switch roles with your partner. When you're on the flip side of the exchange, your job is to listen as deeply and respectfully as you can. Don't engage in dialogue. Keep the focus entirely on your friend, and remain mindful of the image of his or her heart in its exposed vulnerability.

After you've both tried each role, take some time to talk about your experiences. What did you learn about yourselves and each other? How did it feel for you to work with the image of your heart in your hands? Did this image help you perceive a *visceral* reading of your relative safety or discomfort, or did it just freak you out? What was it like for you to imagine your partner's heart beating and exposed in front of you?

Intimacy requires just the right mix of safety and risk. The Open Heart Safety Check can help with this by teaching you to discern the boundary of your emotional safety *before* you overstep it. To illustrate what I mean, imagine that your *intimacy boundary* is like the edge of a cliff. Have you ever experienced the thrill of walking near the edge of a precipitous cliff?

I remember walking along the rim of the Grand Canyon, with its breathtaking drops of a thousand feet and more. Whenever I crept too close to the edge, I felt a compelling urge to jump off and fly. However, I was quite aware that such a flight would be short-

Only the heart knows the correct answer.

DEEPAK CHOPRA

Every time you don't follow your inner guidance, you feel a loss of energy, loss of power, a sense of spiritual deadness.

SHAKTI GAWAIN

Although the act of nurturing another's spiritual growth has the effect of nurturing one's own, a major characteristic of genuine love is that the distinction between oneself and the other is always maintained and preserved.

M. SCOTT PECK

lived—literally. Therefore, I experimented with finding a balance: close enough to stimulate my desire to fly, but not so close that I would succumb to abject terror. After all, I didn't really want to lose my life.

This dance between excitement and fear reminds me of the dance of intimacy. I like to get close enough to someone to feel the intensity of contact, but not so close that I lose my sense of self. The Open Heart Safety Check can help you traverse this edge by showing you when you have enough ground to go forward into self-disclosure—and when you should pull back. You are the only one who gets to decide if, when, where, and with whom to share your heart. Small steps, respectfully taken, will help your safety grow.

THE THREE-DAY WINDOW: SUBSTANCE USE IN RELATIONSHIPS

This chapter is dedicated to my dear friend, Deborah Smith, who was killed by a drunken driver on September 10, 1987.

I've long been aware that my own past use of substances (primarily marijuana and caffeine) affected my mood. Until I stopped using those drugs, however, I didn't fully appreciate the degree to which this mood alteration had affected my behavior and so, my relationships. Also, I didn't realize how much *other* people's substance use affected *me* until my own system was free of all mood-altering drugs—including the stimulant drug caffeine.

Obviously, I'm not the first person to write about the detrimental effects of substances on people and their relationships. For instance, Dr. M. M. Glatt's chart about the progression of alcoholism has become a classic because it so clearly illustrates the personal, interpersonal, and community consequences of this addiction.

Since this kind of general information is widely available, my task lies in a more specific direction: to share my *personal* experience with the effects of alcohol, tobacco, caffeine, and other drugs in the context of relationships. In addition, this chapter examines some of the energetic and behavioral changes I've come to associate with the use of these drugs. Finally, I'll address the *lingering* effects of mood-altering substances, which can last for days.

This is where my concept of the "Three-Day Window" comes in. Generally speaking, I can usually perceive some degree of drug *interference* when people have used alcohol, tobacco, caffeine, or

Addiction is the only disease in the world that convinces the afflicted he does not have it.

KARL TARO GREENFELD

Addiction is not like strep throat. It doesn't go away. Drugs change brain cells in profound, long-lasting ways.

ALAN LESHNER

other drugs within three days of interacting with me. Putting this another way, I've noticed that it takes a minimum of three full days of abstinence (not including the day of contact) for the first level of clearing to occur in most people.

To explain what I mean by drug interference, I'll give you an analogy and then provide more details as the chapter progresses. For now, consider the case of secondhand smoke, the effects of which are well documented. People have even won lawsuits for damages to their health from exposure to secondhand smoke.

Just as secondhand smoke can harm anyone in the vicinity of the smoker, I believe that *all* mood-altering substances can detrimentally affect those who relate to people who have used the substances. Of course, in the same way that secondhand smoke affects different people differently, the impact of one person's substance use on others will vary, depending on the level of exposure and the sensitivity of the other people.

Because I am allergic to tobacco—and because I'm sensitive to chemicals of any kind—I'm like the proverbial canary in a coal mine that warns workers of impending danger before they're able to detect it themselves. Therefore, my perspective may provide valuable information for you, even if you are not as sensitive as I am to the effects of drug interference.

I never give them hell. I just tell the truth and they think it's hell.

HARRY S. TRUMAN

Hopefully, my personal experience will serve to show how alcohol, tobacco, caffeine, and other drugs can impact people and their relationships, *whether they are aware of it or not.* In addition, I'd like to show how you can approach this issue with more clarity, compassion, and care—even if you choose to use mood-altering substances on occasion.

Chemically Induced Personal Space

As I mentioned earlier, I may be impacted by drug interference when I relate to people who have used alcohol, tobacco, caffeine, or other drugs within a few days of our interaction. For one thing, I can perceive a *veil* between us. At times, this veil may feel more like an impervious wall. Either way, this apparent energy block makes it more difficult for me to stay in contact with people's hearts. It's as if there's a protective *force field* around them.

Trust in yourself. Your perceptions are often far more accurate than you are willing to believe.

CLAUDIA BLACK

One of my friends (who uses alcohol, tobacco, and caffeine in small but regular quantities) has heard me talk about these veils, both in relation to him and in relation to others. He has even coined a term, "chemically induced personal space," to describe the self-protective buffer that substances seem to provide.

I think his term is brilliant because it puts a handle on something I've noticed for a long time. That is, I think people use substances for many conscious and unconscious reasons, one of which is to make artificial boundaries between themselves and others when they don't know how to create space for themselves in more proactive and sustainable ways.

Let me give you a personal example. Many years ago when I was addicted to marijuana, I used it primarily for one purpose: to make a boundary around solitary time for myself, during which I would sit in front of my altar and commune with my body, my soul, and the powers-that-be. This communion was my supreme pleasure, so I had a hard time giving it to myself (see "The Five-Minute Switch System" for more about this). Therefore, I used drugs not only to induce an altered state, but also to help me bypass my guilt about giving myself pleasure.

My solitary time of communion was very sacred and it took many forms—writing, drawing, dancing, drumming, singing, chanting, meditating, praying, and doing other kinds of spiritual work. Although this time was well used, it was still drug induced, which meant that there was a *shadow* side operating before, during, and after the experience.

For one thing, I used marijuana's *high* to avoid pain, even though at the time, I thought I was using the drug to "go into" my pain. Secondly, I was less emotionally stable for a few days following my use of marijuana, though it took me a long time to admit this. Another shadow aspect showed itself in the way I was overly protective of my chemically induced personal space.

Once I closed the door to my room, smoked a toke or two, and began my altar time, I couldn't be interrupted without losing that sacred connection to self and cosmos (it took me years after quitting dope to learn how to sustain that connection without drugs). Even when I had gotten to a point in my addiction work where I was only using one toke per week, I would get angry, agitated, or depressed if anyone or anything delayed, interrupted, or prevented my solitary private time.

I've heard similar sentiments from other people when they talk about alcohol, tobacco, caffeine, or other drugs. Sometimes people sound militantly defensive in regard to their habits. For example, someone might say, "My cigarette break is *my* time for *me*, and I have a right to smoke if I want to!" Or, "I like to have a drink or two after work to help me unwind, and it's nobody's business but my own!" Or, "You'd better not talk to me until I've had my morning *hit* of caffeine!"

Here in this body are the sacred rivers; here are the sun and moon as well as all the pilgrimage places....I have not encountered another temple as blissful as my own body.

SARAHA

When will people learn that there is no free lunch? There is a price to pay for every mood-altering chemical people put into their bodies.

ABIGAIL VAN BUREN

The Infant Stage of Addiction: I Want What I Want When I Want It

Sometimes I joke with people that these kinds of self-absorbed statements illustrate what I call the *infant stage* of addiction, which is characterized by the phrase "I want what I want when I want it" and its corollary "If it feels good, do it!"

Of course, it's normal for infants to be completely self-absorbed and to operate from a place of immediate need and instant gratification. No one expects infants to be paragons of virtue who consider the consequences of their actions. After all, they don't even know about consequences yet. On the other hand, no one expects adults to act like infants, either.

Unfortunately, some people get stuck in the infant stage of addiction. They spend their whole lives on automatic, using mood-altering substances to satisfy their short-term desire for pleasure, without any regard to subsequent consequences.

In the case of the self-absorbed statements mentioned above, I sometimes wonder if that kind of militant defensiveness could explain why I often experience drug interference as a kind of *fight* energy. It's as if the chemicals make a force field that is not only protective but *repellent,* creating such harsh boundaries that I feel pushed away.

I'm so sensitive to drug interference that I perceive this "pushing away" at energetic levels, even when people don't act in overtly obnoxious ways. Since I trust my perceptions, I may either speak up or withdraw if I feel this repellent energy. If I speak up—assuming it's with someone who knows about my Three-Day Window concept—I may simply ask if he or she has used any substances in the last few days. What happens next determines whether we have a mutually considerate relationship.

If the other person discounts my experience, or worse, if he or she blames me for being too sensitive, then I'm likely to withdraw (see "My Personal Rules of Respect" for more about withdrawal). However, if the person believes me and takes responsibility for whatever rough edges he or she may be contributing to the field between us, I'll probably feel safe enough to stay.

My favorite people are those who not only believe me and take responsibility, but who actually appreciate my sensitivity to subtle energy shifts. When people are open to my needs as well as their own, it gives me a chance to explore the drug interference *with* them, instead of having to parry the energy all by myself.

Although it's still more work for me to relate to people who have used substances, I appreciate people who are aware enough of

If children don't receive healthy love they search for a love they can control; they develop addictions to gain what wasn't available from parents....

BERNIE SIEGEL

According to a professor at the University of Kansas Medical Center, habitual users tend to fall into two categories— the angry and the lonely.

MIKE MAILWAY

themselves that they can help mitigate the effects of the drug interference if it's brought to their attention. They do this by being compassionate, respectful, and responsible when I say *ouch* in response to any of the behavioral effects outlined in the next part of this chapter.

Behavioral Effects of Drug Interference

I've mentioned some of the ways that mood-altering substances can affect people's energy, in terms of the veils that feel like protective or repellent force fields around their hearts. In addition to these energetic imbalances, I've also come to associate certain behaviors with drug interference.

As you read the following descriptions, please remember that I may notice these behaviors within three days of people using alcohol, tobacco, caffeine, or other drugs. In other words, these kinds of conduct don't only manifest during or immediately after substance use; the effects are more long-lasting.

It's also important to note that people who regularly use the aforementioned substances may exhibit some of these behaviors on a regular basis if they never go longer than three days without their drug of choice. With chronic substance use, people's true personalities may become hidden underneath layers of equally chronic disrespectful behavior, which may be triggered by chemical changes in their brains.

In any case, different people may display varying degrees of the following behaviors, depending on the amount and type of substance they've used, their sensitivity to that particular drug, and how much time has elapsed since they used it. Also, the effects of drugs can be magnified by other stressors in people's lives.

If you use mood-altering substances, and if you recognize any of the following behaviors in yourself, please don't use this list to beat yourself up. Instead, you can use it to become more aware and therefore more able to take responsibility for the consequences of your choices.

Rough Edges/Mean Energy. Although I describe this category in energetic terms, it can show up in any number of speaking tones, gestures, and actions. For instance, those of us who have lived with alcoholics are well acquainted with the way booze can stimulate mean-spirited behavior. In my experience, other drugs—including caffeine and tobacco—can also impact people's behavior in similar ways, causing them to be more easily agitated, quicker to anger, and generally "edgier" to be around.

Be with those who help your being.
RUMI

Alcohol, heroin, cocaine, nicotine, marijuana— all modify dopamine function in similar ways. Initially, people take drugs because they like what it does to their brains, but over time something happens. All of a sudden, you're taking drugs not because you like them but because you must. This compulsion is the essence of addiction.
ALAN LESHNER

Don't drink and drive. It will cost you. You will pay. It might not be today, but you will pay eventually. And it's terrible.
JEREMY REID

Your teen may be drinking more; consider that more than 41 percent of all academic problems stem from alcohol abuse. And as many as 350,000 of the nation's 12 million undergraduates will die from alcohol-related causes while in school.

JEFF LINDENBAUM

Flipping. By *flipping*, I mean that people with substances in their systems can be especially prone to moods and behaviors that run hot and cold. One moment, they'll be warm and welcoming. The next moment, they'll be nasty and abrasive.

No doubt everyone has the capacity to flip, depending on what's happening internally and externally, and depending on the amount of stress they're experiencing. However, I believe that alcohol, tobacco, caffeine, and other drugs can induce this kind of behavior in all but the most evolved humans.

In addition, if someone's personality is such that he or she already shows a propensity for Dr. Jekyll/Mr. Hyde behavior, then mood-altering substances will greatly exacerbate this tendency.

Incongruency/Inconsistency. This means that people may say one thing and do another, or they'll say or do something in such a way that I won't believe the sincerity of their words or actions. For example, someone might say, "You can trust me," but my body says *no way*. When there's inconsistent or incongruent behavior, I experience a discrepancy between the presenting personality and the underlying energy.

Repression of Feelings. Although drugs can make people seem more emotional on the surface, this can be deceptive, because substances often put a damper on people's true feelings. For instance, small amounts of alcohol can temporarily make some people appear talkative and outgoing, when in fact they are quite shy and even afraid of intimacy.

Repression of feelings is one reason that it's unhealthy for me to spend long periods of time around people who have used mood-altering substances within a few days of seeing me. Let me try to explain why this is so.

First of all, I believe that people are interconnected—and I don't think this is merely a metaphysical concept. If you imagine humanity as one body, then I'm like a heart cell in the body of humanity. Whether I like it or not, I'm sensitive to subtle shifts of feeling in the "psychic float," to borrow a phrase from Arny Mindell.

Being addicted is a primary way of being emotionally unavailable.

ROBIN NORWOOD

If someone is *stuffing* their feelings instead of taking responsibility for them, those feelings don't just disappear; they *leak* into the relationship field—the collective "float" of psychic energy that is generated by humans. I don't mean to sound airy-fairy in describing this. It's a palpable phenomenon for me.

Thus, if I'm in the vicinity of someone who is pushing away their feelings through the use of substances, I may end up feeling more than my share of emotions. This can happen despite my best efforts and my good boundaries, the way secondhand smoke can affect anyone in the vicinity of the smoker.

Deflection or Denial of Responsibility. I think that responsibility is the number-one issue in human development. Of course, people have varying degrees of interest and skill in taking responsibility. In general, mood-altering substances *decrease* people's ability to take responsibility for themselves and their behavior.

One exception to this happens when people use certain hallucinogens sacramentally, within strict protocols and under the guidance of a shaman or other spiritual guide. In such cases, the resulting experience, though drug induced, may result in a subsequent increase of personal responsibility (and indeed, this is often one of the intentions).

Obviously, most people don't use drugs in a sacramental, infrequent, and highly disciplined way, nor are most people focused on personal responsibility when they introduce alcohol, tobacco, caffeine, or other drugs into their systems. In any case, deflection or denial of responsibility can show up in many forms, whether verbal, behavioral, or energetic. For example, if I feel hurt or offended by something that was said by a chemically influenced person, he or she may blame me for being too sensitive, accuse me of being controlling, or respond with a responsibility-denying statement such as "I wasn't *trying* to hurt you!"

Last of all, I'll simply mention a few of the more blatant examples of how drugs decrease responsibility at the behavioral level. Statistics about alcohol and drug use in relation to car accidents, criminal violence, and domestic abuse are well documented. In the case of tobacco, there are considerate smokers, but there are also plenty of smokers who believe that their right to smoke is more important than other people's right to breathe clean air.

In regard to caffeine, the use of this stimulant is so rampant in our culture that I can only imagine how many people will read this chapter and continue to deny the fact that caffeine is a drug at all, much less a powerful one that affects their nervous systems, their moods, and their behavior. Yet if caffeine didn't pack a punch, why would anyone use it? The bottom line is, if people won't admit that caffeine affects the way they feel and the way they interact, they won't be able to acknowledge—or take responsibility for—its impact on their personal relationships.

From Infant to Warrior: Substances and Conflict

If you have more conflict in your relationships than you'd like, or if you're tired of watching the same old conflicts replaying endlessly like a bad movie, consider dropping *all* mood-altering substances for at least six months. To be thorough, this would include

Ancient healers dried plants to make medicines. That clarifies why our word "drug" comes from an old German saying meaning "to dry."

Mike Mailway

If you play Trivial Pursuit with crime statistics, your answer is Substance Abuse to any question involving the cause for most crimes.

Roger C. Lake

Alcohol may make you feel sleepy (it's a central nervous system depressant); however, it will actually sabotage a good night's sleep. The reason is that alcohol is known to suppress a phase of sleep known as REM (rapid eye movement), which is the phase when most dreaming occurs. Less REM is associated with a restless sleep caused by more night awakenings.

PAT BAIRD

letting go of alcohol, tobacco, drugs, and all forms of caffeine (e.g., coffee, black or green tea, caffeinated soft drinks, chocolate, and many over-the-counter medications).

When people see that long list of contributors to drug interference, they may reject the idea of taking a six-month break from mood-altering substances. They may rationalize that their morning cup of coffee or their evening glass of wine can't possibly hurt that much, or they may be afraid to face life—and themselves—without stimulants, depressants, or numbing agents.

While these objections are understandable, they are also telltale signs of addiction (see "The Five-Minute Switch System" for more about this). If you associate abstinence with deprivation and discomfort rather than freedom and growth, it may not be time for you to do this experiment. In the end, it comes down to priorities. Is substance use more important than clarity? Are drugs more important than relationship healing? Only you can answer these questions for yourself.

If you do try the six-month experiment, you can certainly learn a lot by doing it alone. However, your time-out will proceed more smoothly if the other person in your relationship also participates, since mood-altering substances can detrimentally affect *both* people, even the one who only experiences their effects secondhand.

The point is, mood-altering substances can be hard on relationships because they cloud perceptions, destabilize the emotional body, diminish personal responsibility, and ultimately decrease the capacity for true intimacy. For these reasons, substance use can trigger or exacerbate conflict.

You don't have to take my word for this. Check out the following four stages of development in regard to substances and relationships. See if you occupy any of these positions on a regular basis. Then, if you want to up the ante for yourself, try moving into the stage *following* the one you usually occupy. By doing this, you'll discover more information about the role of substances in your relationships, and specifically, their role in conflict.

I never drink and I have never done drugs.

TINA TURNER

By the way, I've noticed that for me, there has always been a three-day, three-week, and three-month *window of craving* whenever I have gone through the process of dropping a mood-altering substance (some of them took many tries, so I became well acquainted with these windows of craving). My desire for the drug got much stronger during these periods, and I had to work harder to stay on track. In addition, I noticed that life felt more difficult for a while after letting go of the substance, as my underlying issues made themselves more glaringly apparent.

I mention this to warn you that things may seem worse for a while as the drug(s) clear from your system. You may feel more irritable, confused, or depressed, and your conflicts may increase in frequency, intensity, or duration as your body detoxifies.

Therefore, I suggest that you wait until *after* you've been clean for at least six months before you reevaluate any significant relationships. If you need to take a break from someone during your experiment, you can. However, if a relationship is important to you, I recommend that you wait until your period of *housecleaning* is over before you make any major decisions. What follows, then, is my concept of the four stages of development in regard to mood-altering substances and relationships.

Living on Automatic: The Infant Stage. Earlier in this chapter, I mentioned the mottoes for the infant stage of addiction, namely, "I want what I want when I want it" and "If it feels good, do it!"

When both people in a relationship are at this stage in regard to substances, it's likely that their interactions will consist of mutual *stroking* of each other's automatic behavior. Whether they're in denial of their addictions or just unwilling to work on them, the result is the same: no real intimacy and no real growth.

Waking Up: To Act or Not to Act? At this stage, one or both people begin to wonder if there isn't something more to life than an endless cycle of short-term gratification and patterned responses. This can trigger a dilemma for many people, because if *waking up* is followed by *action*, the relationship will change.

Because change is by nature unpredictable, the relationship may or may not survive if one or both people decide to move toward letting go of habitual substance use. Either way, people who remain at this stage of development may sacrifice awareness and growth for the comfort of a familiar relationship.

Taking Responsibility: The Choice for Loving-Kindness. People at this stage have not only admitted that substances affect their moods and behaviors; they have also decided that the presence of substances in their systems is no excuse for disrespectful behavior. Therefore, if they choose to indulge, they take responsibility for any rough edges that arise as a result.

For instance, two of my good friends (a couple) have said how much they appreciate what they've learned from me about the effects of substance use in the relationship field, because they've applied this information to their own partnership. Now if they hit a snag in a conversation, they often check in about substance use *first,* instead of letting things escalate into a big processing session that may prove unnecessary if they discern the presence of drug interference.

When a meth addict is given the choice between caring for his or her children or taking meth, the meth addict will always pick meth.

ROGER C. LAKE

Fear is a natural reaction to moving closer to the truth.

PEMA CHÖDRÖN

"A clear colorless liquid created as a waste product by anaerobic bacteria"— would you put that in your martini? It's alcohol.

MIKE MAILWAY

When you truly grow up what you will be is free.

EMMANUEL

Since both of these people are committed to the choice for loving-kindness, they have given each other permission to speak up if either of them perceives any kind of *disconnect*. For example, one person might say, "Oh, I just remembered that I ate a chocolate bar (caffeine) this morning, and I'm feeling a little edgy and irritable tonight. Sorry!" Or if one of them feels ambushed by a mean-spirited comment, he or she might gently inquire as to whether the other person used a mood-altering substance within the last few days.

As you can see, this stage of development evolves most easily when both people in a relationship consider the effects of substance use during conflict. Otherwise, one person may end up doing too much of the work, while the other person sloughs off in the personal responsibility department.

Beyond Drugs: The Warrior Stage. People who have reached this stage have grown weary of drug interference, both in themselves and in other people. They consistently choose clarity over short-term gratification, and they cultivate relationships with people who do the same. Although they realize that abstinence from mood-altering substances won't bring an end to internal or external conflict, they know that abstinence will decrease the frequency, intensity, and duration of conflict.

Those who attain this level of personal development are in a unique position to take their growth to deeper levels. They can do this by using what they've learned about substances in order to explore habitual ways of thinking, feeling, and acting—including the effects of these habits on their relationships.

Of course, it's possible and even helpful for people to work on behavioral addictions at the same time they work on substance addictions. However, behavioral addictions will become more apparent—and more available for permanent change—when mood-altering substances are out of the picture.

DISRESPECT AND SUBTLE ABUSE: WATCH OUT FOR THESE CHARACTERS

Most people know what blatant abuse looks like, but they miss the less obvious, though still damaging, forms of disrespect. For example, have you ever felt completely demoralized after an encounter, but you can't figure out why? As one of my friends says, if you feel like you've been *slimed,* you probably have been. To help you get a handle on this and other uncomfortable situations, I've devised an annotated list of twenty different styles of disrespect and subtle abuse. I'll share the list with you in a few moments.

Do you remember my definition of abuse? **Abuse occurs when someone uses another person to meet a need in a way that harms, coerces, or devalues the other person.** While it's true that we all use each other to get our needs met, this should be a mutually respectful experience. The next chapter deals specifically with guidelines for respect. For now, I'd like to share a few tips for working with this chapter's list of *disrespectful* character styles.

First and foremost, do *not* use these labels as weapons to beat people up. It's okay to observe other people's behavior, of course, and you may choose to cut a wide berth around folks who exhibit disrespectful behavior with alarming regularity. In general, however, I'm offering this list so you can use it to clean up *your own* act.

If you're scared to admit that you have any shady characters lurking around in the dark recesses of your mind, take heart. Every one of us is capable of the most horrendous behavior imaginable. The people who scare me most are those who deny this capacity in themselves. On the other hand, I'm more likely to trust people who acknowledge and respect their *shadow* sides.

The shadow is not evil, as some people believe. It is simply the repository of all the disowned parts of the self. As such, it's a tremendous source of power, if the rejected parts can be accepted and expressed in responsible ways.

Some people suffer from the effects of disowning or suppressing their *admirable* qualities, such as sensitivity, intelligence, or

True compassion is not just an emotional response but a firm commitment founded on reason. Therefore, a truly compassionate attitude toward others does not change even if they behave negatively.

DALAI LAMA

Fleas are essential to the health of armadillos and hedgehogs, in that they provide necessary stimulation for the skin. Deloused armadillos and hedgehogs do not long survive.

ASHLEY MONTAGUE

Unmannerly people may not be malevolent, but, as you have discovered, they are callous all the same. The effect of their behavior is not much different than if they had deliberately chosen to be cruel.

JUDITH MARTIN

playfulness. However, most people struggle more profoundly with the so-called negative aspects of their character. The good news is, these qualities are only considered negative because people haven't yet discovered the hidden value of these traits.

Let me give you an example from my own experience. For much of my life, I've rented homes and apartments from various people. There's nothing wrong with renting, of course, but it was never my first choice. In any case, there were times when I chose landlords or landladies who seemed nice enough on the surface. Sometimes, however, when I needed to ask for their consideration about a particular matter, their superficial niceness dissipated like so much dust in the wind. In conflict, their true colors came out, and I found myself holding monsters by their tails.

These situations were complicated by the fact that I often tend to be too *nice*, which made the owners' lack of consideration all the more apparent. Although some people might say that these situations were a reflection of my own inconsideration of others, my consultation work revealed something quite different: These landlords from hell were showing me that the inconsideration that needed to change was my inconsideration of *myself*. I actually needed to be less concerned about other people.

Don't get me wrong. I'm not saying that I want to be a jerk who doesn't care about other people. Frankly, there's probably no chance of that ever happening, because I have always had the opposite problem. I was taught to be so attentive to the needs of others that I sometimes neglect my own needs. In the case of the landlords, I was so afraid of being like them that it took me a while to notice the high side of their obnoxious behavior. The high side, of course, was their unapologetic devotion to self-care. Ironically, I needed to be more like them!

By facing the shadow side of these unpleasant relationships, I turned a monster into an ally. The ally appeared when I wrestled the monster of their total self-absorption to the ground, and claimed its self-loving intent for myself. Gradually, I practiced being more assertive and self-protective in regard to my needs. In other words, my inconsiderate landlords helped me learn to be more considerate of myself, an area in which I still needed improvement.

As this story illustrates, the qualities that repulse me most may hold the biggest jewel hidden behind their fearsome appearance. Their repulsiveness makes me want to get rid of these qualities, but I know that won't work. In the end, if I want the jewel, I must *transform* the repulsive quality.

If you're worried about finding repulsive qualities in yourself, rest assured that you're not alone. Every human heart holds the seeds of every possible thought and action, no matter how beautiful or brutal. As a human being, it's your job to care for these seeds. What will you do with the seed of hatred? How will you find a place for the embryo of cruelty?

Whether you face the shadow side of your psyche with fear or courage is not as important as the act of facing it at all. If you need support to dive into the murky regions of your mind, then by all means, get support and plenty of it. There are no prizes for doing everything yourself. Feel free to enlist the aid of a trusted friend or mentor. For example, I have a great time play-acting my shadow characters with friends. Sometimes the mere presence of another person can make the process more enjoyable and less frightening.

Hopefully, I haven't scared you off with all these precautions about doing shadow work. The truth is, there are few things more rewarding than turning your monsters into allies. Believe it or not, it can even be fun once you get the hang of it. Even so, I'll be the first to admit that whenever I get comfortable with a certain level of shadow explorations, the trickster spirits up the ante. The monsters get bigger or more plentiful, or they appear in even more mysterious disguises. If this wasn't true, it wouldn't be shadow work!

Now, are you ready for my list of disrespectful shadow characters? Don't forget to use this list to notice—and protect yourself from—disrespectful behavior in other people. More importantly, though, I recommend that you use it to help you clean up irresponsible behavior in *yourself*. In addition, see if you can discern the high side of each category.

For instance, can you find the hidden jewel in *know-it-all* behavior? Can you imagine a positive reframe for *Mr. Fix-it* tendencies? Do you know the value of *denial*? If you can separate the wheat from the chaff, you can give these characters new jobs, so to speak. Transform the *energy* of their disrespectful behavior, and use it to be more respectful.

Last of all, if you think I'm being unfairly judgmental in describing these unsavory characters, let me assure you that it takes one to know one. Although I wish I could say that I came up with these labels *only* through diligent observation of other people, the fact is that I've learned just as much about them by witnessing my own worst behavior over the years.

By the way, the apparent gender of these labels is purely arbitrary. These styles of disrespect transcend all categories of race,

Not only are you the shadow that is dancing on the wall, but you are the hand that makes the shadow, and you are the Light.

EMMANUEL

creed, class, culture, gender, and sexual orientation. In other words, everyone is capable of everything!

Here, then, is a list of some common forms of disrespect and subtle abuse. I've arranged them alphabetically except for the last one, which must come at the end.

The Constant Competitor. Constant Competitors are masters of one-upmanship. No matter what you say, they've already done it. Not only that, but they've done it better, longer, further, and faster. These folks are extremely insecure, so they build themselves up by showing you up. Never mind that their inflated stories may or may not be true.

The Enlightened Fool. The Enlightened Fool always has the perfect comeback. However, his pretty words, slick slogans, and metaphysical gobbledygook fall flat, because he's more concerned with *looking* wise than with *being* wise. If he was truly enlightened and not a fool, he'd listen more and speak less.

The Eternal Infant. Eternal Infants spend their whole lives trying to get other people to take care of them. If they don't get what they want when they want it, they bitch and moan, whine and cry, or throw a tantrum. An Eternal Infant will suck you dry faster than you can say "Mom-m-m-m-m-eeeeeeeeee!"

The Evil Eyer. Evil Eyers are likely to deny the abusiveness of their dagger-laden gaze. After all, they didn't actually hit you, and they didn't utter a single word of disdain. How can a *look* be abusive? Well, you've heard the phrase "If looks could kill." Evil Eyers know that they can do great harm with an icicle gaze, because it's designed to shame, criticize, and control you.

The "For Your Own Good" Bully. Alice Miller's book, *For Your Own Good*, opened my eyes to the profundity of abuse inflicted in the name of good intentions. Although the book was difficult reading for me, I didn't have to read every chapter to get the point, which is this: If you impose your will on others, even if you think it's *for their own good*, it's still abuse. If you don't think so, turn the tables and imagine how you'd feel if someone tried to impose his will on you. Parents, helping professionals, and other authority figures may become For Your Own Good Bullies if they believe they have the right to tell others what to do or how to be.

Although it's more than possible to safeguard and nurture the well-being of others without pulling rank or imposing one's will, For Your Own Good Bullies don't have a clue about how to do it. In fact, they actually believe they're being helpful. Because they see their abusive behavior as loving, For Your Own Good Bullies are extremely dangerous.

Real learning comes about when the competitive spirit has ceased.
KRISHNAMURTI

Shallow understanding from people of good will is more frustrating than absolute misunderstanding from people of ill will.
MARTIN LUTHER KING

The Guilt Tripper. Guilt Trippers attempt to manipulate or control your behavior by using guilt-inducing statements, looks, or threats. Their manipulative efforts may be subtle or blatant, depending on their personal style and your willingness to be controlled.

The word *should* is the Guilt Trippers' mantra, and they use it with great abandon, because they believe they know best what you *should* or *should not* do. Another manipulative technique employed by Guilt Trippers is to tell you that you're being selfish, as if this is a sin. It doesn't take a rocket scientist to see that *they* are actually the selfish ones, since they want you to do what makes *them* happy!

The Grand Inquisitor. These characters may seem as if they are deeply interested in you, since they just *have* to know every detail of your life. However, what they really want is control. The more they know about you, the more power they have over you. Grand Inquisitors weasel their way into every nook and cranny of your psyche in order to locate your weak points, so they can use them against you later, when you have moments of vulnerability. On the flip side, they avoid vulnerability themselves by constantly asking questions and by never offering any personal information in return.

The Jugular Jester. This dastardly dude goes for the jugular using humor as his weapon. If you call him on it, he avoids responsibility. "I was only kidding!" he exclaims, as if this excuses his verbal punching. The Jugular Jester also hides behind his other trademark refrain: "Don't take it personally!" In other words, he'll blame you for being too sensitive, rather than face the fact that he's been hurtful.

The "Kill the Messenger" Fanatic. These people don't realize that when they get triggered by someone else's words, it may be because they don't want to hear the message. To deflect their upset, they will criticize, crucify, and sometimes even kill whomever they believe to be the source of their distress.

The King of Criticism. The King of Criticism utilizes many of the obnoxious techniques used by others on this list. No matter what style he employs, however, the unifying characteristic of this royal abuser is his ability to find fault with everything.

If you share joy about a personal success with the King of Criticism, he will burst your bubble by telling you that you'd better not be too happy or something bad will happen. If you do a great job on a project, he'll notice nothing except the one thing you didn't complete to perfection. And if you do something with exquisite finesse, he'll complain that you're too much of a perfectionist.

The Know-It-All. There's nothing wrong with being knowledgeable, but problems arise when Know-It-Alls push their opinions on others without permission. The arrogance of these

When they tell you to grow up, they mean stop growing.
TOM ROBBINS

A truth that's told with bad intent
Beats all the lies you can invent.
WILLIAM BLAKE

characters becomes particularly apparent if the subject of their opinions is *you*.

Know-It-Alls are obnoxious because they don't just consider their opinions to be opinions; they actually believe that their opinions are the only ones that are *right*. In fact, they are so desperate to be right that they can't bear to acknowledge the validity of any position other than their own.

At best, Know-It-Alls may agree to disagree with you, but they'll do this with such an air of condescension that you know they're only doing it to humor you. After all, they believe that anyone who disagrees with them must be feeble-minded or unevolved, and therefore deserving of pity. In any case, Know-It-Alls speak with an overpowering self-righteousness that is obvious to everyone but them.

The Master Blamer. Master Blamers are experts in the dubious arts of deflection, deception, and defamation. No matter what happens, they never take responsibility for anything, even if they must lie or falsely accuse others in order to save their own butts.

The Missionary. The Missionary is a Know-It-All with proselytizing tendencies. If you have the misfortune of exposing your difficulties to these folks, you're in for a sermon based on their favorite book, healer, seminar, tape series, guru, religion, or dietary plan.

Mr. Fix-it. When you tell Mr. Fix-it about a challenge or problem in your life, he will immediately launch into a long litany of what he thinks you must do to fix it. In addition, he will offer his unsolicited advice without first asking what you already know, what you've already tried, or what you need now, if anything, in the way of assistance or support.

As you may have guessed, Mr. Fix-its are closely allied with Know-It-Alls. Unlike Know-It-Alls, who share their opinions no matter what's going on with others, Mr. Fix-its usually require the presentation of another person's problem in order to activate their particular brand of invasive "helpfulness."

The Nicey-Nicey Knifer. A Nicey-Nicey Knifer slips in sweetly. Once your heart is open, she inserts a verbal knife. If you cry out in pain, her standard response is, "I was only trying to help!"

The Patronizing Pollyanna. If you have a major setback in your career, the Patronizing Pollyanna will say, "Count your blessings! You've still got a job!" If your home burns down, she'll say, "Look on the bright side. You can get a whole new house now!" If your lover dies unexpectedly, the Patronizing Pollyanna will hold your

If the only tool you have is a hammer, you tend to see every problem as a nail.

ABRAHAM MASLOW

hand, look pleadingly into your eyes, and say, "Don't worry, honey, you'll fall in love again someday."

Although Patronizing Pollyannas insist that they're trying to make you feel better, they're actually interested in making *themselves* feel better. The point is, they're so afraid of their own pain that they can't tolerate yours.

The Queen of Denial. The Queen of Denial will try to nail you for the same qualities that she herself blatantly exhibits. If you call her on this, she'll feign innocence, question your character, or become downright nasty. In her rulebook, no one is allowed to question the Queen, which conveniently allows her denial to remain intact.

The Slimy Slimer. When you encounter a Slimy Slimer, you may not know what hit you until after you part company. Afterward you feel like hell, but you don't know why. What's worse, you're often left wondering if *you* did something wrong. Slimy Slimers are so good at shaming people that it's second nature to them, like breathing. Wherever they go, they leave a trail of slime behind them.

The Sneaky Sniper. Sneaky Snipers come in a variety of styles, ranging from the well-intentioned For Your Own Good Bully to the arrogantly self-righteous Know-It-All to the maliciously inclined "Kill the Messenger" Fanatic. However, whether they mean well or whether they're just plain mean, Sneaky Snipers are a particularly deadly breed.

Sneaky Snipers have overdeveloped egos and underdeveloped hearts. Basically, they think it's their job to *enlighten* you about whatever ways they think you're falling short of their expectations. They don't care if you're interested in their opinions of you, because they're going to tell you anyway. What's worse, Sneaky Snipers are gutless creatures who always do their dirty work under cover: They rely on anonymity to level their attacks.

Sneaky Snipers love to write letters or send e-mails without signing them, or if they must sign a name or give an e-mail address, they hide behind a phony one. Similarly, if they strike by telephone or by voice mail, they give away their presence by that same telltale lack of identification.

In any case, these abominable creatures rely on your willingness to stay put while they dish out their criticisms of you. They assume that your curiosity will overpower your intuition, which wisely warns you *not* to open that envelope that arrives without a return address—and equally wisely, warns you *not* to listen to that anonymous phone message. The point is, Sneaky Snipers are like sharks in a swimming pool. Your only hope is to get out of the pool as soon as you spot their fins.

People seem not to see that their opinion of the world is also a confession of character.

RALPH WALDO EMERSON

While it may appear to be a bloodless crime, people who destroy the self-esteem of others with cruelty and ridicule are really committing a violent crime. To ignore it or tolerate it is to aid and abet it.

DEAR ABBY

If you're not part of the solution, you're part of the problem.

ELDRIDGE CLEAVER

God is infinite, and his shadow is also infinite.

MEHER BABA

Typhoid Mary. Ram Dass tells the story of an army nurse who ministered to the wounded, not realizing that she was a carrier of typhoid fever. Oblivious to her own toxicity, Typhoid Mary had no idea that she was wreaking havoc on those she meant to help. Even still, the fact that she was ignorant of her effects did not negate the distress of those she touched.

In everyday terms, Typhoid Mary characters often show up as carriers of *emotional* toxicity. Unaware of their own backlog of unprocessed feelings, they *leak* distress to all who come in contact with them.

The Constant Competitor Enlightened Fool Eternal Infant Evil Eyer "For Your Own Good" Bully Guilt Tripper Grand Inquisitor Jugular Jester "Kill the Messenger" Fanatic King of Criticism Know-It-All Master Blamer Missionary Mr. Fix-it Nicey-Nicey Knifer Patronizing Pollyanna Queen of Denial Slimy Slimer Sneaky Sniper Typhoid Mary. There really are people who have *all* these abusive, disrespectful styles lurking around in the pit of their psyches. Sometimes I even catch a glimpse of one of these multi-talented creatures when I look in the mirror!

The point to remember is that everyone is capable of everything. If you get stuck in a swamp when you go wading around in the depths of your psyche, don't despair. Dig your way out! Sure, you may have a shadow, but so does everybody. There's no way around that if you want to stand in the sun. In the end, if you play your cards right, you can make your shadow one of your own best friends.

My Personal
Rules of Respect

Many people object to the word *rule* because of its arbitrary, hard-line approach to behavior. In most cases I share this objection. However, in the area of respect, there are guidelines so inviolate for me that they deserve to be called rules. While there may be exceptions to every rule, I generally treat my personal code of conduct as inviolate, because this reminds me that respectful behavior is not subject to passing whims. I like to honor myself and others to the fullest extent possible in every situation.

In the previous chapter, "Disrespect and Subtle Abuse," I spoke about the opposite of respect, and I described a myriad of character styles that illustrate how *not* to treat people. Now I'll address the flip side by sharing My Personal Rules of Respect with you. Before I do that, though, I'd like to offer a few tips about how to imprint the experience of respect in your body, so you can develop an internal *barometer of respect* to help guide your behavior.

I take readings from my own internal barometer of respect by paying attention to the feelings in my gut. My gut-level experience of respect is difficult to put into words, but I'd say that it makes me feel expansive, buoyant, *straight-across* with people, and free to be me. This feeling of respect arises in my body whether I'm giving or receiving it.

My internal experience of respect is very different from the way I feel when shame, blame, or criticism taint my own or another person's behavior. In such cases, my body might contract with fear or pain. If I'm on the receiving end of the disrespect, I might feel *small*. In contrast, I might feel overbearing or imposing if I'm the one who's being disrespectful. No matter which side I'm on, I notice that disrespect always brings a decrease in my sense of freedom.

Basically, respect makes my body relax, and it makes me feel encouraged. Disrespect makes my body shut down, and it makes me feel disheartened. That last word is key: Respect gives me heart, and disrespect takes it away.

Surround yourself with people who respect and treat you well.
CLAUDIA BLACK

I encourage you to tune in to your own internal barometer of respect. Notice how your gut feels when you feel honored during an exchange, then notice how your gut feels when you don't feel honored. Sometimes your barometer may give you readings that are out of whack in relation to what's really happening, since there may be times when misunderstandings cloud people's true intentions of good will. However, the only way to increase the accuracy of your perceptions is to *trust what you get,* and then build on that.

Begin by paying attention to exchanges where you feel treated in such a way that your self-worth is fostered. In addition, notice how your body feels when you extend respect in such a way that the other person *gets it.* Imprint these experiences by noticing and validating them. Validation can be as simple as acknowledging the sensations in your body that you associate with respect.

For contrast, take note of your gut-level response to being shamed, blamed, or disrespected in some way. Even if other people say they mean to be respectful of you, listen to your own heart about it. If you don't *feel* respected in an interaction, you get to be the final authority about your experience. A true friend will honor your perceptions and try to understand how his or her words and behavior affected you adversely.

In the same way, give others this kind of consideration. That is, if people say they don't feel respected by you, let them make that call. Give them the benefit of the doubt, for their sake and for the sake of your own development. Assume that there is at least some truth in their assessment of your words or actions, and take advantage of the opportunity to polish your rough edges.

Once you've got a handle on your own internal sense of respect, you'll be in a better position to hone your personal code of conduct, which in turn will guide you in your interactions with people. For inspiration, you can check out My Personal Rules of Respect. As you read my guidelines, be sure to engage your own barometer of respect. Find the rules that resonate with you, and make them yours. On the other hand, if something doesn't fit for you, change it or let it go.

First I'll simply list my Rules of Respect, so you can get a sense of them as a whole. Then I'll go through them again one by one, giving additional tips and comments to flesh them out for you. Please note that I have written my rules in a form of *you* statements that sound as if I'm telling myself what to do. Actually, that is precisely my intention. Like many people, I sometimes talk to myself as if I'm another person, because this allows me to coach myself (see Rule #2 for more about this).

My Personal Rules of Respect

1. Take 100% responsibility.

2. Speak in first-person "I" statements.

3. Don't tell others what you think of them, or what you think might help them, without first receiving their permission to do so.

4. When someone else is talking, listen.

5. To practice respectful caring, use Lucia Capacchione's three simple questions: "How do you feel? What do you need? How can I help you get what you need?"

6. Nurture the capacity to ask for help clearly and without expectation.

7. If someone asks you for help, give only what is right for you to give, if anything.

8. Don't attack anyone personally, but feel free to get feisty about ideas!

9. Never criticize anyone for saying "ouch."

10. If you feel hurt or disrespected by someone's words or actions, speak up when appropriate, using "I" statements— or withdraw when necessary.

11. Give yourself and others the freedom to withdraw at any time—for any reason or for no reason—without fear of shame, blame, coercion, or retaliation.

12. Ask trusted friends to speak up if they think you're not walking your talk. If they do offer solicited input, listen carefully.

13. For kick-ass pattern busting, use this daily prayer: "Show me the flip side of my patterns, so I can get to compassion faster."

14. Respect the power of privilege.

15. Trust that people are doing the best they can, given everything.

My Personal Rules of Respect—Expanded Version

1. Take 100% responsibility.

Ihaleakalā Hew Len taught me the following question, which forces me to focus on the only part of a situation I can change, namely, *myself:* "What is going on in me that I have caused this problem, and how can I rectify this problem in me?"

I don't use this question to beat myself up, nor do I use it to excuse other people's bad behavior. For me, taking 100% responsibility is about *cleaning up* whatever form of distress I experience, no matter how or where it appears. As an analogy, let's say I come across a mess in the forest. I can keep walking and ignore it, saying I didn't cause it, so I don't need to clean it up. I can track down the mess-makers and try to persuade them to clean it up. Last of all, I can simply clean it up myself. There's no question that this dilemma can get tricky, depending on the size of the mess and my ability to clean it up alone. However, I trust you get my point.

In interpersonal relationships, the only thing that works for me is to take 100% responsibility for whatever blunders occur. This doesn't mean I don't notice other people's parts in the system, nor does it mean that I don't speak up for myself when I feel disrespected. In point of fact, *not* speaking up for myself may well be the *problem in me* that created the mess.

Ultimately, no matter who does what in a given situation, the only part I can change is my part. When I catch myself obsessing about another person's behavior, it's a signal that I'm avoiding my responsibility to look within for the cause—and the cure. This includes situations of abuse, where it's my responsibility to leave as swiftly and safely as possible.

2. Speak in first-person "I" statements.

In general, *you* statements and *we* statements are justifiable only if I have outright permission from others to speak for them.

One peculiar version of *you* statements is rampant in our culture. It happens when someone speaks about herself as if she's talking about you instead of her. I'll give you an example. Let's say my cat has just died, and I'm all broken up about it. Instead of speaking about it in a first-person *I* statement, I say, "*You* really hurt when *your* cat dies." An even more detached version of the same thing goes like this: "*It* really hurts when your cat dies."

Although some people might think this style of speech helps the listener to feel included, I find it unsettling and sometimes even

I can solve a problem only when I say "This is my problem and it's up to me to solve it."

M. SCOTT PECK

condescending. In the very least, it's presumptuous for someone to assume she knows how I'd feel in her place. At best, it's simply a sign of low self-esteem when someone can't stand on her own and speak for herself in first person.

To be fair, people learn to speak this way because there is a strong tendency in our culture to devalue the self. *You* statements uphold this prevailing tendency by drawing attention away from the self. However, just because this kind of communication is common doesn't mean it's healthy.

There are many other forms of unhealthy *you* statements, like when people try to tell others what to do or how to be. For example, I cringe when I hear parents tell their children, "You need to...." Nobody has the right to tell others what they need! Besides, these kinds of statements are as ineffective as they are insulting.

When someone tells me what I need or how I should be, it engages my *rebel*—the part of me that rightly resists coercion. For those parents (or others) who doubt the seriousness of this offense, I ask them to turn it around. How would *they* feel if their children—or anyone—told them what *they* need, what *they* should do, or how *they* should be?

It's fair to ask for what you want when you need something, as opposed to giving orders or handing down ultimatums. Parents in particular may also want to provide structure by offering choices when they ask for help. For instance, with older children you could say, "I need help with the kitchen cleanup. Would you sweep the floors, or would you rather help me with the dishes?" Whatever words you choose, the important thing is to speak to others, including children, in the same way you would want others to speak to you.

Since I'm childless by choice, parents sometimes dismiss my input about respect as naive, arguing that coercion is a necessary part of child-raising. I do realize that if parents *ask* instead of *demand*, they might be refused. This can be frustrating when they're trying to teach cooperation, chore-sharing, and mutual respect. However, parents can't teach cooperation by imposing their wills. This only creates power struggles.

When a conflict of wills arises—which is probably inevitable—the most compassionate response for parents is to take 100% responsibility for the situation by examining their own behavior first of all. They can't expect respect from their children if they don't model it themselves. In the final analysis, it's the parents' responsibility to be aware of their position of power (see Rule #14), so that their behavior, words, and tone of voice *encourage* respect by *extending* it.

Your child comes to you as a wondrous mirror, as a teacher who says to you, "Remember love. Remember who you are."
EMMANUEL

Dare to be naive.
R. BUCKMINSTER FULLER

Children who are respected can find their way in the world.

J. Konrad Stettbacher

If it seems like I'm coming down hard on parents, rest assured that these suggestions are meant to benefit parents as much as children. The point is, coercive language—as opposed to respectful language—will simply incite more resistance, if not downright rebellion. This, in turn, serves to deepen any power struggles that may arise.

In worst case scenarios between parents and children—when power struggles escalate into displays of threat, domination, or force—nobody wins, especially not the person who *appears* to win. Those who feel vanquished will always rise again in some way, so the struggle for power will inevitably repeat itself. Coercion is not the path of respect.

All these tips about coercive language and parent-child relationships apply to any situation where one person holds more power, privilege, or assumed authority in a relationship. Examples might include marriage or partnership, sibling relationships, helping professional or therapeutic relationships, or relationships where there are imbalances of power due to racial, ethnic, religious, class, gender, or sexual orientation differences.

In all these cases, it's common for the more privileged person to tell those in *one-down* positions what they need to do or how they should be, though this usually doesn't happen in reverse. As I mentioned in the previous example of parents and children, power-imbalanced relationships can give rise to an overuse of *you* statements, if those in power think they have a right to impose their will on others.

By the way, I'm not saying that you can never begin your sentences with the word *you.* All I'm saying is, pay attention to the way you communicate. Speak in first-person *I* statements whenever possible. Avoid using *you* statements, particularly if you use them to manipulate, criticize, or blame people. In addition, watch out for sentences that begin with phrases such as *you need to, you should, you must, you have to,* or any other words that infer you know better than others what they need, what they should do, or how they should be.

...words are more powerful than perhaps anyone suspects, and once deeply engraved in a child's mind, they are not easily eradicated.

May Sarton

As you've noticed from reading this book, there is one exception I make to my own rule about avoiding *you* statements. That is, I use *you* statements to communicate instructions in a direct way when I have the other person's permission to do so. For instance, in "The Body Trust Game," I wrote: "You grasp your partner's wrists, and your partner grasps your wrists." Obviously, I'm telling you what to do in that sentence. However, I'm trusting that you can feel the difference between my use of this style as a coaching technique, versus my use of it as a form of manipulation.

Since you can put this book aside at any time, I assume that you are reading it voluntarily, which indicates permission on your part. Beyond that, I do my best to remind you, here and there, that you are free to do—or not do—anything I suggest. In this book, as well as in my other self-help writing and speaking, I couch my *you* statements with extra helpings of permission to respect you, of course, but also to respect myself.

The truth is, I really have no idea what you need or how you should be, and it would feel strange for me to infer otherwise. Still, I want to share my experience in order to express myself and to share ideas, in case you feel drawn to experiment with anything I've tried. When I use *you* statements, I do it with awareness of the possible pitfalls, but with the hope that you can understand my choice to employ this style of speech in a mutually respectful way.

Once again, I will refer you to your own internal barometer of respect. Sometimes you'll hear people (or yourself) use *you* statements, and your body won't object. Other times, though, you might get a queasy feeling in your stomach, your heart will close down, or you'll just feel mad. At that point, you'll know something's wrong, or at least, that something needs your attention.

You can also use your barometer of respect to check out another potentially devaluing form of speech, namely, *we* statements. In the same way some people use *you* statements to draw attention away from the self, others may speak in plural *we* statements to accomplish the same thing in another way. When one person speaks or writes as if he or she is a group instead of an individual, it gives me pause. Do these people think they have a right to speak for others? Although some people might consider *we* statements to be a good way to make others feel included, I find it patronizing. How can anyone speak for me, much less all of humanity?

In my experience, people often use *we* statements to claim more than their individual share of power or because they don't have the guts to stand on their own. This may sound harsh, but if you like to communicate in the "royal we" style, please consider the following questions next time you find yourself speaking or writing as if you're *plural* instead of singular.

Are you trying to speak for your mate or for someone else? Are you speaking for everyone all over the world and across time? If you are one person speaking for all of humanity, are you trying to make your words sound more important or far-reaching than your own personal scope of power or experience? Are you simply afraid to stand alone in your position?

Believe those who are seeking the truth; doubt those who find it.

ANDRÉ GIDE

If there is righteousness in the heart, there will be beauty in the character.

If there is beauty in the character, there will be harmony in the home.

If there is harmony in the home, there will be order in the nation.

When there is order in the nation, there will be peace in the world.

SATHYA SAI BABA

R-E-S-P-E-C-T.
Find out what it means to me.
ARETHA FRANKLIN

Many couples speak in *we* statements, as if they are a unit instead of two individuals. I don't mind if people speak in third person plural if they're describing factual information such as, "We went to the store last night." However, some spouses and partners use *we* statements to speak for one another at emotional and philosophical levels. Some spouses never speak in first-person *I* statements at all! While some people might believe this is perfectly acceptable behavior for couples, I think it's a telltale sign of serious enmeshment.

In the 1970s, I had a wonderful boss who introduced me to the pomposity of *we* statements. Whenever he caught me using "we" statements, he would stop me with a big grin and say, "What? Do you have a mouse in your pocket?" It was great!

If *we* statements and *you* statements make up a large part of your speaking or writing style, you might have trouble making the switch to first-person *I* statements. It's not unreasonable to expect this transition to take many *years*. During the changeover, you might feel terribly narcissistic if you don't draw attention away from yourself by speaking in *you* statements or *we* statements. My father actually told me once that I shouldn't write sentences that begin with the word *I*, so you can imagine how hard it's been for me to learn how to communicate in first-person statements.

I still get scared sometimes when I speak in first person. It's as if a part of me is afraid that all those childhood admonishments will turn into giant vultures that swoop down and carry me off to the abyss, where they'll eat me alive for committing such flagrant acts of verbal self-centeredness. However, I honestly believe that if people think my first-person statements sound narcissistic, this is better than sounding pompous or presumptuous, which is how I feel when I speak in second or third person. In the end, I choose to err on the side of speaking directly from my own truth, letting the chips fall where they may. How will you choose?

3. Don't tell others what you think of them, or what you think might help them, without first receiving their permission to do so.

The most unwelcome advice is that which is unasked for, so volunteer your information only when asked. The exception would be a life-threatening situation.

ABIGAIL VAN BUREN

This is really quite simple. If someone doesn't want my input, it's up to me to keep quiet. Period.

I do make one exception to this rule in life-or-death situations. For example, if someone is about to step in front of a truck, and he or she is looking the other way, I'd yell "WATCH OUT!" without asking permission before offering my input. My personal gauge for when to do this is to ask myself if I would want someone else to do it for me, if I was the one in danger.

4. When someone else is talking, listen.

This means that I don't interrupt, swipe the focus from the speaker, or offer unsolicited advice. Listen means listen.

I make an exception to this rule in two cases. First, I sometimes encounter people who would speak until the end of time if I continue to listen in my fully attentive way. Second, there are times when someone's words feel disrespectful or abusive to me. In these cases, I may use whatever means at my disposal to extricate myself from the situation as elegantly and effectively as possible.

For example, if I don't like how someone is treating me, I may interrupt by making a "time-out" signal with my hands—the way referees do in sporting events. If the other person stops being disrespectful and we can work it out, great. On the other hand, it's not my job to take whatever someone wants to dish out, just so I can be a good listener (see "The Anger Primer" for more help with abusive situations).

When someone you love has difficulties, listen. When you're feeling terrible that you can't provide a cure, listen. When you don't know what to offer the people you care about, listen, listen, listen.

BERNIE SIEGEL

5. To practice respectful caring, use Lucia Capacchione's three simple questions: "How do you feel? What do you need? How can I help you get what you need?"

Capacchione is the author whose nondominant hand books I mentioned in the chapter called "Joy: A Warrior's Path." She encourages people to use these three questions when they dialogue with their inner selves through the use of their nondominant hands. These questions are so basic, so respectful, and so helpful that I like to use them when I relate to others, as well as to myself.

Of course, the first and most important tip about using these questions is to *really listen* when the other person answers you. Some people find it difficult to be truly open to another person's feelings and needs, without trying to fix or change them. On the flip side, the people you ask might not know—or feel safe to say—what they need or how they feel. In such cases, it's especially important that you don't rush in and fill the space for them, no matter how awkward you or they might feel about the silence.

One of my close friends and I started practicing with these questions in the late 1980s. In the beginning, it was sometimes startling for me to realize that she was actually *interested* in my answers, and that she wouldn't jump in and answer the questions for me if I couldn't come up with anything. As it happened, my friend and I realized that we both had the same tendency of fear operating for each of us. When we talked about this, we discovered ways that our past experiences had contributed to this fear.

Since she and I both came from family situations where our feelings and needs (as children) were overridden and devalued in

People need a lot of caring support before their suffering can turn into compassion.

PEMA CHÖDRÖN

many ways, it took time and patience for us to feel safe exposing these kinds of intimacies to each other. She was afraid that I would *rob her process* if she shared her innermost thoughts, because that's what often happened in her family. My fear was that she would use my self-disclosures against me if I allowed her to *see* me.

Thus, if you use these questions when talking to others—or even to yourself—be sensitive to the possibility that you may not be accustomed to this kind of respectful caring. If the questions trigger old fears, take it slow. Give yourself and others plenty of time and space to answer—or not answer—according to individual levels of comfort with this kind of intimacy.

I'd like to call your attention to the third and last question in Capacchione's series, namely, "How can I help you get what you need?" Notice that this question does *not* say, "How can I give you what you need?" This is an important distinction, especially in a culture that has elevated *caretaking* to a high, though very pathological, art.

If I tell you what I need, it's not your job to give it to me. If you are a friend and you would like to help in some way, then you can certainly ask if there is some way you can help me get what I need. However, the operant word here is *ask*. Although you might be brimming with ideas about what *you* think I should do, it's more respectful for you to ask me what *I* think about the kind of help I need. In the end, if I ask specifically for your help, you can still say *yes* or *no* to anything that involves you.

It is not easy or comfortable for us to consider that selfless behavior, "being good," and efforts to help may actually be attempts to control, and not be altruistically motivated.

ROBIN NORWOOD

Sometimes I may simply want you to hear my feelings and needs, and I won't want anything else. If I do want more support, I'll feel more empowered if you encourage me to figure out for myself how you or anyone else might assist my efforts. No matter how much you care about me, or how much you'd like to help, I'll trust you more if you don't use *my* needs to fulfill *your* desire to help.

6. Nurture the capacity to ask for help clearly and without expectation.

The first part of this rule—the part about asking for help *clearly*—can be problematic for those of us who were taught that it's a sign of weakness to ask for help at all. If you're scared to ask for help, it will be even scarier for you to be blatant about it. As a result, you might mumble (literally) when you solicit support, or you might beat around the bush until the other person guesses what you need, and perhaps even offers to give it to you.

Maybe you have no fear about asking for help, so you've never tried to manipulate others into giving you what you want via indirect forms of communication. I wish I could say the same thing about myself, but the truth is, *asking for help* was considered so shameful in my family that I'm still honing my capacity to ask for what I need clearly and directly.

If you have trouble with this like I do, consider the other side of the equation. Think about how you feel when someone asks you for help. Can you tell when someone is trying to manipulate you? Even if this happens because the other person is afraid to ask directly, it still feels awful on the receiving end, doesn't it? How about when you can't even figure out what other people want, because they're being so indirect? Or how about when people send others to do their asking for them? That's about as indirect as you can get! The point is, if you remember how helpful it is *for you* when people are direct, you might feel more comfortable about being direct when you're in the asking position.

Now for the other part of this rule—the part about asking for help *without expectation*. The bottom line is that it's my job to see that my needs are met, now that I'm an adult. This doesn't mean I can't ask for help. Quite the contrary. I'm only too aware that my survival is completely interdependent with everyone and everything else. I need and receive help constantly, just to stay alive. Much of this support is given freely by the natural environment around me, or else I exchange some effort to obtain what I need. Sometimes, however, I have to ask for help in specific ways.

Expectations create suffering.
Ram Dass

When I ask people for help, it's essential for me to realize that they are not *obligated* to assist me. It's up to them to decide what, if anything, is right for them to give. If one person can't help in the way I need, then it's my responsibility to ask someone else—and yet again someone else—until I get what I need, or until I realize that's not quite what I need anymore.

By the way, this rule applies to couples, too. People in relationships often fall prey to the idea that it is their partner's job to satisfy all their needs and desires, and vice versa. I call this *turning your partner into your parent*. In other words, if I think it's my partner's job to take care of all my needs, then I'm acting like an infant who expects him to be my parent. Yuk!

Truth be told, I've known plenty of couples who think this is actually a good arrangement, so they have a hard time understanding how they disempower themselves and their partners by doing this. They figure it's a fair trade to be someone's *supplier,* if they can rest assured that their demands will always be met in return. To me, this is dependency, not interdependency.

Obviously, if I'm in a partnership where I do all the giving without ever receiving any support, then I might need to make a decision about whether or not to stay. However, it's still not my partner's job to take care of me, even if I end up leaving because of a significant imbalance in this department.

If there is enough love and enough motivation in a relationship, then I encourage couples to find a way for both people to get their needs met in ways that allow each person to feel responsible as well as respected. One direct route to this goal is to nurture the capacity to ask for help clearly and without expectation.

You can take this goal one step further by extending it beyond partnership (or marriage) to include your relationships with everyone—friends, family members, acquaintances, business associates, and even strangers. Whomever you ask for help, it's always good to be clear, direct, and willing to take *yes* or *no* for an answer. This style shows self-respect as much as it shows respect for other people.

7. If someone asks you for help, give only what is right for you to give, if anything.

This is a constant challenge for me in life, because *overgiving* is one of my most stubborn scripts. While I value my inherent spirit of generosity, it doesn't help anyone if I give in such a way that I end up depleted.

As the decades pass, I'm gradually learning my signals—both physical and emotional—that show me when I'm giving and when I'm overgiving. Basically, healthy giving makes me feel expansive and energized, while overgiving makes me feel angry, exhausted, or depressed. Of course, there are a million gradations on this continuum, but I've learned that the best approach for me is to avoid *all* overgiving, because I so easily slip into this self-diminishing script. Needless to say, my intention to avoid overgiving merely moves me in the *direction* of greater self-care. I recognize that this will probably be a lifelong myth for me to unravel.

In addition to learning my signals, I try to get better at catching these signals in the moment, so I can adjust my behavior sooner rather than later. I don't like it when I wait until I've collapsed on the floor before I realize I've overdone it again. Even still, I do give myself permission to clean up my act after the fact, if necessary. In other words, if I make a commitment to someone and then realize that I've overextended, I'll go back to that person and admit my mistake. I'll do this even if it means that I must make other arrangements to help him or her get the support that I originally promised to deliver myself.

There is no better looking glass than an old friend.

THOMAS FULLER

When one is pretending the entire body revolts.

ANAÏS NINN

Since I was raised to always do what I say I'm going to do, it's not easy for me to tell people that I need to rescind my offer. Even still, I notice that true friends respect this kind of self-care. In addition, they know that I give them the same permission to change their minds if they find themselves overextended in relation to me. My friends and I don't make a habit of renegging on our agreements, but it's good to have this option in emergencies. At any rate, my goal remains the same: Never sacrifice self-care in the name of altruism.

8. Don't attack anyone personally, but feel free to get feisty about ideas!

There's a big difference between saying, "How can you be so stupid as to think like that?" as opposed to saying, "I don't agree with your thinking about that." Once again, I refer back to my idea about the internal barometer of respect. If I'm honest, I can tell when I'm blasting an idea and when I'm blasting a human being. This gets tricky, of course, since many of us identify strongly with personal beliefs. However, it's possible to enjoy passionate and even heated discussions without significant mishap, as long as everyone keeps an eye on their own barometer of respect.

9. Never criticize anyone for saying "ouch."

If people express hurt in relation to my words or actions, it's my responsibility to respond with kindness. It's not okay for me to say I was "just kidding" or that they were being "too sensitive." Such responses are extremely discounting, if not downright shaming. Another disrespectful response is the phrase "Don't take it personally!" In my experience, the only people who use this phrase are those who don't want to take responsibility for how their words or actions have hurt another person.

Sometimes it's hard to face the fact that I've been an agent in other people's pain, but the truth is, this may happen despite my best intentions. If I can get out of my ego and into my heart, it's easy to drop my perfectionist pride and focus on the problem. I assume that if people say *ouch* in relation to me, there is something I need to examine in myself, even if it's not exactly the same thing they see. This doesn't mean that their perceptions aren't valid, only that their perceptions may not match mine.

Sometimes things simply look different from different angles. However, this doesn't give me the right to deny anyone's pain. Thus, the first step for this rule is to listen very carefully to other people's distress in relation to me, as long as they communicate respectfully. I can then offer my respect in return by thanking them for their honesty—even if I feel bad about contributing to their pain.

It is possible to be different and still be all right. There can be two—or more—answers to the same questions, and all can be right.
ANNE WILSON SCHAEF

My religion is very simple—my religion is kindness.
DALAI LAMA

I know it's not always easy for people to speak up and say *ouch*. I also know that other people give me a gift when they do this. The gift is an outside perspective. If I trust this gift and take their concerns seriously, I can benefit from the opportunity to soften yet another of my rough edges. In addition, I get a chance to validate other people's perceptions, and I learn more about how to be compassionate with their vulnerabilities.

10. If you feel hurt or disrespected by someone's words or actions, speak up when appropriate, using "I" statements—or withdraw when necessary.

This is the flip side of the previous rule. A big part of self-respect is ensuring that others treat me respectfully. Since I can't control the way other people act, all I can do is speak up whenever my internal barometer of respect registers a problem with the way they're treating me. As always, it's important for me to state my objections in first-person *I* statements.

If my needs fall on deaf ears and I continue to feel disrespected, it's up to me to take care of myself by withdrawing from the situation. Also, there are times when I may not wish to speak up, but may choose to withdraw instead. Either way, I'm in charge of honoring my comfort level in all interactions.

11. Give yourself and others the freedom to withdraw at any time—for any reason or for no reason—without fear of shame, blame, coercion, or retaliation.

This rule is inviolate for me. I even extend this right to those who use withdrawal as a form of punishment. It doesn't matter to me. Besides, I don't have to take their withdrawal as punishment, even if that's what they intend! I might be perfectly thrilled about their withdrawal, for all I know. In any case, I'm a big advocate of withdrawal as a tool for self-care. The truth is, even those who withdraw to punish others remove the opportunity for direct abuse (by them or others). This in itself is helpful.

Of course, if I'm in a relationship with someone who always and only withdraws during conflict—and never stays put long enough to talk things through—I may need to make a decision about whether or not I want to continue that relationship. On the other hand, if each of us uses withdrawal judiciously as one of many options for self-care, then I'd be more likely to hang in there with that person.

Let me give you an example by telling you about Amy and Steven (not their real names). At the beginning of their relationship, Amy struggled with the desire to run away, even though Steven never gave her any reason to do so. Amy had been in an abusive marriage

People's demands are inversely proportional to their respect.
Cat Saunders

before she got together with Steven, so her fear of commitment was pretty extreme. She didn't have much faith in her own—or anyone's—ability to build a long-term relationship.

Fortunately, Steven never pressured her. He let her run as much as she liked. He didn't judge her for withdrawing, and apparently, he wasn't threatened when she did. He just encouraged her to take care of herself, and he told her he'd be there if she wanted to come back. He didn't say *when,* either; he said *if.* Gradually, Amy felt safer and safer with Steven, because the kind of love he extended to her was about *freedom.* He loved her the way you love a butterfly— with an open hand. Butterflies must be free to fly!

The truth is, everyone must be free to fly. Coercion has no place in a loving relationship. Speaking from my own experience, I sometimes get scared when people withdraw from me. I may think they don't love me anymore, or that they're leaving forever. However, I truly believe that these fears are my problem, not theirs. I deal with my fears internally, or I express them if it feels appropriate. Despite these fears, I always encourage my friends to do whatever they need to do for themselves.

If I love you, it means that I want you to take care of yourself first of all, even if you must go away from me. If you do go away— even forever—I'll still love you, because my love is not dependent on you being there for me in a particular way. To me, love is about respect more than anything, and respect must include the right to withdraw.

12. Ask trusted friends to speak up if they think you're not walking your talk. If they do offer solicited input, listen carefully.

There are few things more valuable to self-development than the honest reflections of trusted friends. No matter how much I work on myself alone, there is no substitute for outside perspectives. It's easy to fool myself about the clarity of my character if I operate in a vacuum. It's not so easy to fool myself if my allies report any inconsistencies they see.

Although my close friends have my blanket permission to speak up if they think I'm out of line, I also solicit their input regularly. I *ask* for their input because I want it, obviously, but also because I know it's not always easy for friends to comment on my behavior. They're a pretty respectful lot, and they tend to accept me, foibles and all. Therefore, I take special care to show my sincerity in *seeking* their perspectives, so they can feel more comfortable about speaking up.

One way I show my sincerity is by listening carefully when they do respond to my request for input. It's not fair for me to pounce on them by *criticizing their criticisms* of my behavior. Even if I feel

There can be no friendship where there is no freedom.
WILLIAM PENN

Could a greater miracle take place than for us to look through each other's eyes for an instant?
HENRY DAVID THOREAU

For the truly loving person the act of criticism or confrontation does not come easily; to such a person it is evident that the act has great potential for arrogance.

M. SCOTT PECK

embarrassed, ashamed, or defensive about what they say, it's my responsibility to focus on their concerns. I can always express my feelings later, if necessary. The main thing is to learn as much as I can about their points of view. When they're done, I might ask questions, paraphrase what I've heard, and make sure that *they* think I get what they're saying. Afterward, I like to thank them for their ideas and their honesty—even if I don't like what they say about me!

Later, I take their information to heart and sit with it. If it resonates with my own knowing, I can make choices about how to adjust my behavior in the future. This feedback process will then repeat itself when I check back with them to see if *their* perceptions of my progress match *my* perception of it.

By the way, there's a hidden bonus when you solicit input from friends. That is, if you *ask* for their opinions of you, it gives you a chance to open your heart to receive the information. Needless to say, this is more self-respectful than allowing people to ambush you with their opinions, when you haven't given them permission to tell you about you.

13. For kick-ass pattern busting, use this daily prayer: "Show me the flip side of my patterns, so I can get to compassion faster."

This is a foundational prayer for me, which means that I've put all my spiritual helpers on notice that I actually *want* whatever experiences will help me blast any patterns that stand in the way of deeper compassion. Because I've asked for this, it's up to me to remember my prayer whenever a piece of the proverbial shit hits the fan.

And of all glad words of prose or rhyme,
The gladdest are, "Act while there yet is time."

FRANKLIN P. ADAMS

This prayer requires me to *look within* for the source of the problem when I notice any kind of distress in my life. This doesn't mean I blame myself, nor does it mean that I deny other people's responsibility for their own actions. However, I can't control other people's behavior. The only part of any situation that I can change is my part. Besides, if I'm the one who's distressed, it's my distress! Therefore, it's up to me to take 100% responsibility for the distress by doing everything in my power to clean it up.

For example, let's say that I'm having trouble in a relationship with a woman friend. Maybe I think she has mistreated me, and I'm upset about it. If I remember the prayer, then my first step is to take some time alone to sit with my feelings. As I contemplate the situation, one question that arises from the prayer is: *How is this situation showing me my own patterns?* When I consider this question, I may remember a time when I mistreated my friend (or someone else) in a similar way to what I'm experiencing in the current situation.

On the off chance that I can't recall an instance of similar misbehavior on my part, I'll go deeper in my meditations until I encounter an aspect of my character that is *capable* of perpetrating this behavior, and I identify with the flip side of the situation that way. Since I'm pretty friendly with my *shadow* at this point, it usually doesn't take long for me to come up with multiple points of identification with the woman who is mistreating me now.

Once I connect with my own bad behavior, it softens my self-righteousness. This softening, in turn, allows me to bridge the gap of separation that arises in my heart when I delude myself into thinking that *I could never do that*. With my self-righteousness at bay, I can begin forgiveness work. As you may know from reading my two chapters on forgiveness, this is multi-layered work for me. It involves forgiving myself, forgiving others, and forgiving everyone and everything back to the beginning of time.

The bottom line is that I can't possibly know who or what contributed to every pocket of pain that I encounter in life. God only knows! Therefore, when a chunk of distress crosses my path, all I can do is take responsibility and start cleaning it up. To stop a pattern of distress, I must first remember my all-too-human capacity to perpetrate it. With this humility, I can move from blame to compassion, which gives me the opportunity to seek and offer forgiveness for the distress.

Last of all, my prayer to know the flip side of my patterns requires me to put my spiritual work into *action* by making amends for any past transgressions I uncover during my reflections. In addition, I must act on this prayer by working to avoid distress-causing behavior in the future. This is easier said than done, I realize, but it's my intention, and my pattern-busting prayer helps me stay on track.

14. Respect the power of privilege.

Those who are not aware of their position of power are likely to abuse it, however unintentionally. This applies to all types and levels of relationship: racial, sexual, familial, cultural, socio-economic, physical, emotional, intellectual, spiritual, professional, political, environmental, and even interspecies. If there's a possibility for relationship, there is a potential for power imbalance and abuse. You can even abuse power in relation to yourself!

It's been said that those who are oppressed know more about their oppressors than their oppressors know about them. I agree. Those who are oppressed *must* know everything they can about their oppressors in order to survive. On the other hand, the ones *on top* enjoy a level of impunity that allows them to operate oblivious

You know, we live in a moral universe after all. What's right matters. What's wrong matters. You may keep things hidden, but they don't disappear into the ether. They impregnate the atmosphere.

DESMOND TUTU

When our models of who we are fall away, we are free to simply meet and be together.

RAM DASS

to the needs of those they treat as if they were *beneath* them. Generally speaking, those in power aren't motivated to understand the people they oppress, since this would only upset the balance of power that supports the status quo, which in turn supports the privileges they (the ones in power) enjoy.

In contrast, people who are oppressed will always seek to upset the status quo that keeps them disempowered. It's human nature to rebel against *any* form of bondage, including the invisible bonds that pervade personal and interpersonal relationships at every level of society.

Unfortunately, it's also human nature to switch from *oppressed* to *oppressor* whenever the dominant power structure is overturned. This vicious cycle of abuse can only be stopped through awareness. Usually, this awareness comes from the minority voices—from those who have been oppressed—because they have the most to gain from stopping the abuse. Sometimes, though, awareness may come from members of the dominant group who are sensitive to the double-edged sword of privilege.

Let me bring this philosophical discussion down to earth by telling you a story about something that changed me forever. It happened in 1987, when I was 33 years old. I had just left a short, abusive marriage. In order to leave that relationship, I had to let go of my home, which also housed my counseling office. I was emotionally exhausted and unable to work for a while, but I was fortunate to have a network of friends who "passed me around" from home to home over a period of two years, while I got back on my feet. One of these generous souls was a woman I'll call Arianna, to whom I owe a great debt, not only for giving me shelter, but also for teaching me about the power of privilege.

One day Arianna and I were hanging out, talking, when the conversation shifted to race relations. Arianna's black and I'm white. At some point in the conversation, she launched a direct verbal attack on me as a white woman. Arianna talked passionately and at length about how I've always had privileges as a white woman that she has never had—and may never have—in her lifetime as a black woman.

I don't know how I had the grace to keep my mouth shut while she raged at me, but I did. In retrospect, I think that I was able to listen without defending myself because she was RIGHT. Arianna didn't speak in generalities. She talked about *me* and *her*. She went into detail about how my skin opens doors for me—the same doors that slam shut in her face. She made my position of privilege clear to me in a way that no one ever had before. I mean, I'd been intellectually aware of my white privilege, but Arianna's expression of rage helped me see how my *personal* use of this power—however conscious or unconscious—made me one of the *white oppressors*. It also made me one of *her* oppressors.

Before that conversation, I'd always fancied myself to be a racially hip liberal. *Bigot* was not a label I would ever have applied to myself. However, Arianna taught me something about the shadow side of bigotry, namely, that bigotry is also perpetrated each and every time I take advantage of privileges that others don't have.

For example, it would be impossible for me to separate my white skin from the education I received. I grew up in primarily white neighborhoods, and I attended primarily white public schools. Then I won a small scholarship from a primarily white company, which allowed me to use the money at any college I chose. As it happened, I started my college career at a primarily white university in Oregon.

In those days, I didn't pay much attention to the lack of color around me, because I was used to swimming in an ocean of whiteness, the way a fish swims in water. Whiteness was ubiquitous, and I was swimming along okay, so what was the problem?

The problem, obviously, was that I was living without awareness, and I was blithely taking advantage of privileges every single day that millions of people don't have even for a moment. Do you think Arianna had the same opportunities I had? Do you think she could have gone to my schools and enjoyed the same ease of interaction? Do you think she would have been considered for the same scholarship made available by that white male construction company? Do you think she would have felt at home on the campus of that pearly white university at a time (in the early 1970s) when race awareness was even less developed than it is today?

I'm not suggesting that Arianna would even *want* to attend the same schools I attended or pursue the same activities I pursued. I'm only saying that she didn't have the same ease of opportunity to do so. What for me was a *given*, for her was an effort. **This is what privilege is about: when one person has to struggle for something another person takes for granted.**

I suspect that many—if not most—white people rarely even consider the issue of privilege. If they do consider it, they might even hold fast to the belief that the privileges they enjoy are actually *rights*—but woe unto those who want a piece of the action! Whenever I encounter this attitude, I'm ashamed to be white, even though I realize that my shame may be perceived as yet another white liberal attempt to be politically correct.

But it is not really difference the oppressor fears so much as similarity.

CHERRIE MORAGA

You've gotta pass through Race Place in order to make it to Can We All Get Along, but most everybody is looking for a shortcut.

LONNAE O'NEAL PARKER

You know, it's not the world that was my oppressor, because what the world does to you long enough and effectively enough, you begin to do to yourself.

JAMES BALDWIN

Never doubt that a small group of thoughtful, committed citizens can change the world. Indeed, it is the only thing that ever has.

MARGARET MEAD

I must admit that I do wish I could banish all traces of my own covert bigotry—the hidden traces of fear and judgment that arise in me via cultural and familial conditioning. Although this is a valid wish, I know that it would be virtually impossible for me to remove all the subconscious and irrational messages about skin color that I've absorbed into my psyche over time. Therefore, I can only do the next best thing, which is to *own* and *process* my hidden streaks of racism as I become aware of them—and to do my damnedest not to act on them.

This means listening carefully when people of color talk about their oppression, knowing that I am one of the oppressors. It also means that I must face and work with my grief about this role, without expecting forgiveness from those I oppress. As I mentioned, I must also follow the threads of my inner work into outer action, in terms of *not* acting on the hidden bigotry I discover in my psyche. This is easier said than done, I realize, but my *intention* to be alert to my own covert racism does influence the way I experience any given situation, and therefore, this intention positively influences the way I interact with others.

Last of all, taking responsibility for my covert racism means that I walk the line between hopelessness and hope. I know I'm only one person, and there is so overwhelmingly much to do about racism that it's easy to fall into despair. Even still, I choose hope over hopelessness, not because I'm just some bleeding-heart liberal, but because the alternative is unthinkable to me. Thus, I choose to believe that each person *can* make a difference, and that *I* can make a difference. I realize that change can only come one step at a time— one hidden streak of bigotry uncovered and examined at a time, one shadow effect of my privilege acknowledged and ameliorated at a time.

Arianna's teaching about privilege yielded an additional gift for me. It allowed me to build bridges to men who deny their position of power in regard to women. Since I'm white, it's impossible for me to conceive of the double whammy of racism and sexism that Arianna has known her entire life. However, I do know what it's like to deal with men who are oblivious about their *personal* contribution to gender oppression. Some men deny their role as oppressor because they fancy themselves to be *sensitive* males, just as I once believed that I was not a member of the white oppressor class, since I don't commit racist hate crimes or act in blatantly intolerant ways.

I've shared the story of Arianna's anger with some of these so-called sensitive men in my practice as a counselor. These men would become indignantly incensed when their female partners raged at them about their male privilege, just as Arianna had raged at me about my white privilege. The men were honestly puzzled by their partners' anger because, frankly, they were in denial of their own power as men.

Because they refused to recognize their gender privilege, they were unable to acknowledge all the countless ways they *personally* contributed to women's oppression in general—and to their partners' oppression in specific. As long as they refused to acknowledge their *personal* role in this oppression, their ability to hear their partners' pain was compromised by their desire to defend their innocence. They maintained that their partners' rage was misplaced: that it belonged to men as a *collective*, maybe, but not to them *personally*. As if they weren't men!

What's worse, some of these men expected their female friends to soothe their (the men's) woundedness related to the burdens of manhood, even though they had a hard time seeing how those same burdens had also benefited them in ways their female partners were denied. Ironically, their desire for sympathy was an indirect admission of their position of power.

Unfortunately, these men were primarily interested in describing how the stresses of this power position had hurt *them*. Needless to say, their arguments about the burdens of manhood went nowhere with their female partners as long as they (the men) would neither acknowledge the oppressiveness of their power nor find a way to empathize with the disempowerment experienced by women.

If you think I'm being too hard on men, you may be right, but I didn't think Arianna was being too hard on me. I'll shoulder any accusations of being too hard-line about power imbalances, because I *am* hard-line about this issue. I certainly won't deny the detrimental effects that inevitably come to those who hold more than their share of power.

However, I feel strongly that it's the responsibility of those with privilege to listen *first* to those with less privilege, not the other way around. In addition, those with less privilege cannot be expected to entertain stories about the oppressors' pain until they (those with less privilege) are ready and willing to do so. There are many reasons for this, but since that would take another book, let me just give you a simple analogy.

Let's say that you are a perfectly healthy individual of average height and weight, and let's say that I'm a six-foot, six-inch, 550-pound professional wrestler. Now, it doesn't take too much imagination to see that if I decide to sit where you're sitting, you'll

Doing the best at this moment puts you in the best place for the next moment.

Oprah Winfrey

get crushed. Maybe you could cause me some pain if you sink your teeth into my back side as I settle my bulk on your lap, but even then, I wouldn't be nearly as compromised by the situation as you would be. Clearly, my impressive size would tip the balance of power in my favor. You'd be crushed long before I lose much blood from your bite.

Obviously, this is a very simple analogy, but you get my point. As the 550-pound top dog, it would be silly for me to expect you to listen to me whine about my pain from your bite. I may be hurting, but you can't even *breathe*. Therefore, if I want to have any kind of meaningful dialogue with you, I must make the first move. In this case, I need to get up, back off, and give you some space. I also need to realize that even if you wanted to, you probably could never overpower me the way I could overpower you. Therefore, if we do try to engage in a straight-across dialogue, I must remain aware of the fact that for you, I'll always be a 550-pound giant who could easily crush you.

When I'm in the power position, it can be awfully tempting to enjoy the privileges accorded me without acknowledging the effects of my actions on those who don't enjoy the same privileges. Even still, I know how uncomfortable it feels to identify with the power side of a situation, since the power side is often seen as the oppressor or the abuser (i.e., the *bad guy)*. However, if I can't identify with the shadow side of whatever kind of power I hold, I'll never be able to truly understand how my choices and my actions contribute to the pain of those who are not empowered in the same way. Ultimately, if I can't see how my position of power affects others detrimentally, then I'm likely to keep perpetrating some kind of hurt, however unintentionally.

In my practice as a counselor, I've learned a lot about my blatant and subtle abuse of privilege. It took me a long time to realize that my clients almost always perceive some degree of power imbalance in our relationship, even when I do my best to relate to them as equals. The truth is, the person who holds the *most* power in any given situation is usually the one who experiences the imbalance the *least*.

Paradoxically, I've always had issues around claiming my own authority, so it is sometimes startling for me to realize that clients see me as an authority figure, even when I don't always see myself that way. It's important for me to remain mindful of their perception of me as an authority figure. Otherwise, I run the risk of discounting their experience, which would only add to the power imbalance.

As I gradually became more aware of the issue of privilege (and as clients felt safer with me), I would encourage them to speak up if they felt disempowered in any way. If they have the guts to do this, it's my job to listen carefully, validate their concerns, and ask for their ideas about how I can address these concerns in ways that are meaningful for them. In addition, I try to stay sensitive to their vulnerability by doing role reversals in my mind: by remembering how I feel when I'm the client. Even though I have a Ph.D. myself, I sometimes struggle to feel empowered with doctors and other professionals when the roles are reversed. While this is somewhat embarrassing to admit, I like that it helps me stay awake to the issue of privilege.

Aside from power imbalances related to racism, sexism, and professional status, there is another huge group of people who regularly abuse their position of privilege, both knowingly and unknowingly. If you guessed *parents*, you got it right. However, I've already addressed a number of potential problem areas in regard to parenting, both here and in other chapters. Therefore, I'll simply call attention once again to the fact that parents have an awesome responsibility to be aware of their privileged position, so that they use their power wisely and not abusively.

If you have a hard time identifying with your own position of power or privilege in any area of life, keep working on the flip side. Think about situations or relationships where you feel (or have felt) one-down, discounted, or less powerful than others. Have you ever related to a mother, a father, an older sibling, an elder friend, a boss, a teacher, a religious mentor, a doctor, a counselor, a coach, or some other authority figure who abused their position of power in regard to you? Did someone ever act toward you in such a way that they assumed it was your job to defer to them, simply because they were bigger or older—or because they had more status, more money, more credentials, or more whatever?

If you've had this experience and struggled with it, you may be able to avoid repeating this kind of power abuse yourself by opening your heart to the distress *you* felt while in one-down positions. Do you want others to feel that way in regard to you? If not, then do some troubleshooting. Are there any roles in your life where others might see you as more powerful, even if you don't see yourself that way? If so, can you imagine yourself in their position and see how they might be deferring to you because of a role you play in their lives? Can you think of ways to soften any power imbalances you discover?

If you have trouble coming up with anything, ask a trusted friend to help you brainstorm potential areas of power imbalance.

There is no better and ultimately no other way to teach your children that they are valuable people than by valuing them.

M. Scott Peck

I don't find a conflict anymore between my contemplative side and my activist side. I think that they feed off each other, perhaps even need each other.

Alix Kates Shulman

Nearly everyone holds a position of privilege in regard to someone else, even if it's just your little brother or that kid down the street. Most of us go in and out of power positions all day long, depending on what's happening and who's involved.

For instance, partners in a marriage might pass the *power baton* back and forth unconsciously, depending on the subject of conversation or the situation at hand. In other cases, like at work, a complex pecking order of power may determine people's behavior. In the world at large, countless issues of privilege arise constantly in regard to race, gender, class, and other individual differences. If you truly want to respect the power of privilege, the opportunities are endless.

15. Trust that people are doing the best they can, given everything.

Albert Einstein said, "The most important question all of us must answer is whether the universe is a friendly place or not." How you answer this question will determine your experience in life. Personally, I choose to believe that the universe is a friendly place—even allowing for the existence of pain, suffering, and death.

In the context of a friendly universe, I choose to regard everything as helpful, even though I must sometimes meditate long and hard to understand *how* certain things are helpful. Believe me, I don't always come up with answers. Fortunately, though, my decision to regard everything as helpful is not dependent on my understanding. In fact, my understanding of any given situation is so limited that it would be silly for me to base my belief system on it. Do you want to know why I choose to regard everything as helpful? Because I find it helpful!

Despite this bias, I sometimes have to work hard to apply it when people act in ways I don't like. Obviously, it's no one's job to please me. Therefore, when I encounter situations where I feel disrespected or hurt, I have to find some way to reconcile this with my choice to regard everything as helpful. My first step is to give people the benefit of the doubt, which is to say, I trust that they are doing the best they can, given everything.

Of course, I can never really know that other people are doing the best they can. It's my choice to take this view and I do it for one simple reason—because I find it helpful. If I trust that others are doing the best they can, this frees me up to consider my own responsibility in the situation. On the other hand, if I obsess about other people and their motives, I get stuck in an endless mental runaround. I don't find that very helpful.

The greatest application of power is in restraint, not in application.

JAN SCHLICHTMANN

If you're going to care about the fall of the sparrow, you can't pick and choose who's going to be the sparrow. It's everybody.

MADELEINE L'ENGLE

Even though I choose to believe that people are doing the best they can, this doesn't mean I can't speak up for myself and ask for something different when I feel mistreated. Sometimes my input provides new information that allows others to *better* their previous *best*. However, if a situation continues to be untenable for me, it's up to me to remove myself from whatever interaction is contributing to my distress. Thus, one way that disrespectful treatment is *helpful* is that it allows me to differentiate between situations that nurture my well-being and those that don't.

The high side of judgment is discernment. Judgment says people themselves are bad when they act like jerks. Discernment says that people may *act* badly, but this doesn't necessarily mean they're bad people. This kind of discernment is helpful because it allows me to respect people's inherent worth, while still making choices about how to take care of myself in regard to their behavior. Ultimately, my decision to separate the person from the behavior makes it possible for me to experience the deepest level of respect for each of us as human beings. It's the best I can do, given everything.

I use the following mantra to handle most conflicts. Be nice, forgiving, tough and clear. Be nice at the first stage of conflict, forgive if the other person cooperates in solving the problem, be tough if he or she escalates the conflict, and always be clear with the person and yourself about what you are doing.

Jennifer James

The Group as Healer: Adding Power to the Punch

SECTION FIVE

WHAT'S SO GREAT ABOUT A GROUP?

These days, it seems like there's a group for every purpose under the sun. Here I'd like to focus on groups related to healing. Before I mention some of the advantages of groups, however, I want to raise the question of whether or not it's necessary to do group work in order to heal.

The answer to such a question must be *no,* for at least two reasons. First, there are as many paths to healing as there are people, and a path that doesn't include group work deserves as much respect as a path that does include it. Second, there are some people who have suffered such severe abuse or neglect that a group setting will never feel safe to them. To say that such people are barred from healing would be presumptuous, judgmental, and downright cruel.

With the understanding that groups aren't right for everyone, I'd like to say a few words about the many benefits of groups. For one thing, groups can deepen and accelerate the process of personal development. I've witnessed group-triggered growth spurts in countless clients and friends, and I've experienced them myself.

Another benefit of groups is that they can ease the pain of isolation. Many families have a rule (whether spoken or unspoken) that says, "Don't talk about the family outside the family." As a result, some people grow up thinking they're the only ones with problems, which can lead to the belief that their problems are somehow shameful. When people feel shame, they tend to *hide out* even more, which only compounds their sense of isolation.

On the flip side, isolation that arises from hiding one's problems can result in an interesting situation, namely, a feeling of specialness based on one's pathology. In other words, some people regard personal pain as the only thing that makes them unique. If so, they may fear that if they share their pain and discover that others have similar experiences, their specialness will be lost. If people organize their lives around pain and identify with it as the hallmark of their individuality, they may be invested in staying isolated. While this may be understandable, it is also crippling.

There is nothing so moving—not even acts of love or hate—as the discovery that one is not alone.

ROBERT ARDREY

We meet ourselves time and again in a thousand disguises on the path of life.

CARL JUNG

The idea that the whole world is within us is no longer simply a transpersonal or archetypal belief; it is a practical and political necessity.

ARNOLD MINDELL

Hopefully, a well-chosen group can provide enough safety and support to help isolated individuals build bridges to other people. Although participants may initially form relationships based on shared experiences of pain, this can evolve as the group progresses. Over time, people will more than likely discover that their specialness can go far beyond an identification with pain.

Another quality that makes groups powerful is their inherent capacity to stimulate *mirror* experiences. Basically, a mirror experience happens when someone or something triggers strong feelings for you in such a way that your patterns are reflected back to you. This can occur in many different ways, such as when a person in a group reminds you of someone close to you.

Most of us have internalized images of important people in our lives: parents, siblings, children, lovers, friends, enemies, teachers, healers, saints, and shadow figures. When you participate in a group, it's likely that someone will remind you of one of these internalized images. Such a mirror-person might look, act, smell, sound, or move like one of the important people in your past or present life. For example, someone in your group might remind you of your father, and before you know it, you might find yourself acting like a little kid when you interact with him.

This kind of situation is rich material for learning, especially if the group is set up to help people work through old patterns. Whether you process a mirror experience in the group or wait until you're alone, the point is to focus on *your* behavioral patterns. No matter how much the other person triggers your *father stuff*, it's still your stuff! It's not the other person's job to change anything. If you need ideas about how to work with your emotional patterns in a responsible way, please refer to relevant chapters in the section called "The Heart of the Matter."

Whether a mirror experience triggers conflict *within* you or *between* you and another person, groups offer extraordinary opportunities for growth precisely because they can stimulate so many kinds of conflict. Basically, conflict may arise when there are differences between individuals or between factions of people. *Webster's* defines conflict as "emotional tension resulting from incompatible inner needs or drives."

Depending on the people involved, conflict can be appreciated and resolved, resisted and avoided, devalued and denied, or any mix of these options. At best, conflict can help people explore and integrate the differences it reveals. This gives people an opportunity to become more tolerant as they entertain, and perhaps even embrace, alternate viewpoints. It may help to remember this advantage of group conflict if you have fears about it. In addition, you can soften any fears you might have by accessing and encouraging the part of you that is open to—and excited about—change.

Working with conflict in the presence of ten, twenty, or a hundred people can definitely accelerate personal growth. Groups give you a chance to witness (or join) all kinds of challenging interactions, which means you can learn vicariously as well as through direct participation. Either way, you can use situations of group conflict to work on yourself.

For instance, if one participant gets into a heated argument with someone else, try focusing on your inner experience while they hash it out. How do you feel when other people butt heads? Is it exciting for you? Is it scary? Do you feel disgusted? Do you feel angry? Sad? Numb? If you do feel something, where is the feeling in your body? Do you notice any sounds, images, or sensations associated with the feeling? If you let the emotion shift into the realm of movement, how would you move? These are just a few questions that you might use to help you learn more about yourself when you are witnessing conflict between other people.

To expand this inner work into the realm of relationship now, notice which of the arguing people seems more appealing to you. Do you identify with this person more than the other one? If so, what is it about the person that appeals to you? Does he or she have qualities that remind you of you—or of someone you like? Does the person have attributes that you admire?

After you consider your identification with the person who initially appeals to you, turn your attention to the other person. Can you find a way to identify with him or her? If not, do you have a sense of why it's hard for you to assume the role of someone who seems different from you? Is he or she a mirror-person who reminds you of someone you don't like? What might happen if you identify with someone you don't like?

Follow these questions as long as they interest you, and then shift your focus to the conflict itself. Do you have fantasies about what the people will say before they actually say anything? What if the conflict becomes more intense? Do you get turned on by *fight* energy? Do you get terrified? Do you want to *fix* things? Do you want to run away?

What if the conflict doesn't get resolved within the allotted time period? Can you tolerate a lack of resolution? If not, how will you handle your distress? Can you let go of the intensity when you leave the room, or will you need time to process your feelings afterward? Be sure to take care of yourself at all levels. Pay attention

Just as we have two parents and four grandparents, back a mere 20 generations we've each got more than a million direct ancestors—at a time when the world population was less than 500 million. At that rate, you quickly discover that just about everyone is family.

ASTA BOWEN

We are the hurdles we leap to be ourselves.

MICHAEL MCCLURE

to whatever gets stimulated for you—emotionally, mentally, physically, sexually, spiritually, even politically. Milk the conflict for all it's worth!

Let's say the conflict does get resolved. How do you feel when this happens? Are you relieved or exhilarated, exhausted or overwhelmed, disappointed or depressed? Not everyone likes resolution. If all the group members go away satisfied with the outcome, do you wish another conflict would come in and stir things up again?

If you're the one who's directly involved in a conflict, as opposed to witnessing it happen between other people, it may be more difficult to stay focused on your own experience. Many people *lose themselves* in the heat of the moment. Instead, they respond to conflict impulsively by falling into automatic patterns of behavior. While this style isn't inherently wrong, it's often messy. When people act without awareness and responsibility, there's a greater potential for disrespectful or abusive results.

Vengeance destroys those it claims and those who become intoxicated with it. It seems clear that if we don't deal with deep conflicts, they don't disappear. You can't cover over the cracks forever.

DESMOND TUTU

I know some people who are usually respectful, yet they seem to *go unconscious* during conflict. Instead of blaming themselves for this occasional lack of clarity, they simply reflect later on the words and actions that came out of them during the conflict. Once they've sorted through their feelings and considered the way they behaved, they make choices about how to act more responsibly in the future. If appropriate, they will also go back to the other person and make any necessary amends. In this way, they work toward integrating higher levels of respect over time.

In addition to the personal growth benefit that can arise out of group conflict, there's another way groups can accelerate your process, namely, through expanded levels of acknowledgment and support. To get a sense of what I mean, think of a time when you felt totally understood and validated by a friend, then multiply that feeling by a factor of ten, twenty, or a hundred. When you have the focused attention and support of an entire group, it can be extremely transformative.

The simple experience of being fully *heard* by large numbers of people can in itself be very healing. It takes a great deal of courage for people to reveal themselves in a deeply intimate way in the presence of others. If you've ever taken this risk, only to be lovingly acknowledged by dozens of people simultaneously, you know how groups can push the envelope of your growth.

Because group healing can be so potent, people are sometimes seduced into thinking that a single group experience can permanently overcome twenty or thirty years of ingrained habits and emotional patterns. While this may happen sometimes, I think it's unwise to expect it. Family patterns don't develop overnight, and they rarely disappear overnight. Even when a particular pattern is dealt a death blow by a powerful group experience, follow-through is still necessary to effect change in daily life. Ongoing support groups can help to ground the *highs* that sometimes occur in short-term workshops and intensives, thus providing a way to translate insight into action over time.

To conclude, I want to state the obvious: *The whole world is a group*. Our lives are crisscrossed by groups. Whether or not you ever set foot inside the boundaries of an organized group, you have the biggest group of all available to you constantly. It's called humanity!

Aside from being a member of the human race, each of us can claim membership in a wide array of subset groups. For example, you're a member of your family, even if you disown them or they abandon you. You're a member of a group where you work and where you play. You're a member of an ethnic group and a member of a particular culture. You're also a member of various groups referenced by gender, skin color, and spiritual orientation. You're even a member of a group based on what you do in the bedroom!

Groups are an unavoidable part of being human. Whether you choose your groups with intention or let life choose them for you, groups can help you grow. To support this growth, the following chapters are devoted entirely to groups. If some of the exercises seem mundane or unsophisticated at first glance, don't be deceived. Groups pack a powerful punch, and these techniques are simply designed to set the stage and get the ball rolling. After that, the mysterious forces of human nature will conspire to stimulate and transform a thousand different parts of you.

Check out the chapters that call to you, and see what juicy experiences await you when you multiply the human factor.

It does not astonish or make us angry that it takes a whole year to bring into the house three great white peonies and two pale blue iris....Yet in our human relations we are outraged when the supreme moments, the moments of flowering, must be waited for... and then cannot last.

MAY SARTON

It doesn't matter what you do in the bedroom as long as you don't do it in the street and frighten the horses.

MRS. PATRICK CAMPBELL

The Talking Circle

When I was in graduate school, I did ghostwriting for a few students. One of my favorite clients was a Navajo man, whom I will call Running Wolf. Running Wolf facilitated alcoholism seminars for people of all colors, and he incorporated this work into his master's program. Since he used certain rituals in his seminars, he chose to teach me some of these rituals, so that I would be in a better position to help him translate his experience into writing.

One of the ceremonies Running Wolf taught me is called the "Talking Circle." Before I pass it along to you, I'd like to briefly address the issue of disseminating tribal teachings. Since I am part Cherokee through the bloodlines of my father, I could (technically) claim the right to teach various rituals of my own tribe, if I was guided to do so. However, I don't teach the Talking Circle because of my American Indian heritage. Rather, I share it because certain shamanic rituals and techniques are universal. They don't belong to any one tribe; they belong to the *human* tribe.

As I see it, it's robbery to transmit a particular tribe's traditions unless you are a member (or at least a designated honorary member) of that tribe. However, some rituals are so widespread among native cultures that they truly belong to everyone. The Talking Circle is one such ritual.

The objects required for this ceremony are simple: a feather, sage grass and matches, and a small container for burning the sage. If you don't have a feather, you can use a stone, a bowl, or a decorated stick. To burn the sage, you can use an abalone shell or a clam shell, a ceramic bowl, or a fireproof dish.

Traditionally, eagle feathers are used for this ceremony. However, it's illegal to have an eagle feather unless you can claim religious rights to its possession by virtue of being an American Indian. I urge everyone to respect the laws that protect this magnificent bird. As an alternative, many people use turkey feathers for this ritual. If you can't find a turkey feather through other means, they can be legally purchased.

Sage grass is a plant often used for cleansing the air of impurities, both literally and symbolically. Sage also protects against the undue influence of other people. It's readily available through mail order supply houses, metaphysical bookstores, and some herb stores. Be sure to get the kind of sage that's used for ritual work, as opposed to the kind that's used for cooking. There are several varieties of ritual sage, such as white sage, which is a favorite of mine. You may want to experiment with different kinds to see how they're unique and how they affect you personally.

If you like, you can gather sage grass by hand in the desert. If you do, please be respectful. Don't tear off entire branches, and don't rip whole bushes from the ground. *Tune in to the plants*. Ask to be led to the sage plants that are willing to give a few leaves or twigs for sacred purposes. Take only what each plant is willing to give, if anything, and never take more than you need. After removing a leaf or a twig, express gratitude to the spirit of the plant for its gift to you.

If you think it's crazy to listen to plants, I suggest that you forego picking the sage yourself. On the other hand, if you find this instruction intriguing, but you're just not sure you can do it "right," go ahead and trust your intuition. Listen as best you can to the plants. It takes a lot of practice to hear plants—usually years of practice. However, you have to start somewhere. If your intention is sincere, the plant spirits will help you.

Once you bring the sage home, bundle the branches loosely and hang them up, or lay them on absorbent paper, so they can dry slowly. Once dry, you can make bundles (smudge sticks) by wrapping thread around the branchlets or leaves of sage. You can also leave it loose in unsealed paper bags. Either way, make sure the sage is completely dry before you bundle or package it. Otherwise it will become moldy, and you won't be able to use it.

Here's a word of caution about burning sage (I'll get to the burning part of the ceremony in a moment). That is, be sure all the embers are completely extinguished before you leave your ritual space. Smudge sticks in particular can smolder indefinitely, so I like to turn them upside-down and bury the hot tip in a bowl of sand or dirt. If I'm burning loose sage in an abalone shell, I use my fingers or a small stick of wood to tamp down the edges of the leaves that are smoldering.

Now that you know what materials you need and how to proceed safely, I'll tell you how you can do the Talking Circle with a group of friends. Begin by placing a small pile of sage grass in a shell, a ceramic bowl, or a fireproof dish. Light it with a match, and

Our lives are like islands in the sea, or like trees in the forest, which co-mingle their roots in the darkness underground.
WILLIAM JAMES

A shift in awareness is the first change.
DEEPAK CHOPRA

DR. CAT'S HELPING HANDBOOK

gently blow on it to get it started. Next, use the feather to softly fan the sage, so that the leaves smolder around the edges. Don't worry if you have to relight the sage grass a few times. It may take some practice to develop your technique. Even when you become adept at this, some sage can be temperamental and tough to burn.

I remember one time many years ago, I was lighting sage to smudge a client and myself before doing a soul retrieval for him. He watched as I patiently lit and relit the sage a few times, then he said, "I've heard that it's a bad sign if you have to relight sage more than three times."

I laughed and told him that I call that kind of thinking *uptight* shamanism. I also told him that I don't subscribe to that kind of thinking. I must confess, it was a little embarrassing for me to have trouble with the sage, because I could tell he was watching with a critical eye. However, for all I know, the trickster spirits could have set up the whole situation so I could increase my humility and he could loosen up his rigid rules about shamanism. Who can say? Either way, the sage brought unexpected teachings that day.

In any case, once the sage is lit and smoking around the edges, you're ready to begin smudging. Move slowly around your circle of friends, holding the shell or dish of sage in front of each person, one by one, while you fan the cleansing smoke toward him or her. Give people a chance to *catch* the smoke and swirl it around their bodies with cupped hands. Of course, it's also okay for people to sit quietly and receive this acknowledgment without any active participation.

To complete the smudging, you can lightly touch the tip of the feather to people's foreheads, and then to their hearts. This symbolizes the wisdom that comes from the union of heart and mind. By the way, be sure that you get smudged, too. Once you've fanned the cleansing smoke around everyone else, ask someone to smudge you in the same way.

Occasionally, someone in a group may have severe allergies that preclude the burning of sage grass. Interestingly, sage smoke doesn't always bother those of us who are challenged by hypersensitive immune systems. Because sage is unique in this way, I encourage allergic individuals to experiment with sage, rather than assume it will necessarily hurt them. Of course, this choice must be left up to the people involved. Thus, it's a good idea to ask if anyone objects to the sage smoke before you begin the ceremony.

If someone objects—for any reason or no reason—honor that person's need by finding an alternative. Perhaps he or she could leave the room during the smudging portion of the ritual (be sure to air out the room before they return). As an option, the group could

The makers of the rules would never admit it, but they'd perish without the breakers of the rules.

Rob Brezsny

Tell the truth and you won't have to remember anything.

Dale Turner

do the smudging symbolically, without actually lighting the sage. Whatever you decide, come to a decision by group concensus, so the person who objects can still feel valued and respected. Also, if people do leave the room, be sure to smudge them symbolically upon their return.

After everyone has been smudged, it's time to begin the second part of the Talking Circle. For this, the feather is passed around the circle, person to person. Whoever holds the feather is allowed to speak without interruption. If someone does not wish to speak, he or she still receives and then passes the feather. In fact, if a person wants to sit in silence for a while, that's perfectly okay.

Running Wolf said that in traditional Talking Circles held in teepees, the elders of the tribe would sometimes speak for hours on end. No one was permitted to leave while a person was speaking— not even to relieve themselves! In my workshops and groups, I usually ask people to say whatever feels most important in a spirit of brevity and focus. Even with this more limited approach, the ceremony still holds tremendous power.

Curiously, the power of the Talking Circle does not diminish when used with small numbers of people. I've used this ritual to begin sessions with just one client, giving us each a chance to smudge, hold the feather, and speak. I've also found it useful in couples counseling. A lot of couples don't know how to listen to each other without interrupting, so the ceremony helps them practice this vital skill. Obviously, you don't need a feather to practice good listening skills, but a sacred object can serve as a gentle reminder of respect.

One of my personal variations is to do the Talking Circle alone. If you want to try this, here's what you do. First, light the sage and smudge yourself. You can also smudge the space and the objects around you. Next, hold the feather and speak from the heart. Don't worry if you feel silly. No one's watching! An empty room makes a first-rate witness: guaranteed to listen without interrupting. Say whatever you need to say. By speaking out loud, the energy of your thoughts can move and release more easily.

Whether you use the Talking Circle alone, with one other person, or with a group, it's a potent way to honor the sacred beauty of each person's presence. Use it often and use it well. Ho!

The question is laid out
For each of us to ask;
Whether to hold on
Or to drop the mask.

MARTHA BOESING

In my workshops I often ask people to guess how much time the average married couple spends talking to each other each day. People usually guess anywhere from 5 minutes to 20 minutes. The right answer is 12. What amazes me is that people come so close!

CECILE ANDREWS

THE GROUP STROKE

This urge to make everything profound. What nonsense!

HENRY MILLER

If you attend a lot of group meetings, or if you need a good trick for energizing yourself and others, you might like a technique I call the "Group Stroke." Even the most stimulating discussions can give way to periods of ebb within the flow. People may get tired or restless, or the topic may be so emotionally charged that people space out and become virtual zombies. It happens to the best of us.

Here's one solution. First, ask those who are shy about touching to watch the rest of the group for a few minutes, so they can observe before deciding if they'd like to participate. Then ask everyone else to stand up and form one large circle facing the center. Next, have people turn to the right, so they're all facing the same direction. At this point, each person should be facing another person's back. Finally, ask everyone to stroke the back of the person in front of them, using an upward motion. That is, beginning at the waist, gently brush the person's back in strokes that move toward the neck.

This is not meant to be a massage. If you're doing it right, it will feel almost effortless. You can make it real easy by using only the tips of your fingers to brush the other person's back. It's the upward motion that counts, not the vigor with which you do it. In fact, don't be vigorous! You're working with *energy*, not muscle tissue. Soft, subtle strokes are best.

After a few minutes, tell the group to reverse positions, so the person who was giving the strokes will now receive them. Let people continue for a few minutes again. When it appears that everyone is feeling a little more revitalized, you can see if they're ready to return to whatever you were doing before. Good luck getting them to stop!

I first learned this technique in the mid-1980s from a man who was teaching a workshop at Unity Church in Seattle. I can't remember his name, but I remember him talking about the four main ways to stimulate endorphins. Do you know about endorphins? They're chemicals that are released from the brain under certain circumstances. Basically, they make us feel *good*. Endorphins can sometimes generate such powerful feelings of pleasure that they can even block out pain.

The workshop leader said that the four best ways to stimulate endorphins *naturally* are: singing, dancing, laughing, and stroking the back up. Whenever you need a boost, you can experiment with these four methods. If you're feeling so bad that you can't bring yourself to laugh, dance, or sing, maybe you can at least ask someone to stroke your back up.

Whenever I introduce the Group Stroke in a workshop, people always laugh because the name sounds a little obscene. Then when they try it, they usually laugh some more simply because it makes them feel good. When people laugh while stroking each other's backs, two of the four main natural endorphin stimulators get activated at the same time. If you and your fellow group members are really creative, perhaps you can invent a way to laugh, dance, sing, and stroke each other's backs simultaneously.

You can do the Group Stroke on a smaller scale with individual friends. Tell them what I just told you about endorphins, and teach them how to do the upward back stroke. As an option, you could surprise your friends by doing it next time you hug each other. In other words, you can do this technique face-to-face as easily as you do it face-to-back (as previously described for larger groups). Play with each approach, both as the stroker and as the receiver, and find out if you prefer one or the other—or both!

One thing I love about this technique is that you have to ask for help. Unless you're some kind of contortionist, you can't brush your own back all the way up. Even if you could, the effect is not as stimulating as having someone do it for you. In addition, the act of asking for help can itself be stimulating, though perhaps in a different way. Since many people are afraid to ask for help, it's great to practice doing it by asking for an upward back stroke, because when someone strokes your back, the endorphin rush can smooth away your fears about asking for help. What a bonus!

The trick in asking for help is to keep asking people until you find someone who says *yes*. It's important not to expect any one person to satisfy your wants and needs, because that encourages infancy-level dependency, as opposed to adult-to-adult relationships (see "My Personal Rules of Respect" for more tips about asking for help responsibly).

What I mean is, if I *expect* a particular person to satisfy all my requests, then I'm essentially acting like a six-month-old who wants a mother who will take care of her. Needless to say, this is a setup for the replay of old patterns. While it's certainly okay to ask for what you want, I recommend that you cultivate a spacious heart when you do this, so that you can hear *yes* or *no* with equal grace.

All sanity depends on this: that it should be a delight to feel heat strike the skin, a delight to stand upright, knowing the bones are moving easily under the flesh.

DORIS LESSING

Leave undone whatever you hesitate to do.

YOSHIDA KANKO

Other people have the right to choose whether or not they want to give you what you request of them. Besides, in the case of the Group Stroke, do you really want people to touch you if they don't want to touch you?

Whether you practice the upward back stroke with just one friend—or with a hundred others—I think it's sweet that nature requires at least two people to activate this natural endorphin stimulator. You can laugh and dance and sing alone, but for this one, you need help. Could this be by design?

PICTURE
STORYTELLING

You can do Picture Storytelling alone or with a friend, but it's especially intriguing to do it in groups. Picture Storytelling is simple, yet the results can be profound. There are many ways to do it, so I'll suggest a few, and then you can play with your own improvisations.

To do Picture Storytelling with a group of people, you'll need several pairs of scissors, along with a big stack of magazines that are ready for recycling (don't use anything you want to save). Magazines that have a lot of photographs, graphics, or art reproductions are best.

Let each person choose a few magazines to peruse for pictures. Give everyone plenty of time to flip through the pages, so they can cut out anything that catches their interest. At this point, people will be working playfully and relatively quickly to accumulate a pile of pictures that the whole group will use later. Therefore, it's fine for people to select photos that might stimulate other people's imaginations, even if they themselves might not choose it for storytelling.

Pictures that arouse strong feelings are good choices, as are pictures that draw you in and make you wonder *what happened before* or *what will happen next*. Pictures with people or animals often stimulate stories more easily than pictures without them. However, photos of landscapes and certain objects can trigger powerful responses in some people, so the trick is to trust your gut response. Follow your hunches. You don't need to have reasons.

Encourage people to cut out a wide variety of pictorial subjects. The bigger the selection, the more options your group will have to generate stories. Once you've accumulated a large array of photographs and graphics, it's story time! First, lay all the pictures out on a table or on the floor, so everyone can choose one. Next, go around the circle, and give each person a chance to tell a short story about their chosen picture. To keep the flow going, you might want to agree on a three- or five-minute time limit before you get started.

Every child is an artist. The problem is how to remain an artist once she grows up.

PABLO PICASSO

We have to develop not only compassion, an awareness of suffering and the will to do something about it; we must also develop our sensuality, our utter enjoyment and celebration of the beauty of this world.

SAM KEEN

Suppose someone were to say, "Imagine this butterfly exactly as it is, but ugly instead of beautiful."

LUDWIG WITTGENSTEIN

So you see, imagination needs moodling—long, inefficient, happy idling, dawdling and puttering.

BRENDA UELAND

The idea is to inspire people to *wing it*—to say the first thing that occurs to them. Give people permission to be wild and wacky, or subtle and serious. Anything goes!

Whether or not you set a time limit, every effort should be made to give each storyteller the group's complete attention. Practice your best listening skills, and show respect for each person's contribution. *Judgment and criticism are verboten.* Even praise can be distracting. Instead, a thoughtful nod or a simple expression of thanks can provide a note of acknowledgment after each story.

A second method for Picture Storytelling is to agree on a certain time period (ten or fifteen minutes is usually sufficient), then let everyone write a short story on their own. When the time is up, people who want to read their stories out loud can do so, one at a time. Be sure to allow enough time for everyone who wants to read, and make it clear that sharing is optional. Some stories are important to write, but too private to tell. No one should be pressured to talk, even if everyone is dying to know what the shy person wrote.

Another storytelling technique is to let the group select one magazine picture as the subject for everyone's story. Start with one person, who will begin the story by making up one or two sentences to go with the picture. Another person can then add a couple more lines to the tale. Continue in this way, creating a story through successive contributions by various group members. You can go around the circle in order, or let people add to the story randomly. Either way, the story will be complete when no one has anything else to add. This particular method is fun because it gives people the opportunity to experience the act of creation together. It can also lead to some pretty lively debriefing discussions afterward.

A fourth kind of Picture Storytelling again focuses on one photo selected by the entire group. In this case, however, everyone takes ten or fifteen minutes (in silence) to write a story about the same picture. After people are done writing, those who want to share can do so. When you listen to each other read, I bet you'll be amazed to see the similarities and the differences in stories generated by the same picture.

If you do this last method of Picture Storytelling with the same group on different occasions, it may be interesting to note any changes in the *energy* of the group itself, based on the pictures selected over time. Do the pictures and stories somehow represent any themes in the evolution of the group? Perhaps someone could keep a pictorial journal of the chosen photographs, or better yet, the group could create a book of everyone's stories.

Each chapter might begin with the picture of the day, followed by a collection of everyone's stories (minus those withheld for the sake of privacy). When the book feels finished, perhaps someone could volunteer to make copies for everyone. Then you could arrange a special meeting, so people could pick their favorite stories to read again. In any case, such a book would be a work of art. It would also be a symbolic representation of the group's unfolding.

In conclusion, there are many reasons I include Picture Storytelling in this section. First of all, many people are attuned to the visual mode, so pictures are a great way for them to access their thoughts and feelings. In addition, Picture Storytelling allows people to sidestep their fears about exposing themselves directly. After all, they're only telling a story about someone or something else, right? Well, yes and no.

Inevitably, people reveal themselves in their writing, even though there may be no direct relationship between their stories and their real lives. Whatever the case, don't pry. People will offer what they want you to know. This is storytelling time, not the inquisition!

Ultimately, storytelling is an art, though I think it's an art that runs deep in our blood. Verbal transmission of stories has been a primary means of human communication for millennia, long before written history began. If you want to take Picture Storytelling to the limit, gather up your friends, your supplies, and your camping equipment, and take a trip into the wilds of nature.

During the day, cut out pictures and write stories together, but don't share them. Then when night falls, build a big fire—following all the safety protocols, of course—and sit in a circle around it. Pass a flashlight around the group, and read your stories aloud to each other. Invite the spirits of the ancestors to join you in the magic, and see what happens next.

All creative artists, whether they are making a book, a painting, a pot, or a life, are extremely connected to the wider world....Art is a response to our collective being, a response that is sent out into the community, and to which the community responds, in turn.

SATISH KUMAR

DRAWING IN GROUPS

Beauty is something everyone longs for, needs, and tries to obtain in some way—whether through nature, or a man or a woman, or music, or whatever. The soul yearns for it.

JAMES HILLMAN

I f you'd like to draw with a group of friends, the first step is to gather materials. The possibilities are endless, limited only by your imagination, finances, and availability of supplies. Some basics might include: rolls of newsprint or big pads of drawing paper, construction paper, crayons, oil pastels, charcoal, chalk, colored pencils, felt-tip pens, fingerpaints, drawing pencils, fountain pens, and ink. You can be plenty creative with one drawing medium and some all-purpose paper, so don't feel intimidated by all these options. It's fine to start simple.

Once the materials are ready, group members can choose a subject of their own to draw, or everyone can draw the same subject. In this case, I'm not talking about drawing from models. Instead, I'm suggesting that people choose an idea, feeling, or image to draw from their imaginations. If you need help with topics, there's a list of ideas for you at the end of this chapter.

As an alternative, people can draw spontaneously, without focusing on any particular topic. Either way, let everyone decide in advance how long they'd like to draw. Be sure to allow ample time, so that no one feels rushed, but not so much time that people get bored. When you set a time frame, try not to be too strict about it. Time limits provide structure, which is helpful, but rigidity can kill the creative spark.

Once you've chosen a subject and a general time frame, place all the materials in the center of the room, so everyone has access to them. Then encourage people to find their own space to draw. Some people like to draw without being observed, or at least, without having their drawings visible to others. Hopefully, the place where you meet will be large enough to accommodate people's needs for privacy as well as community.

After everyone is done drawing, some people might like to show their work to the rest of the group. As I said in the previous chapter, sharing must always and only be voluntary. Don't ever pressure anyone to share. Perhaps even more than stories, drawings can be

I paint not by sight but by faith. Faith gives you sight.

AMOS FERGUSON

deeply personal. Some people may need to keep their art to themselves. That's okay.

If people do want to show their drawings to the group, the next question is whether or not they want a response, and if so, what kind. It's best if the person with the drawing can clearly state his or her preferences about this. Others can help by waiting for a go-ahead from the artist before they comment in any way. Be sure everyone knows it's okay for people to show their drawings, even if they don't want any feedback.

If you want the group to respond to your drawing, ask specifically for the kind of feedback you desire. I stress this point because a lot of people have been hurt in regard to their creativity. Perhaps someone laughed at their artistic efforts, or told them that they have no talent. Unfortunately, this kind of shaming is all too common, and it can leave deep wounds. The last thing anyone needs is more wounding. Therefore, when people show their drawings, it's important to remember that criticism of any sort is forbidden. Even praise can make people feel uncomfortable, for a variety of reasons. But if criticism and praise aren't helpful, what's left?

I recommend simple acknowledgment, which comes in many forms. In cases where people have been brutalized around their creativity, the act of letting others see their work can bring up a whole barrage of feelings and fears. For such people, it can be healing for them to simply have their drawings witnessed, without any exchange of words at all. Group members can support wounded artists by quietly communicating—through their sincere interest and their gentle presence—that *it's safe to be seen*. Beyond that, I encourage you to let the artist take the lead. Don't offer any feedback unless it is directly solicited. While this approach is especially helpful for wounded artists, it also works well in general.

The main thing to remember is to treat people and their art tenderly. The fires of creativity can be doused by a single thoughtless remark. If you can't decide whether your comments will feel like criticism to the artist, don't take a chance. It's better to err on the side of restraint, rather than risk hurting the inner muse of another person.

If you feel troubled or restimulated by someone else's drawing, and you don't know how to deal with your feelings, *ask permission* of the artist to talk about your experience. If it's not okay with the artist or with the group, take a raincheck with your heart. That is, set aside some time later to work with your feelings, either alone or with someone you trust. If it's not appropriate for you to share your experience with the group, this doesn't mean you should repress

Sometimes a cigar is just a cigar.
SIGMUND FREUD

The artist never finishes his work. He only abandons it.
CHUCK JONES

When we lose a sense of beauty, our souls die of starvation.
SATISH KUMAR

your feelings. You might just have to be a little more creative about how and when you express them.

When you're the one who is showing your drawing to the group, treat yourself with as much kindness as you show others. Give yourself permission to be witnessed silently, if that's all you want. On the other hand, if you want to invite comments, be sure to stay tuned to your own sense of respect as you listen to people's responses. Generally speaking, feedback that is truly supportive will make you feel more expansive and creative.

In contrast, critical comments—no matter how carefully worded or supposedly well intended—will probably make your body *shut down* in some way. You might get a queasy feeling in your stomach, or you might find yourself wanting to hide or run away. If you notice anything that seems the least bit distressing for you, ask people to stop commenting. It's their job as fellow group members to be respectful, and it's your job to take care of yourself by being your own gatekeeper during the input.

You don't have to have a reason for wanting to stop. You can just ask people to stop. However, if you're interested, you may want to take a few moments to check in with yourself to see if something painful has been triggered, or if you've simply reached your limit of self-exposure for the time being. Whatever the case, ask yourself what you need *now*. Then do what you can to get what you need before the group proceeds.

By the way, if you were raised on a steady diet of criticism, you may be so accustomed to it that your body might not register any signals of distress when you're treated disrespectfully in present time. I'm not saying that your body doesn't notice, only that your emotional armor may be so well-developed that it protects even you from knowing what's happening.

If this is true for you, you may have to learn how to recognize disrespectful comments by noticing what's *missing* from them, since your distress signals may be shut down from years of overload. That is, if you *don't* feel more expansive, more excited, and more inspired when you listen to other people's comments about your art, take this as a sign that you may not be getting the kind of support you need.

Occasionally, I've run across people who were so traumatized as children that they can't feel *anything*. They can't feel anything when others are genuinely supportive, and they can't feel anything when others are mean. It's as if these people have retreated deep within their core in order to keep their souls safe from attack. If this applies to you or to a fellow group member, practice your sweetest

Useful criticism ultimately leaves us with one more puzzle piece for our work. Useless criticism, on the other hand, leaves us with a feeling of being bludgeoned.

JULIA CAMERON

The job of the artist is always to deepen the mystery.

FRANCIS BACON

levels of compassion. Proceed slowly and listen as best you can to your heart. Ask yourself (or the other person) what's needed, and err on the side of saying too little, rather than too much.

Even with all these precautionary measures, there may be times when you (or others in the group) feel disrespected, hurt, or scared, despite everyone's best intentions. This can happen for a variety of reasons, one of which is that the *language of shaming* is both universal and unique. What I mean is, there are forms of communication that would hurt almost anyone, while there are other forms of communication—words, tones, or gestures—that might feel hurtful to some but not to others.

This doesn't mean that it's okay to discount other people's pain, only that it's virtually impossible to keep from causing pain sometimes. Therefore, if your comments offend or wound someone in the group, validate that person's perceptions by listening respectfully and by doing your best to understand. Own your part in the system and don't be afraid to apologize—even if your intentions were good, and even if you were misunderstood. After all, if you're dancing and you step on your partner's toes, I assume you didn't do it on purpose! Nonetheless, you caused someone's pain, and you can apologize for that. The same principle applies more broadly to all interactions, and it certainly applies when you're commenting on other people's art.

An apology is a good way to have the last word.

DALE TURNER

If I seem overly protective of people's artist-selves, that's okay with me. It breaks my heart to think of all the people I've known who stopped drawing, dancing, writing, singing, or doing some other kind of art because a mean-spirited or oblivious person stomped on their inner muses. I've even done shamanic soul retrievals for people in regard to this issue.

It does no good to say that people's inner artists should have tougher hides. That's like saying spider webs should be made of thick jute, instead of silken threads. If a spider web was made of jute, it might not be so fragile, but it wouldn't be exquisitely sensitive, either. In fact, if it wasn't so sensitive, it couldn't do what it was designed to do.

I learned to trust my obsessions. It is surely a great calamity for a human being to have no obsessions.

ROBERT BLY

The same thing is true about the artist in you. The sensitivity that makes your artist-self fragile is the same sensitivity that feeds your capacity to create. If you give your inner muse the care and protection it needs, it will grow more sensitive, and therefore, more able to express the vast expanse of your soul. Any accompanying fragility is best addressed through tenderness and good boundaries, not judgment.

Artists who seek perfection in everything are those who cannot attain it in anything.

EUGÈNE DELACROIX

When you draw in groups, remember that the goal is *not* to produce great works of art, although that might happen. Neither is it appropriate to use the group as if it's some kind of professional critique service. Instead, the goal of an informal drawing group is simply to create a safe environment for people to be creative and to *be witnessed* as artists.

To help you get started, I'd like to offer that list of topics I promised you earlier. You can use the following ideas to inspire your drawings or to brainstorm ideas of your own.

- Your favorite dream
- Your grief, fear, anger, or joy
- Your family
- Your family's number-one rule
- Your father
- Your mother
- Your sibling(s)
- Your childhood home
- Your dream home
- Your addictive habit(s)
- You with all your addiction(s)
- You with no addiction(s)
- Your favorite place in nature
- Your life on another planet
- You as an infant or a child
- You as a teenager
- You as an elder
- You as a person of the opposite sex
- You as a person of another race
- Your worst concept of yourself
- Your best concept of yourself
- Your most positive quality

- Your darkest secret
  - Your innocence
    - Your inner tyrant
    - Your concept of love
    - Your concept of death
  - Your feelings about death
- Your fantasy of your own death
- Your ideas about what happens after death
  - Your favorite sexual fantasy
    - Your worst sexual experience
      - Your scariest thought
        - Your sweetest sense of compassion
        - You as an animal
    - You as an element of nature
  - Your worst fear about the world
- Your highest hope for humanity
- Your image of Mother Earth
  - Your concept of Divinity, God/dess, or the Void

PASS THE BODY

The name of this game may conjure up images of adolescent Halloween parties, where people are blindfolded and they pass around pseudo body parts, such as peeled grapes for eyeballs. Instead of being an exercise in the macabre, however, this game of "Pass the Body" is actually an exercise in trust.

The only thing this game has in common with the Halloween original is that they both tend to stimulate fear. Hopefully, though, my version will help you discover something Fredric Lehrman once taught me, namely, that "fear is fun in disguise." In other words, if you can use this game to contact the *excitement* underneath your fear, you'll be well on your way to a deeper relationship with trust.

To play Pass the Body, you'll need at least nine people. If your group is quite large, it's best to form smaller groups of nine to twelve people. To begin, everyone will make a circle around one person, who will stand in the center. Next, people in the circle will move closer together, almost shoulder-to-shoulder, so there are no gaps between them. Everyone needs to stand close in order to work together to support the weight of the person in the middle, who will be gently *passed* around the circle in a particular way.

Let's assume that you'll be the first person to take the center position. Your job is to keep your body rigid, with your arms held close to your sides. It helps to imagine yourself as the upright trunk of a tree. Next, imagine that there is a swivel at the base of your "trunk," just above ground level at your ankles.

With this image of a swivel at your ankles, and with your body held stiff like a tree, you can see how the slightest leaning of your body will make you fall one way or the other. Of course, you can decide in advance which way you'd like to lean. When you're ready, choose which direction you want to fall, and let your body slowly lean that way. You can keep your eyes open or closed while you tip and sway.

As you allow yourself to lean in one direction, two or three people in the circle will rally together to catch you with their hands. The people who are closest to the direction you're falling will be the ones who catch you. Those who brace your fall will then push your body back up to a standing position. As an option, they can pass you to the arms of the group members to their immediate left or right. Either way, people will somehow manage to do all this without saying many words, though they may make a lot of other sounds!

If you've never played this trust game, it's best to begin by asking circle members to stay close to you. This will allow you to become more comfortable with the process of falling, and it will allow other people to practice supporting you. After you get used to the experience of being passed around, you can increase the distance between you and the other circle members. Increasing the distance will probably increase your fear as well as your excitement. Take it a step at a time.

You can also increase the risk factor by asking group members to speed up the rate at which they pass you around the circle. If you do increase the speed or the distance of your fall, I recommend that you alternate these risk increases with alternate periods of slower pacing and shorter fall ratios.

If you have concerns about the size, shape, weight, or feel of your body, it might help to troubleshoot some ways to make the game feel safer for you. For instance, if you're playing with a support group, you might request a few moments to talk about your concerns. It's a good bet that others will have similar fears. Sometimes if one person can muster the courage to speak up, it can alleviate some of the tension for the whole group.

If your fears seem insurmountable, and you can't bring yourself to mention them, please don't *force* yourself to take the role of the person in the middle of the circle. In the short run, it might seem courageous to do something that terrifies you. In the long run, however, I don't think it works to *blast* your fear.

Fear dissolves best in an atmosphere of kindness and acceptance. Imagine fear as a rock, which can be gradually worn away by the powerful—yet relatively gentle—forces of wind or water. Obviously, a rock can also be blasted away with dynamite. In that case, you'll certainly get the job done with great speed, but you might get hurt in the explosion. At the very least, you'll have to deal with a big mess! On the other hand, if the rock is eroded over time, the tiny particles of dissolving rock can blow or wash away without a trace.

Thus, if you feel reticent to play Pass the Body in the center position, *follow* this reticence until it shifts, if indeed it does. You can still participate in the game by joining the circle and supporting others. As you watch people take turns falling into the arms of friends, their enjoyment may be just the stimulus you need to

Taking a risk often turns out to be the safest measure.
ARNOLD MINDELL

Taking a new step, uttering a new word is what people fear most.
DOSTOEVSKI

If you fall flat on your face, kiss the ground.

Cat Saunders

At every step the child should be allowed to meet the real experiences of life; the thorns should never be plucked from the roses.

Ellen Key

overcome your fear. In any case, you'll know when it's right for you to try falling, because your excitement will overpower your fear.

If you'd like to try an alternative that lies somewhere between all or nothing, consider the following moderate approach. First of all, tell your friends that you'd like to try falling, but only within certain parameters. Ask them to stay close, so you won't fall very far. In addition, tell them that you'd like to do one fall at a time, instead of being passed around at the whim of the group.

This means that each time you lean into a fall, the group will catch you, and then bring your body back to an upright position in the center of the circle. This will limit the speed of the game, and it will eliminate the uncertainty that comes from not knowing where you'll be passed next. Hopefully, this will reduce the intensity of the falling experience, so you can gradually become more comfortable with the balance between control and letting go. Experiment with the choice to *risk* versus the choice to *rest*. Both are necessary components in the dance of trust.

Whether you have fears about falling because you don't want people to feel the weight of your body, or because you're just plain scared you'll hit the floor, the way to build more trust is always the same: *Do it slowly!* Take it a step at a time. When you're ready, ask your friends to move a little farther away, and see how it feels to risk a bit more.

If worse comes to worst and you fall to the ground, you'll probably discover that it's no big deal. In fact, it can be kind of fun to fall all the way down to the ground while your friends surround you and cushion your fall. It's like riding a wave onto the beach! In all the times I've played Pass the Body, I've never seen anyone get hurt, though I have seen people laugh themselves silly.

Since this is a trust game, please remember that your capacity to risk and trust may fluctuate depending on the situation, the people involved, and your present state of mind. You might be tired, distraught, premenstrual, overstimulated, or a thousand other possibilities. Along the same lines, it's good to remember that other people's trust levels—and support skills—may also fluctuate. This is a reflection of life.

Occasionally, people may try to shame you for "not trusting enough," as if you can flip a switch in your belly button and suddenly become the King of Confidence. Don't be swayed by this kind of misguided criticism. You can only be who you are at any given moment, and the only way to move from a position of mistrust to a position of trust is to accept yourself in the mistrust first.

Trust begins with trusting *yourself,* and this includes trusting your fear. While it's certainly okay for people to reassure you that they'll do their best to catch you, it's not okay for them to cajole you into doing something that you're not ready to do. As always, listen to your own heart, and let it tell you when to *risk* and when to *rest.* With patience and practice, your trust will bloom and grow.

We learn to do something by doing it. There is no other way.
JOHN HOLT

MANY HANDS
MAKE YOU LIGHT

*In the difficult are the
friendly forces, the hands
that work on us.*

RAINER MARIA RILKE

Like the previous chapter, this one offers another game for experimenting with risk, excitement, and trust. To play, you'll need at least seven people, although eight or ten would be better. You can play inside or outside on a soft surface such as carpet, sand, or grass. To start, one volunteer will lie down on the floor or on the earth, face up. The rest of the people will divide themselves into two groups, each of which will form a line along either side of the volunteer. Everyone will then kneel down, spacing themselves evenly along the length of the volunteer's body.

To make the rest of this explanation simpler, let's say you're the first volunteer. Once you're lying on the ground with a support team along both sides of you, the teams will now place their hands (or their forearms and their hands) underneath your body in preparation for lifting you. Please note that everyone on the support teams should pay careful attention to the placement of their hands, so that you feel comfortable, safe, and respected.

When you say you're ready, everyone will lift you up high in the air. As you are lifted, people will need to quickly reposition their hands, move closer together, and do whatever it takes to keep you aloft. This may sound difficult, but it's surprisingly easy. *Many hands make you light!*

Once you're up in the air, you can stay there as long as you like, or until the group gets tired, whichever comes first. If you'd like to be carried around while you're up there, be sure to ask for that. When you're ready to come down, let your friends know, so they can lower you to the ground slowly and gently.

After you've come back to earth, take a few moments to rest and to savor the experience. Did you discover anything new about risk and trust? Did you notice anything interesting about the relationship between fear, excitement, and pleasure? Is there anything you'd like to do differently next time? Would you like to find ways to up the ante of intensity? Conversely, did you find yourself wishing it was over as soon as it started? However you respond to these questions, go *underneath* your answers if you find fears or concerns that need attention. Find out what this game may be trying to teach you about yourself.

For example, when I first played this game in the early eighties, I was anorexic. Because of my distorted body image, it was scary for me to even *think* about letting people lift me up. I didn't want them to feel the weight of my body. Not only did I have a lot of shame about my body, but I was actually afraid that my body would be too heavy for people to lift. I didn't see myself as I was: skinny. I thought I was huge!

Despite my fears, however, I was curious about the exhilaration that I saw on the faces of others when they were held aloft by friends. They sure seemed like they were having a good time up in the air, whether or not they had any fears initially. At some point, my own fear gave way to curiosity, and I volunteered for the airborne position. To my amazement, my shame and fear were quickly overwhelmed by a tidal wave of pleasure, which swept through me when people lifted me up with their hands.

I couldn't help but notice that it was truly easy for people to lift me. This forced me to reassess my grossly inaccurate body image. It's not that my distorted thinking vanished forever, never to return. It's more that the game made a *dent* in my misperceptions. If you know anything about anorexia, you know that any shift in the "crazy thinking" is valuable, even a small shift.

For people on the flip side of the weight issue, this game can be equally challenging. In addition, those of us who have survived sexual or physical abuse may have fears about being touched by other people, whether they are family, friends, or strangers. If these kinds of fears make you reticent to play, perhaps you could ask group members to address your concerns by opening a general discussion about issues related to touch.

People who have not been abused can sometimes overcome their fears through a simple process of inner dialogue—that is, by giving themselves a pep talk. Others may require a few extra helpings of outside encouragement to help them join the game. Whether you need a little or a lot of support around fear, there are several other chapters in this book that provide detailed information to help you work with this powerful emotion. Therefore, I'll just say once again that *whatever you need* in relation to your fear is absolutely okay. Your task is *not* to make your fear wrong, but to treat it with compassion and respect.

Even those who have no deep-seated body fears (or touch issues) may discover a few unexpected pockets of intensity when they play

There is something else you can do with fear's incredible vitality. Give it another label. Call it excitement. Look how much more energy you suddenly have. Another piece of you has been remembered.

EMMANUEL

The next time you encounter fear, consider yourself lucky. The trick is to keep exploring and not bail out, even when you find out that something is not what you thought. Nothing is what we thought.

PEMA CHÖDRÖN

Spirituality must also be sensuous. A spiritual person is one who lives fully in the body.
Deepak Chopra

this game. For instance, when was the last time—maybe it was also the first time—you got lifted up above other people's heads? You were probably an infant, right? You might not remember this when you play the game, but your *body* may remember. As a result, you might be flooded with sensations that you can't describe in words, since you didn't know words the first time you felt that way. These sensations could be pleasurable or distressing, depending on what kinds of memories are stimulated for you.

Strange as it sounds, many people have as much trouble with pleasure as they do with fear. If this is true for you, you might want to read more about the fear of pleasure in the chapter called "Joy: A Warrior's Path."

Whether you struggle with fear or cruise through it, physical trust games are a good way to practice new ways to relate to this primal emotion. Paradoxically, fear sometimes means STOP, but sometimes it's trying to tell you to FEEL THE EXCITEMENT AND GO FOR IT! By tuning into your body, you can learn *when* to do *what* with your fear.

If you understand that fear is a signal that needs your attention, as opposed to a demand that requires an automatic response, you can use it to open doors to a more expansive life. Where there is fear, there is opportunity for growth. Let it be your ally on the path to deeper trust.

THE LEAP OF FAITH

In the early 1980s, I was introduced to firewalking by a man I'll call Michael. Michael opened up a whole new world for me: the world of treating fear as a friend. Michael was a tall, shy man with a heart as big as the sky. His method of teaching people to walk on fire was not the typical mind-over-matter approach, which is about control. Instead, he encouraged people to make a conscious choice to trust their bodies and to surrender to the ultimate safety of the universe.

When I met Michael, I was struggling with the last vestiges of a fifteen-year dance with anorexia. If I had to describe anorexia in one word, I'd say that it's about *fear*. Anorexia is about fear of the body, fear of feelings, fear of pleasure, fear of womanhood, fear of power, fear of passion, fear of intimacy, fear of self-expression, fear of life, fear of almost everything. When everything inside and outside the self is scary, life becomes increasingly limited.

Eventually I realized that it didn't work for me to treat fear as an enemy. I wanted to try something different, so I was intrigued when I heard about Michael's way of approaching fear as a friend. Also, I figured that if I could walk on fire and still be safe, then I'd have to consider the possibility that food could be safe, feelings could be safe, and perhaps even life itself could be safe.

My plan succeeded. I can't say it was firewalking that did the trick. Firewalking was merely the punchline to the hours we spent creating a new relationship with fear. The punchline was necessary, of course, in the same way a joke falls flat without the final clincher. I must admit, it was pretty amazing to walk barefoot over a long bed of coals hot enough to melt aluminum. In fact, it was so amazing that I had to do it nine or ten times over the next few months, just to prove to myself that it wasn't a fluke.

It wasn't a fluke. Michael had effectively demonstrated a way to walk on fire that changed the way I looked at life. More than the

And the trouble is, if you don't risk anything, you risk even more.

ERICA JONG

Faith is the bird that sings to the dawn while it is still dark.

KABIR

He who is conscious of danger creates peace for himself....

THE I CHING

Radical is nice, but sometimes radical has to bow to practical.

DAN SAVAGE

firewalking itself, it was Michael's style that made the difference. With gentleness, humor, and respect, he taught us wonderful trust games, a few of which are described in this section. He also helped me learn *practical* ways to tune in to my body's own knowing.

Before I share another one of his trust games with you, I'll tell you my favorite of his practical techniques for accessing the body's knowing. Not only is it a great tool for ensuring safety while firewalking, it's also applicable to decision-making in everyday life. You can experiment with it when you play what I call the "Leap of Faith," which I'll describe to you in a moment.

No matter how much inner preparation I did in relation to fear before the firewalk, there still came that moment of truth when I had to decide: Is it time to walk right now, or isn't it? This is a pretty intense question when you're faced with the prospect of roasting your tootsies on a bed of hot coals. I was well aware of the fact that people can and do get burned—sometimes badly—when they walk on fire. I wasn't interested in hurting myself, but how would I know when to step forward and when to hold back? I mean, it wasn't like I had a good track record up to that point, in terms of knowing how to trust my body.

Michael gave us a simple tool. He said to pay attention to whether my body relaxes or contracts when I ask myself, "Is it time to walk right now?" If my body contracts, it's not time. On the other hand, if my body relaxes and goes *ahhh*, then it's time to go for it.

This simple tip kept me safe during all my firewalks. Despite my relatively disconnected anorexic state, I found this technique easy to use and exceedingly clear. I especially like the part about waiting until my body goes *ahhh* before I act. Needless to say, this technique has a scope of application that goes far beyond firewalking. You can use it anytime you need to decide whether a particular action is right for you at a given moment in time.

Now, are you ready to try another of Michael's trust games? To play this one, you'll need at least eight people in addition to yourself. Ten or twelve friends is better, so people can rotate out of the game when they get tired. You'll also need a sturdy platform strong enough to hold the full weight of one person. The platform should be well balanced, so someone can stand on the edge of it, without tipping it.

The top of the platform should be at least waist high and not more than chest high. The height is very important: The feet of the person standing on the platform should be approximately level with the waists of the people on the ground. A heavy picnic table works great. At one of Michael's firewalking workshops in the North Cascade Mountains in Washington, we improvised by using a huge boulder for our platform. Feel free to be creative, but make sure that the ground around your platform is soft and safe.

The next thing to do is to form the ground crew, which will be comprised of six people. These people will form two lines, parallel to and facing each other—like a double receiving line, with three people on each side. These two groups of people should position themselves so the lines they form are perpendicular to the edge of the platform, from which the *leaper* will fall into their arms. If this sounds confusing on paper, don't worry. It will make more sense when you actually do it.

When the ground crew is in position, each group of three will be standing shoulder-to-shoulder, with their feet solidly planted about shoulder-width apart. Now everyone will join arms with the person directly opposite them on the other side of the receiving line. People should use a trapeze grip to join arms, which means that everyone will grasp their partner's wrists with their hands, and vice versa. This kind of grasp is very strong—good for catching a falling body!

It's imperative that the people on the ground take their roles seriously. The trust game itself is scary enough for most people; no one needs to up the ante by heckling the leaper in any way. If someone in the receiving line thinks it's funny to taunt the leaper, it's best to ask that person to watch for a while. Another option might be to let the mischievous person be the first leaper, so he or she can discover the importance of a supportive ground crew.

When the receiving line is ready, it's time for someone to be the first leaper. Let's say it will be you. You won't actually be leaping, but rather, you'll be *leaning* into a gentle fall. To do this, you can either fall face first into the arms of your friends, or you can turn around and fall backwards. People have different fears about falling either forward or backward. I recommend that you try them both at least once, starting with the one that feels the *least* scary. You can also experiment with keeping your eyes open or closed.

When you're ready, move toward the edge of the platform, and position your feet in a way that feels comfortable for you. If you like, you can ask your friends to reassure you that they'll catch you no matter what. It's important for them to be honest about their abilities, and to act accordingly. For example, if one of the leapers happens to be particularly large or tall, your friends might want to add a fourth person to each side of the receiving line. In addition, a fourth person per side can be helpful if the leaper has a lot of anxiety about the game.

One does not discover new lands without consenting to lose sight of the shore for a very long time.

ANDRÉ GIDE

Remember, you won't actually be leaping; you'll be leaning into a fall. I only use the word *leap* to emphasize your active willingness to step into your fear. To leap, pretend that you're a tree in the same way I described in the chapter called "Pass the Body." That is, keep your body rigid, your legs together, and your arms flat against your sides. Then allow yourself to tip over slowly, pivoting from your feet, as if you have a swivel in your ankles. Lean toward the open arms of your friends, and let go. Don't forget to keep breathing! Breathing helps the body integrate strong emotions, such as fear and its counterpart, excitement.

Most people who try the Leap of Faith become enamored with it quite quickly. In fact, I'd wager that people will get tired of serving as the ground crew long before everyone gets their fill of falling into each other's arms. Be sure to give everyone at least one chance to *leap* before allowing anyone to make a repeat performance. However, some people may prefer to stay on the ground. They may not feel ready, willing, or able to be a leaper. Nonetheless, the support position can still provide plenty of opportunities for working with issues of trust and fear.

For example, can you trust yourself to catch another person? Do you feel physically and emotionally strong enough to do it? Do you feel comfortable working as part of a team? Do you trust others to do their part? What if you drop someone? Does that possibility bring up fear or shame for you? Also, can you trust yourself to stop when you're tired, even if everyone else wants to keep playing? This last question is very important, because it clearly illustrates the relationship between self-care and care for others. If you overextend yourself to please others, you or they might get hurt.

When you participate in this trust game, please play it safe. Take care of yourself and don't overextend. In addition, I recommend that you follow all the basic guidelines. Be sure to have at least eight teammates besides yourself. Use a strong platform that won't tip when someone stands on the edge. Play the game on a soft surface, such as grass or sand. Never play this game over concrete or a hard floor. If you play inside on a plush carpet, it's a good idea to lay down extra cushions or mats, just to be on the safe side.

The purpose of trust games is *not* to court disaster. Rather, the purpose is to provide an *edge* of fear, so people can explore their ability to trust themselves and others. If someone gets really scared or overstimulated, *stop the game* and take time to support that person. Ask what he or she needs, and see what can be done to meet those needs before continuing the game.

You can't cross a chasm in two steps.

RASHI FEIN

There are three kinds of people: those who make it happen, those who watch it happen, and those who wonder what happened.

WILLIAM LEVINSON

Hopefully, I haven't frightened you by outlining all these safety precautions. My intention is simply to encourage you to create a safe environment, so that you can explore the continuum between trust and fear. As strange as it sounds, it's best to learn about fear in an atmosphere of safety. Here's the bottom line: *If you're not having a good time when you play trust games, you're pushing too hard.* Play involves risk, but you shouldn't be terrified. Keep it fun.

When you're falling through the air, heading for the arms of your friends, imagine how your life would feel if you surrendered all your actions to that much trust. *Ahhh!*

Courage is fear that has said its prayers.

ANONYMOUS

THE GIFT CHAIR

The "Gift Chair" encourages you to ask for what you want in the presence of people who may be willing and able to fulfill your wish. Here's how you play. First, you'll need a group of at least two people, although in this case, bigger is definitely better. More people will bring more opportunities for pleasure. After you get a group together, you'll need to designate a Gift Chair. A pillow or even a special spot on the floor will do in a pinch.

Whoever sits in the Gift Chair gets to ask for anything he or she wants. Everyone in the group can take turns in the chair as the spirit moves them, or people can go around the circle one by one, in order. As for time parameters, you can play until everyone is satiated, or you can set a time limit and take first come, first served.

When you're in the Gift Chair, it's best to ask for something the group can provide. However, you can express your wildest dreams, if you simply want to be witnessed and supported. Whether or not the group can satisfy your request, the act of asking for what you want may feel risky. Many of us were taught that it's socially incorrect, if not downright rude, to state your desires openly and directly. Some of us grew up in families where covert manipulation and overt demands were the typical means by which people got their needs met.

Apart from cultural and familial conditioning against asking for what you want, there is also the matter of vulnerability. That is, when you ask for what you want, you risk self-exposure as well as rejection. While this rejection may simply be a rejection of your request, some people may experience this as a *personal* rejection.

In any case, fear of self-exposure and fear of rejection are powerful motivators that may prevent people from asking for what they want. When you take a turn in the Gift Chair, then, you may experience some degree of these fears. On the flip side, however, it can be exhilarating to step into these fears, ask for what you want, and be met with support instead of rejection.

At one of my workshops sponsored by Unity Church of Seattle, a couple had traveled by ferry from the San Juan Islands in Puget Sound. A few minutes before we started the seminar, they told me that they didn't have enough money to get home on the ferry afterward. They asked if I could help them. Knowing we would play the Gift Chair later in the day, I told them not to worry. Briefly, I described the game and encouraged them to ask the group for help. I assured them that they would probably get more than they needed for their return trip.

When it came time to play, the shy couple sat in the Gift Chair together. They spoke about their need, and they asked for small contributions. As I predicted, the couple got more than they needed. It was sweet to see their embarrassment melt into wide-eyed amazement and gratitude. It was equally sweet to watch the group's delight at being able to help. Everybody won.

One of the most popular requests from people in the Gift Chair is to receive a group massage. At my workshops, people have always done this with their clothes on, although a more risqué version might be fun among close friends. Either way, group massage can be given by any or all who want to provide the recipient with a luscious treat. Believe me, it's incredible to be massaged by five or ten pairs of hands simultaneously. If you try it, I recommend that you breathe deeply and continuously. You may be surprised to discover how hard it is to stay conscious in the face of that much pleasure!

Once in Los Angeles, I was working with a group comprised solely of women. We started playing the Gift Chair about half an hour before the scheduled lunch break, and everyone got carried away exchanging group massages. An hour and a half later, we were all reduced to putty. No one complained about being late for lunch.

In most of the seminars I've facilitated, participants take to this game like kids to candy. It's as if people are hungry for permission to indulge themselves. Occasionally, however, I run across people who require repeated coaxing to play. While it's not uncommon for one or two people in a group to need extra encouragement, I once encountered an entire group of people who sat paralyzed with fear when I introduced the Gift Chair. No one wanted to take center stage. Apparently, the prospect of asking for what they wanted terrified them. It was heartbreaking. Needless to say, I had to do an extra pep talk that day to entice them to play.

Ironically, the same people who deny themselves the opportunity to *receive* may have no trouble *giving* to others. It's as if they've taken that old maxim, "It's better to give than receive," to its furthest

Look and you will find it— what is unsought will go undetected.

SOPHOCLES

It is one of the most beautiful compensations of this life that no man can sincerely try to help another without helping himself.

RALPH WALDO EMERSON

Those who are unable to receive are actually incapable of giving. Giving and receiving are different aspects of the flow of energy in the universe.

DEEPAK CHOPRA

Your heart will give you greater counsel than all the world's scholars.

TALMUD

extreme. As a recovering overgiver myself, I can personally attest to the pervasive power of this conditioning. Just because something is pervasive, however, doesn't mean it's healthy.

A friend once explained to me that if I'm not willing to receive, then I'm blocking the natural flow of the universe. For example, if I refuse to receive from other people, I deny them the opportunity to give. My friend suggested that if I couldn't receive for the sake of my own pleasure, then perhaps I could do it for the sake of others. She knew this would appeal to my humanitarian sense of fairness. Essentially, she *tricked* me (in a good way) into realizing that I also give by receiving.

On the flip side, I'd like to say a few words about giving. In general, I recommend that you give *only* when you genuinely want to give. Don't force it. Consider this: If you're on the receiving end, how would you feel if you knew that someone had forced herself to give to you? I don't know about you, but I hate it when people give because they think they *should* give (see "Guilt Could Mean You've Done Something Right"). When people give to me because they think they should, or because they feel obligated, I feel patronized, pitied, or insulted.

Some say that people must be goaded or guilt-tripped into giving. If the rules of obligation are removed, they say, no one would give. I think the opposite is true. That is, I believe the human heart is giving by nature. The pressures of guilt and obligation actually *constrict* the heart's natural desire to share. If I think I *should* give, it sets up resentment in the part of me that doesn't like to be told what to do. Ultimately, if my giving is tainted by resentment, my efforts may do more harm than good.

Obviously, my suggestion that you only give when you genuinely want to give carries with it the hope that you'll tune in to your heart in order to make this determination. It takes practice to discern what is right for you in any given situation. For instance, I might not feel like giving in a particular way, at a particular moment, to a particular person. Yet when I take some time to sort through my thoughts and feelings, I might discover a hidden desire to give in a way I hadn't previously considered. On the other hand, I might find myself automatically offering something, only to realize later that I overextended by not checking in with myself first.

Thus, there are many styles and degrees of giving. When you don't feel like giving, it may only mean that you or others are *expecting* you to give. If you can remove the expectations about if, when, what, where, how, why, and to whom you think you *should* give, then maybe you'll be able to explore your true desire to give.

Instead of operating on automatic, which results in giving out of obligation, take the time to ask what's right for you in any given situation. When people ask you for something, first see if you have the energy and the inclination to give at all. Then check in with your heart to see if the particulars of their request sound like something you can offer. A true gift will feel good to both you and the recipient.

Sometimes when people play the Gift Chair game, a participant will ask for something that no one wants to give. While this may stimulate some embarrassment for everyone, it provides a great opportunity to validate the idea that it's always okay to ask for what you want—and likewise, it's fine if no one wants to respond to a particular request.

Be really whole,
And all things will come to you.
LAO TSU

In such cases, it may help to acknowledge the awkwardness. Perhaps someone in the group could offer a few words of appreciation for the Gift Chair person's courage. Maybe someone else could describe how it feels to be disinclined to give, particularly if someone is left wanting. Nothing has to be done to change or fix the situation. Honest acknowledgment of *whatever is happening* can be powerful in and of itself.

If the person in the Gift Chair is not granted a first request, he or she might want to make another request. In my experience, no one has ever left the Gift Chair without receiving some kind of support. The truth is, the only "problem" I've had with this game is getting people to stop once they start.

Too much of a good thing is
wonderful!
MAE WEST

Come to think of it, it might be fun *not* to stop. Maybe you could start a Gift Chair group, so you could get together with friends every week to play. Nurture each other like crazy, and push the limits of your pleasure. Go for it!

Guided

Meditations:

Calling the

Spirit Within

SECTION
SIX

How to Use
These Meditations

There are a number of ways to use the three meditations in this section. One of the best ways is to ask a friend to read one of them to you while you do it. This method is especially helpful, because a friend can tune in to you and pause from reading now and then, allowing you more time to relax and visualize.

To make it easier for another person to know when to pause, I've inserted a notation called an ellipse (…) at various points throughout the meditations. Of course, there are no hard-and-fast rules about when to pause, so the reader can let his or her intuition be the guide. Generally speaking, it's probably best to allow a little too much time between suggestions, rather than too little.

If you don't have someone to help you, or if you prefer to work with these meditations alone, you can make an audiotape of the script using your own voice. Again, allow ample time between each successive part of the meditation. Since you know yourself better than anyone else does, you'll know whether you like short or long pauses between the sentences. You can also experiment with your speaking style, your tone, and the speed of your reading. Feel free to add some soft background music, if you like. Once you get your audiotape into a form you enjoy, save it for repeated use.

Another way to make your own tape is to slowly read the meditation straight through, without adding any pauses in the script. Then when you use the tape, sit or lie down near the pause button on your tape recorder, so you can stop the tape whenever you want more time. The disadvantage of this method is that you have to stay conscious enough to deal with the tape machine. The advantage is that you can give yourself as much time as you need by varying the length of your pauses each time you do the meditation.

A final technique for using these visualizations is to read the entire script all the way through before you begin. Once you have a good sense of it, get comfortable and do the meditation from memory. You might not remember all the steps exactly as they were written,

Solitude grants the possibility of uninhibited thought.
Alix Kates Shulman

I learned to meditate by doing something my father ordered me to do: "Sit down. Shut up. Listen."

IYANLA VAN ZANDT

Every feeling, thought, movement, and encounter is simultaneously an inner and outer event. Thus, meditation or innerwork is a form of worldwork, just as world events are also personal ones.

ARNOLD MINDELL

but that's okay. I'll bet you'll remember as much as you need to remember—and your improvisations might be fantastic!

Whether you read through the meditation in advance or make your own tape, you'll know how the script ends. If you're concerned that this might detract from the spontaneity of your visualizations, don't worry. In my experience, foreknowledge usually enhances the effect. For example, I've often used the Three-Door Meditation in my addiction workshops. People who have taken this workshop more than once report that they received new insights each time they did the meditation. Apparently, knowing what's coming helped them relax and enjoy the ride more fully.

By the way, you might like to share the details of your inner journeys with a trusted friend. If so, be sure to request the kind of listening you want. Be honest and direct about whether you'd like comments. If not, let your friend know that you'd simply like to be heard. Another person's perspective can add a valuable dimension to your understanding, but *unsolicited* feedback—no matter how wise or well intended—can feel invasive or offensive. This is particularly true if you're feeling vulnerable about disclosing a soulful part of yourself.

Aside from sharing your visualizations with a friend, you can also bear witness to them by journaling. This will give you a chance to reflect on your experiences over time, so you can acknowledge and appreciate all the nuances of change as your process unfolds.

If you do write about your meditations, I suggest a three-part approach. First, before you begin your visualization, write down the focus or purpose of your work that day. Then, after you come back from your inner journey, record as many details as you can. Finally, take a few moments to do a brief synopsis (a few key phrases or a short paragraph) that captures the essence of what you learned from the meditation. Also, make note of any actions recommended by your inner guidance, and of course, be sure to *take action* based on the information you receive. Keep your journal handy, so you can refer back to it for inspiration and support.

Whether you keep your meditation writings private or share them with a friend, remember that you are the first, last, and best authority on your own experiences. No one knows better than you what is right for you. Even when your inner knowing feels inaccessible, it's still there in your heart. Everything you need really does lie within. As Ram Dass says, "The next message you need is always right where you are."

Let the meditations in this section help you find the next message you need—and the next, and the next.

THE THREE-DOOR MEDITATION

This meditation was inspired by a guided journey I originally learned from an Oneida medicine man in Tucson. It is so effective as a tool for releasing addictive energy that I later incorporated my own version into workshops. Every time I listen to people share their insights from this meditation, I'm amazed by its transformative power.

Before you begin this inner journey, take a few moments to consider which of your habits or addictions feels the most harmful or challenging for you (see "The Five-Minute Switch System" for tips). Perhaps you struggle with a substance addiction to drugs, alcohol, tobacco, caffeine, or food. Or maybe you're repeatedly stymied by unhealthy relationship patterns, obsessive ways of thinking, or self-destructive behaviors, such as caretaking or overworking. Whatever the case, be as honest as you can when you name your habit. Call a spade a spade, so to speak, and acknowledge what is really happening. This is the first step in healing.

I do yoga every day, but I've never made a habit of it.
KRISHNAMURTI

Once you've selected an addiction as your focus, find a comfortable spot to sit or lie down. Take a few minutes to look around, quiet your senses, and do whatever it takes to bring your awareness into present time. When you're ready, gently close your eyes. As you gradually turn your awareness inward, imagine that all your random thoughts and concerns have somehow slipped away far beyond the reach of your mind. For now, all you have to do is breathe. There's nothing else you need to do right now except breathe. That's all. Just breathe....

As you continue breathing, imagine that the air around you is somehow taking on a color...and a temperature...and perhaps even a special aroma that calms...centers...and comforts you. This wonderful air swirls around you and comes softly into your mouth or your nostrils on its way to your lungs…where it will nourish you.

Feel the temperature of this air as it comes inside your body. *See* the air as it takes on one of your favorite colors and becomes visible in its swirling patterns around you. *Smell* its special scent as you inhale and receive all the air that you need…without effort…without pressure…without hurrying in any way at all.

As you continue breathing…always breathing…gently roll your eyes up in their sockets. Let them roll up as far as they can go now…and then slowly allow your eyes to roll around to the right…and now let them roll down toward the bottom of your eye sockets. As you continue breathing, let your eyes continue to roll from the bottom of their sockets over toward the left now…and then up and around to the top. When your eyes have followed this circular path back up to the top, let them relax back into their natural resting place again.

As you continue breathing…gently breathing…roll your eyes up in their sockets again once more. Let them roll up as far as they can comfortably go…then let them roll softly around to the left now…and then down to the bottom of your eye sockets. As you continue breathing, allow your eyes to continue to roll from the bottom of their sockets over toward the right now…and then upward again to the top. When your eyes have followed this circular path up to the top again, let them ease back into their natural resting place once more.

With your eyes resting comfortably now, focus again on your breathing. Let the air come in softly as you continue to breathe in whatever way feels easy. In a moment, when you're ready, you can begin an inward journey now…going a little deeper…and a little deeper still….

Take some time now to imagine a place in nature where you would like to go. Perhaps it's a place where you've been before…or maybe it's a place in your imagination where you go when you want to be alone. Wherever you choose to go, be sure that it's a place where you feel safe and secure. Let it be a place where you can relax and be yourself…a place where you can return again and again, whenever you need to refresh and renew your spirit. Go to this place now…in your imagination…and find a good spot where you can sit and watch the sky….

As you sit…watching the sky above you…begin to tune in to the earth beneath you. Feel the weight of your body as it rests on the earth…and feel the weight of the earth as it presses back up against you. Notice how the planet gives you this massive support all the time…for free. You don't have to do anything except receive this support.

Power is born of relaxation.
GEORGE LEONARD

It's a gift…a constant gift available to you anytime…all the time….

Now, from where you sit with the earth beneath you and the sky above you…breathing deeply…let your imagination drift once more. Imagine now that three doors somehow appear out of nowhere. It doesn't matter where they came from or where they're going…and it's okay if they look a little out of place there in your quiet spot in nature. Just let these three doors appear as if by magic.

These magic doors are doors to your inner world…doors to your deepest imagination. These three doors will give you visions of possible futures…specific futures that could happen for you. These doors appear before you now…there in your sacred place. They are waiting to lead you deeper into yourself…into the realm of possibility.

When you're ready…slowly get up from where you're sitting (there in your imagination) and walk over to the first door. Stand in front of it now, and imagine that behind this door there is an image of yourself five years from now…perhaps ten years from now…maybe even twenty years from now.

What you will see behind this door is an image of yourself, if you were to indulge in your chosen addiction with complete abandon. This image will show you a possible future self that does your habit even more than you are doing it now…taking it to its fullest and most intense extreme for many years to come….

As much as you can, look at this image of yourself without judgment or criticism or fear. When you gaze at this possible future self, keep breathing, and allow your heart to open to its teaching. Look closely at the image for the sake of information and learning.

With the curiosity of a child, open your eyes wide to see what you might look like if you completely surrender to your chosen addiction. In this possible future, your addiction has overtaken your life…it has overtaken every nook and cranny of your existence. There is nothing but your habit…and everything you do is focused on supporting this addiction for years on end….

As you continue breathing, fix your gaze on this image for a few more moments. Learn as much as you can by looking at this possible future. Ask the image if it would like to say anything to you from its position in the realm of possibility. If the image speaks to you, listen carefully to whatever it wants to tell you….

When this image of possibility is finished saying whatever it wants to say, thank it for its words, and for sharing its vision with you. Take your time, so you can feel complete….

When you're ready, say goodbye to this possible future self…and now…close the door between you and it. Once you close the door, the image will go back to the realm of possibility. This future may

Always play your options.
JOHN GIOVINE

Why do you hasten to remove anything which burns your eye, while if something affects your soul you postpone the cure until next year?

HORACE

or may not manifest, depending on your choices as time unfolds. For now, this image has vanished…and the first door has vanished along with it.

In a moment or two…go stand in front of the second door. Behind this door there will be an image of yourself in five years…ten years…perhaps even twenty years. It will be an image of yourself, if you were to continue to do your chosen addiction in a middle-of-the road way…not excessively…but never giving it up, either. This image will show you a possible future self that never gets free of this habit…but never becomes entirely enslaved to it, either. In this future, you stay on the fence with your addiction….

When you're ready, open the door and look at this future image…this possible future image of yourself. As much as you can, look at this image of yourself without judgment or criticism or fear. When you gaze at this possible future self, keep breathing, and allow your heart to open to its teaching. Look closely at the image for the sake of information and learning.

With the curiosity of a child, open your eyes wide to see what you might look like if you hold onto your chosen addiction and never let it go. In this possible future, your addiction stays with you…always there in the background. You keep doing your life with this chosen habit always by your side. This addiction never overtakes your existence, but neither does it ever let you go free….

As you continue breathing, fix your gaze on this image for a few more moments. Learn as much as you can by looking at this possible future. Ask the image if it would like to say anything to you from its position…there in the realm of possibility. If the image speaks to you, listen carefully to whatever it wants to tell you….

When this image of possibility is finished saying whatever it wants to say, thank it for its words, and for sharing its vision with you. Take your time…so you can feel complete….

When you're ready, say goodbye to this possible future self…and now…close the door between you and it. Once you close the door, the image will go back to the realm of possibility. This future may or may not manifest, depending on your choices as time unfolds. For now, this image has vanished, and the second door has vanished along with it.

In a moment or two, walk over to the only remaining door, the third and last door. Behind this last door, you will see an image of yourself in five years…or ten years…or maybe twenty years into the future. It will be an image of yourself if you completely let go of your chosen addiction. This image will show you a possible future

The past does not equal the future.

ANTHONY ROBBINS

self that lives totally free of your chosen habit. You've now let go of your addiction once and for all. In this future image, you are free....

When you're ready, open the door and look at this future image...this possible future image of yourself. As much as you can, look at this image of yourself without judgment or criticism or fear. When you gaze at this possible future self, keep breathing, and allow your heart to open to its teaching. Look closely at the image for the sake of information and learning.

With the curiosity of a child, open your eyes wide to see what you might look like if you completely let go of your chosen addiction and live free of it from this day forward. In this possible future, your addiction is just a memory...something you needed in the past...but something you outgrew as you became stronger and more self-aware. You live your life now free of this chosen habit. You're in charge of your life now...you're totally free....

As you continue breathing, fix your gaze on this image for a few more moments. Learn as much as you can by looking at this possible future. Ask the image if it would like to say anything to you from its position...there in the realm of possibility. If the image speaks to you, listen carefully to whatever it wants to tell you....

When this image of possibility is finished saying whatever it wants to say, thank it for its words and for sharing its vision with you. Take your time...so you can feel complete....

When you're ready, say goodbye to this possible future self...and now...close the door between you and it. Once you close the door, the image will go back to the realm of possibility. This future may or may not manifest, depending on your choices as time unfolds. For now, this image has vanished, and the third and last door has vanished along with it.

In a moment or two, walk back to the spot where you were first sitting when you arrived at your sacred place in nature. Go there now and sit down again...or lie down on your back...and rest for a little while. Let your attention drift as you watch the sky above you. Take your time....

Let your mind reflect on the gifts of vision that you have just received from behind the three doors. Remember the visions of those three possible futures...futures that may or may not manifest, depending on your choices as time unfolds. Remember the details of these images as you get ready to return from your inner journey. Remember all you have learned, and say a word of thanks to your imagination for its generosity toward you....

As you continue breathing, tune in to the beauty that surrounds

The moment one definitely commits oneself, then Providence moves, too. All sorts of things occur to help one that would never otherwise have occurred....Boldness has genius, power, and magic in it. Begin it now.

GOETHE

you there in nature. Drink it in, and carry it with you in your heart, as you prepare to return to your everyday awareness. Gradually bring your breathing back into focus now, as you begin to feel the weight of your body against the floor again...as you begin to feel the support of the earth beneath you....

Now...whenever you're ready...wiggle your toes and move your fingers. Stretch your hands...and take a few deep breaths up high into your chest. Allow your breathing to speed up ever so slightly now as you continue to stretch your hands...and your arms...and your legs...and all your limbs now...one by one...as you feel the energy of movement return to your body.

Stretching and moving and breathing naturally...the energy of movement comes flowing back into your hips...and your torso...and your shoulders...and now into your neck...and your head. Your whole body becomes enlivened again, as you continue to breathe...and stretch...and move in whatever way feels good to you....

Slowly, gently, quietly...imagine that little sparks of energy are waking up all the cells in your body. Bit by bit, your body stretches into a state of readiness and wakefulness as these sparks of energy light up your cells like stars in the night....

As you continue to breathe, these sparks of energy stimulate your mind...bringing it into a state of relaxed, alert clarity. And now...when you're ready to bring your awareness all the way back into present time...you can open your eyes slowly...letting them close, and then open again...close, and then open again...as you become accustomed to the light once more....

With your eyes open now...give yourself some time to adjust to your surroundings in present time. Take a look around...and reorient yourself in whatever way you need....

Breathe deeply...and remember the visions that you saw behind those three doors. Carry these gifts of knowledge forward with you as you return to your everyday awareness...sensing the realm of possibility opening before you....

THE TEACHER MEDITATION

One of my deepest aspirations is to *constantly* regard everyone and everything as a teacher. With this perspective, every person brings a message, and every experience bears a gift. When I see everyone and everything as helpmates, it's easier to treat difficult people and challenging situations as opportunities for reflection and growth.

Whether or not you live according to this philosophy, I trust that you've had some important teachers in your life—teachers who have inspired you, guided you, or helped you find your way. These teachers could be people, animals, spirit beings, dream figures, or even special objects or power places. The form of these teachers is not as important as their impact on your life. If someone or something *feels* like a teacher to you, that's good enough.

The following meditation is designed to honor your teachers, past or present. It doesn't matter if you still have contact with these teachers, because this meditation will allow you to access their wisdom and guidance at any time, through the vehicle of your own imagination. Your imagination, in turn, will connect you to the vast network of collective information that surrounds and sustains us all.

What lies behind us and what lies before us are tiny matters compared to what lies within us.
RALPH WALDO EMERSON

To begin this meditation, find a quiet place where you will not be disturbed. Be sure to turn off any technological contraptions that might be lurking nearby. You won't be needing the telephone, television, radio, stereo, or computer during your inner journey. Disconnect the phone lines and free the machines from their power source, so you won't be distracted by their insistent rings, hums, and whirs.

Once you've quieted the space, find a good spot to sit or lie down. Get comfortable, and begin to quiet your senses now by taking one last look around you, making sure that everything is in its place.

The best teachers are those who refuse to stop learning.
ANDREW VACHSS

A sheltered life can be a daring life as well. For all serious daring starts from within.

EUDORA WELTY

The life of the spirit entails a continuous alternation between retreating into oneself and going out into the world: it's an inward-outward journey.

SAM KEEN

When you're ready, close your eyes and turn your attention inward. Allow the rhythm of your breathing to come into your awareness. Without trying to control or change anything, let your breathing become your total focus as you continue to turn your attention inward....

Just breathe naturally...because whatever way you are breathing is perfectly okay. Just follow your breath in...and out...one breath at a time in one long, continuous circle...one long, continuous rhythm...in...and out...however you want....

As you continue breathing, slowly bring your attention to your body. Feel the weight of your body against the chair...or the floor...or the earth...wherever you are sitting or lying down right now. Feel the massive support that your body is receiving...support that you are receiving from the earth beneath you. Feel this deep, strong, solid support...the support of a massive planet that sustains you, all beings, and all things equally, without judgment. You are receiving this massive, constant support simply because you are alive.

In whatever way you can, imagine yourself surrendering to this support as you continue breathing. With each in-breath, you can feel this support a little more deeply. With each out-breath, you can relax into this support a little more fully....

Now, in a moment, get ready to go a step further in your inner journey by imagining a place in nature, a place where you can go when you want to connect with your core...your truest self. Wander to that place now...in your imagination. Go to that sacred place in nature...a place where you feel safe and warm and comforted. It can be a place where you've actually been...or it can be a place you envision in your mind right now, for today. However this place appears to you, let it be everything you want it to be.

As you continue to breathe naturally, let your awareness focus more intently on your surroundings, there in your sacred spot. What can you see? Are there trees around you? Are you in a meadow? Can you see mountains? Is there a river nearby...or a lake...or a beach...or the ocean? Is the sky above you clear and sunny...or is it full of billowing clouds...or can you see the subtle colors of twilight coming up on the horizon?

Take your time as you drink in the view around you. Let all the details of your personal power spot become vivid for you...so you can feel its support a little more with each breath. Continue to breathe naturally, as you focus your awareness on the beautiful landscape that surrounds you....

Now…gradually shift your attention from your eyes to your ears. Notice the sounds around you there in nature. When you listen, what do you hear? Can you hear the wind? Is there a crashing surf in the background? Do you hear the murmur of a nearby stream…or the rustle of leaves…or the creaking of tall trees as they sway in the wind? Can you hear birds? Perhaps there are no sounds at all. Perhaps it's night and everything is quiet.…

Now…slowly…let your awareness drift, and then gradually focus on the air around you. As you continue to breathe in whatever way feels right to you…notice the *temperature* and the *feel* and the *scent* of the air. Is it humid? Is it dry? Is the air electric with the energy of a passing thunderstorm?

Let your nostrils come alive as you breathe in the air around you. Can you smell flower blossoms? Do you smell the salty air of ocean fog? Perhaps there is a campfire nearby. Is there a smoky aroma of burning wood and pine needles? Whatever you smell…take a few moments now to savor the air…your invisible *oxygenated* friend that sustains you and gives you life.…

When the flower blooms the bees come uninvited.
RAMAKRISHNA

Breathe the air deeply…and when you're ready…gradually let your attention shift once again, as you begin to turn your awareness inward. Tune in to your heart, and let your memories of special teachers begin to surface in the reflective pool of your mind. These teachers could be people…or animals…or spirit guides…or dream figures…or perhaps even a sacred object or a power spot.

Begin by thinking of the teachers in your life right now…in present time…and then slowly…go back in your memory, until you remember teachers further back in the past. Think about those special beings who changed your life in some way. Ask your memory banks to call up any experiences that will help you remember your teachers. Bit by bit, let these memories surface for you now, as you recall those who supported you, taught you, and helped you become who you are today.

Slowly, keep going back in your memories…year by year…remembering the points in your life that were transformative for you. As you go back in time, remember all the teachers who assisted you in these transformations, who acted as a catalyst in your growth…who taught you about unconditional love by giving it to you…who brought you lessons of compassion and wisdom by showing you how to act, or by showing you how *not* to act. As you watch these teachers pass before your eyes…acknowledge their presence and their gifts…and thank them…one by one.

To confront a person with his own shadow is to show him his own light.
CARL JUNG

People are like stained-glass windows. They sparkle and shine when the sun is out, but when the darkness sets in, their true beauty is revealed only if there is a light from within.

ELISABETH KÜBLER-ROSS

Now...when you're ready, begin to narrow the focus of your attention until you are able to single out two or three teachers who are especially significant to you. Gradually allow these important teachers to emerge into the foreground...and let them come clearly into focus now....

When you can clearly see these two or three teachers...choose one of them to be the teacher with whom you will spend time today. Don't worry about choosing *the* most important teacher of your life, because there may be more than one of them. Simply choose one of your most significant teachers to spend time with today. Trust your intuition...and let that one teacher come into focus....

As you continue breathing...notice that your teacher is coming toward you now...there in your quiet place in nature. Notice how your heart opens as you see this special being approach you. As your teacher comes closer...remember the experiences that have made this being important to you. Let your face show your gratitude as you come together and greet each other....

Acknowledge your teacher or show your affection in a way that feels right for both of you. Then, when your teacher asks why you have called...say that you would like some help. Tell your teacher that you have a particular problem, challenge, or concern that requires careful attention. You've been thinking about it, and perhaps struggling with it...and now you'd like to ask for your teacher's perspective and guidance.

Maybe you've been worried about a certain relationship...or maybe there's a difficult situation at work that's been hanging heavy on your mind...or perhaps you had a powerful dream or a nightmare that needs interpretation...or maybe you feel overwhelmed by pain or illness...or perhaps you are unclear about your goals or your purpose in life....

Whatever you choose as your focus of attention...take a few moments now to clarify your question...so you can articulate it to your teacher in simple terms. When you are ready, state your concern and ask your question. Don't worry about doing it perfectly. Just do the best you can, knowing that your teacher accepts you and understands you....

If there is a particular way you'd like your question to be answered, be sure to say so. Perhaps you'd like to request a symbolic gift...something that could help you gain insight into your problem, challenge, or concern. Maybe you'd just like to hear your teacher talk about your question, rephrasing your words in such a way that you begin to see your situation in a new way.

If a conversation or a gift doesn't feel quite right, then perhaps your teacher could take you on a journey into your own imagination…to give you an experience that will shed light on your problem. Maybe your teacher will call up a memory from your past or show you a dream from your future. However your teacher answers you, the important thing is to pay close attention…because whatever happens after you ask your question is part of the answer. Notice *everything* your teacher says and does and shows to you.

As you continue breathing naturally…focus your entire awareness on your teacher's message. Listen carefully…watch carefully…and open all your senses to receive your teacher's gift of wisdom. When your teacher is done sharing with you, make sure you understand what has been imparted to you. Tell your teacher what you have perceived. Ask if your understanding is correct. If not, take a few moments now to seek clarification. Keep going until you and your teacher agree that you fully understand the message….

When you and your teacher have finished with your work…spend a little more time together…so you can savor each other's presence for a few moments longer. Thank your teacher for today's answer to your question. If you like, you can also express gratitude for anything else your teacher has given you. Then, when you're ready…say goodbye for now…knowing that you can always come back here to your place in nature. You can always come back and ask for your teacher's help anytime you like….

After you've said goodbye…watch as your teacher moves away from where you've been standing together. Watch until you can no longer make out the outline of your teacher's form. As you watch your teacher disappear into the distance now, remember the message that you've received today.

As you remember the message and hold it in your heart, begin to gradually bring your awareness back to your breathing now. Allow your attention to slowly return to your body, as you continue to breathe naturally. Start to notice the weight of your body against the floor again, as you feel the support of the earth beneath you….

Now…whenever you're ready…wiggle your toes and move your fingers. Stretch your hands…and take a few deep breaths up high into your chest. Allow your breathing to speed up ever so slightly now, as you continue to stretch your hands…and your arms…and your legs…and all your limbs now…one by one…as you feel the energy of movement return to your body.

Stretching and moving and breathing naturally…the energy of movement comes flowing back into your hips…and your torso…and

Think for yourself and question authority.
TIMOTHY LEARY

I don't consider myself a teacher. I consider myself a friend and that's the way I have always dealt with people. I look at it this way, one on one, that's where something happens.
JOE MILLER

Do something awesome instead of waiting for life to do something to you.

ARNOLD MINDELL

your shoulders...and now into your neck...and your head. Your whole body becomes enlivened again as you continue to breathe ...and stretch...and move in whatever way feels good to you....

Slowly, gently, quietly...imagine that little sparks of energy are waking up all the cells in your body. Bit by bit, your body stretches into a state of readiness and wakefulness, as these sparks of energy light up your cells like stars in the night....

As you continue to breathe, these sparks of energy stimulate your mind...bringing it to a state of relaxed, alert clarity. And now...when you're ready to bring your awareness all the way back into present time...you can open your eyes slowly...letting them close, and then open again...close, and then open again...as you become accustomed to the light once more....

With your eyes open now...give yourself some time to adjust to your surroundings in present time. Take a look around...and reorient yourself in whatever way you need....

Breathe deeply...and remember your teacher's message. Carry your teacher's message forward with you...holding it gently in your heart as you go about your day....

THE BIG QUESTION MEDITATION

There are many big questions worth pondering, but there's only one I want to talk about in this final chapter of the book. That is, "What is your purpose in life?" Some people pose this question by asking themselves, "Why am I here?" or "What did I come here to do?" or "What is my true calling?" No matter what words you choose, I encourage you to ask yourself this question. Actually, I suggest that you go *beyond* asking. I'd like to give you a way to *remember* your purpose in life. Let me explain.

I struggled unsuccessfully with the Big Question for many years until my soul retrieval mentor, Sandra Ingerman, mentioned in a telephone conversation that I could journey shamanically to *remember* my purpose. She said that everyone is born with a purpose. Therefore, people don't need to find, create, or design a purpose; they simply need to remember what they already know.

Sandy's reframe made total sense to me. After all, I'd long believed that everyone is born with a purpose programmed into their cells. However, I'd never taken this belief to its logical conclusion, namely, that I merely had to remember what I already knew somewhere deep inside. When I followed Sandy's instructions for the journey, it yielded the answer to my question quickly and easily. Years of struggle went *poof* in a matter of moments, and my purpose made itself exceedingly clear.

I don't know how other people relate to their life purpose, but for me, it's like a powerful litmus test against which I can measure the *alignment level* of all my choices and actions. When I don't know what to do, I consider my options and ask myself: "Will this lead me toward my purpose or away from it?"

For example, my purpose is to LIBERATE MY HEART, which is expressed by the symbol of a winged heart flying into the sun. Apparently, it doesn't matter if I write books, clean floors, or ride Harleys in the desert, as long as it helps me liberate my heart.

This may sound pathetically self-absorbed, but I believe that if I do what I came here to do, it will benefit the whole as much as it

If we have our own why of life, we shall get along with almost any how.

FRIEDRICH NIETZSCHE

Tell me what is it that you plan to do with your one wild and precious life?

MARY OLIVER

Any path is only a path, and there is no affront, to oneself or to others, in dropping it if that is what your heart tells you.

CARLOS CASTANEDA

In the middle of difficulty lies opportunity.

ALBERT EINSTEIN

benefits me. How this plays itself out is not my affair. My job is to keep my nose to the grindstone—or rather, to keep my ear to my heart. If this sounds easy, I assure you that it's not. All day long I must ask myself, "Will this help me liberate my heart or won't it?"

Remembering to ask this question is only part of the process. The real work comes when I must follow through and *act* on the information I receive. Many times I get answers I don't expect, since liberation is often a matter of taking the unexpected course. In other words, it's generally not very liberating to do what everyone else has always done—or even what I have always done. More often than not, liberation is about blasting patterns and blazing new trails.

As you may imagine, this can be scary. In point of fact, it can be scary to work with your purpose no matter what it is. Why? Because if you use your purpose to evaluate and choose all your actions, it will repeatedly push you to your limits and test your commitment. Frankly, if your purpose *doesn't* push you, it probably isn't your purpose.

Your true calling will bring you face to face with your biggest fears, and it's likely to do this in increasingly difficult ways the deeper you go with it. This isn't necessarily bad news, since challenges always bring opportunities for growth. Besides, living according to your purpose isn't only about doing battle with your fears. The truth is, if you follow your bliss, it will lead you to experiences of grace and contentment that may be unavailable by any other means.

Even if you already know your purpose, is it phrased in a crystal-clear way, so you can hold it before you like a lantern to light your way? I know people whose statements of purpose sound more like dissertations than succinct phrases. It's tough to get a handle on a long, drawn-out treatise. Life is confusing enough without having a confusing mission statement. If your purpose is supposed to help you stay clear, then the first step is to have a clear purpose.

In the previous chapter's Teacher Meditation, I mentioned that you can ask your teacher about your purpose in life. This meditation will address that question, and then go a step further with it by adding specific details to help you *remember* the purpose you were born with. In addition, this meditation will use Sandy's tips for getting this information in a simple form. That way, you can hold it in your heart as you go about your day.

For this meditation, I will follow the same format as the Teacher Meditation, except for one difference. That is, when it comes time to ask your teacher for help, I'll give you a carefully worded question that's designed to elicit specific information about your purpose in life. I hope that the familiar structure of the previous meditation will allow you to journey inward even more swiftly and surely, so you can receive your answer to the Big Question more easily.

To begin this meditation, find a quiet place where you will not be disturbed. Be sure to turn off any technological contraptions that might be lurking nearby. You won't be needing the telephone, television, radio, stereo, or computer during your inner journey. Disconnect the phone lines, and free the machines from their power source, so you won't be distracted by their insistent rings, hums, and whirs.

I shut my eyes in order to see.
PAUL GAUGUIN

Once you've quieted the space, find a good spot to sit or lie down. Get comfortable, and begin to quiet your senses now by taking one last look around you, making sure that everything is in its place.

When you're ready, close your eyes and turn your attention inward. Allow the rhythm of your breathing to come into your awareness. Without trying to control or change anything, let your breathing become your total focus as you continue to turn your attention inward....

Just breathe naturally...because whatever way you are breathing is perfectly okay. Follow your breath in...and out...one breath at a time in one long, continuous circle...one long, continuous rhythm...in...and out...however you want....

As you continue breathing, slowly bring your attention to your body. Feel the weight of your body against the chair...or the floor...or the earth...wherever you are sitting or lying down right now. Feel the massive support that your body is receiving...support that you are receiving from the earth beneath you. Feel this deep, strong, solid support...the support of a massive planet that sustains you, all beings, and all things equally, without judgment. You are receiving this massive, constant support simply because you are alive.

For the human soul is virtually indestructible, and its ability to rise from the ashes remains as long as the body draws breath.
ALICE MILLER

In whatever way you can, imagine yourself surrendering to this support as you continue breathing. With each in-breath, you can feel this support a little more deeply. With each out-breath, you can relax into this support a little more fully....

Now, in a moment, get ready to go a step further in your inner journey by imagining a place in nature, a place where you can go when you want to connect with your core...your truest self. Wander to that place now...in your imagination. Go to that sacred place in nature…a place where you feel safe and warm and comforted. It can be a place where you've actually been…or it can be a place you envision in your mind right now, for today. However this place appears to you, let it be everything you want it to be….

As you continue to breathe naturally, let your awareness focus more intently on your surroundings, there in your sacred spot. What can you see? Are there trees around you? Are you in a meadow? Can you see mountains? Is there a river nearby…or a lake…or a beach…or the ocean? Is the sky above you clear and sunny…or is it full of billowing clouds…or can you see the subtle colors of twilight coming up on the horizon?

Take your time as you drink in the view around you. Let all the details of your personal power spot become vivid for you…so you can feel its support a little more with each breath. Continue to breathe naturally, as you focus your awareness on the beautiful landscape that surrounds you….

Now…gradually shift your attention from your eyes to your ears. Notice the sounds around you there in nature. When you listen, what do you hear? Can you hear the wind? Is there a crashing surf in the background? Do you hear the murmur of a nearby stream…or the rustle of leaves…or the creaking of tall trees as they sway in the wind? Can you hear birds? Perhaps there are no sounds at all. Perhaps it's night and everything is quiet….

Now…slowly…let your awareness drift, and then gradually focus on the air around you. As you continue to breathe in whatever way feels right to you…notice the *temperature* and the *feel* and the *scent* of the air. Is it humid? Is it dry? Is the air electric with the energy of a passing thunderstorm?

Let your nostrils come alive as you breathe in the air around you. Can you smell flower blossoms? Do you smell the salty air of ocean fog? Perhaps there is a campfire nearby. Is there a smoky aroma of burning wood and pine needles? Whatever you smell…take a few moments now to savor the air…your invisible *oxygenated* friend that sustains you and gives you life….

Breathe the air deeply…and when you're ready…gradually let your attention shift once again, as you begin to turn your awareness inward. Tune in to your heart, and let your memories of special teachers begin to surface in the reflective pool of your mind. These teachers could be people…or animals…or spirit guides…or dream figures…or perhaps even a sacred object or a power spot.

Begin by thinking of the teachers in your life right now…in present time…and then slowly…go back in your memory, until you remember teachers further back in the past. Think about those special beings who changed your life in some way. Ask your memory banks to call up any experiences that will help you remember your teachers. Bit by bit, let these memories surface for you now, as you recall those who supported you, taught you, and helped you become who you are today.

Slowly, keep going back in your memories...year by year... remembering the points in your life that were transformative for you. As you go back in time, remember all the teachers who assisted you in these transformations, who acted as a catalyst in your growth...who taught you about unconditional love by giving it to you...who brought you lessons of compassion and wisdom by showing you how to act, or by showing you how *not* to act. As you watch these teachers pass before your eyes...acknowledge their presence and their gifts...and thank them...one by one.

Now...when you're ready, begin to narrow the focus of your attention until you are able to single out two or three teachers who are especially significant to you. Gradually allow these important teachers to emerge into the foreground...and let them come clearly into focus now....

When you can clearly see these two or three teachers...choose one of them to be the teacher with whom you will spend time today. Don't worry about choosing *the* most important teacher of your life, because there may be more than one of them. Simply choose one of your most significant teachers to spend time with today. Trust your intuition...and let that one teacher come into focus....

As you continue breathing...notice that your teacher is coming toward you now...there in your quiet place in nature. Notice how your heart opens as you see this special being approach you. As your teacher comes closer...remember the experiences that have made this being important to you. Let your face show your gratitude as you come together and greet each other....

Acknowledge your teacher or show your affection in a way that feels right for both of you. Then, when your teacher asks why you have called...say that you would like some help. Tell your teacher that you have a particular concern that requires careful attention. You've been thinking about it, and perhaps struggling with it...and now you'd like to ask for your teacher's perspective and guidance.

Tell your teacher that you would like help to *remember* the purpose you were born with. Let your teacher know that you realize your soul has always known the nature of your true calling, but somehow, your conscious mind seems to have forgotten this essential information...or at least, you've forgotten how to express it in a clear way....

If you don't know where you are going, you will probably end up somewhere else.

LAWRENCE J. PETER

It is better to know some of the questions than all of the answers.

JAMES THURBER

Dreamers die, but the best parts of their dreams need not die with them.

JERRY LARGE

When you're ready, approach your teacher now with this direct request: *"Help me remember the purpose I was born with. Show me a symbol or a simple phrase that expresses this purpose, my true purpose in life."*

State this request a few more times now to help you clarify and focus your intention: *"Help me remember the purpose I was born with. Show me a symbol or a simple phrase that expresses this purpose, my true purpose in life."*

Remember…remember…remember your purpose in life now, as this essential information becomes clear to you with your teacher's help. Remember your purpose as it's expressed in a symbol or in a simple phrase that you can carry in your heart….

As you continue breathing naturally…focus your entire awareness on this symbol or simple phrase. Open all your senses to receive this gift of wisdom about your true calling in life. Take your time…repeating your request as often as you like to keep your focus clear and your intention strong. Keep asking until you receive your answer in a way that you understand….

Your teacher may answer you immediately by showing you a symbol or by telling you a simple phrase that describes your purpose. Or your teacher may prefer to work more slowly, allowing the symbol or the phrase to emerge from the background of your own awareness…drifting upward from the depths of primal memory…gradually becoming clearer and clearer to your conscious mind…until finally, you can now see the symbol or hear the simple phrase that represents your purpose in life….

When your teacher is done sharing this information with you, make sure you understand what has been imparted to you. Tell your teacher what you have heard and seen and understood about your purpose in life. Ask if your understanding is correct. If not, take a few moments now to seek clarification. Keep going until you and your teacher agree that you have gotten the message about your true purpose, represented by a clear symbol or a simple phrase.

When you are certain of this symbol or phrase, engrave its memory in your brain, so you will always remember it…no matter what. Your true purpose will always be clear for you now, from this day forward….

When you and your teacher have finished with your work…spend a little more time together…so you can savor each other's presence for a few moments longer. Thank your teacher for the answer to your question. If you like, you can also express gratitude for anything else your teacher has given you. Then, when you're ready…say goodbye for now…knowing that you can always

---

The acorn theory says that there is an individual image that belongs to your soul.

JAMES HILLMAN

come back here to your place in nature. You can always come back and ask for your teacher's help anytime you like....

After you've said goodbye...watch as your teacher moves away from where you've been standing together. Watch until you can no longer make out the outline of your teacher's form. As you watch your teacher disappear into the distance now, remember the symbol or the phrase that you've received today.

As you remember this symbol or simple phrase that represents your purpose, gradually bring your awareness back to your breathing now. Holding this symbol or simple phrase in your heart, allow your attention to slowly return to your body, as you continue to breathe naturally. Start to notice the weight of your body against the floor again, as you feel the support of the earth beneath you....

Now...whenever you're ready...wiggle your toes and move your fingers. Stretch your hands...and take a few deep breaths up high into your chest. Allow your breathing to speed up ever so slightly now, as you continue to stretch your hands...and your arms...and your legs...and all your limbs now...one by one...as you feel the energy of movement return to your body.

Stretching and moving and breathing naturally...the energy of movement comes flowing back into your hips...and your torso...and your shoulders...and now into your neck...and your head. Your whole body becomes enlivened again, as you continue to breathe...and stretch...and move in whatever way feels good to you....

Slowly, gently, quietly...imagine that little sparks of energy are waking up all the cells in your body. Bit by bit, your body stretches into a state of readiness and wakefulness, as these sparks of energy light up your cells like stars in the night....

As you continue to breathe, these sparks of energy stimulate your mind...bringing it to a state of relaxed, alert clarity. And now...when you're ready to bring your awareness all the way back into present time...you can open your eyes slowly...letting them close, and then open again...close, and then open again...as you become accustomed to the light once more....

With your eyes open now...give yourself some time to adjust to your surroundings in present time. Take a look around...and reorient yourself in whatever way you need....

Breathe deeply...and remember your purpose...remember the symbol or the simple phrase that reminds you of this purpose. Carry your purpose forward with you now...holding it gently in your heart as you go about your day....

The fabled musk deer searches the world over for the source of the scent which comes from itself.

RAMAKRISHNA

Live your questions now, and perhaps even without knowing it, you will live along some distant day into your answers.

RAINER MARIA RILKE

Be Here Now:

What's Next?

SECTION
SEVEN

BIBLIOGRAPHY: HELPMATES ON THE PATH OF COMPASSION

Countless books have passed through my hands, contributing a seemingly endless supply of ideas and support. For years, I happily allowed these books to accumulate, spilling over onto shelves in every room of the house. Eventually, I began to wonder if my penchant for books was at least partly fueled by an egotistical desire to appear more well read than I actually was. After all, I owned books I'd barely opened, books I hung onto "because I might read them someday," and books I kept simply because they looked impressive. Somehow, it felt almost sinful to get rid of a book, as if I were turning a friend out into the cold.

The truth is, books *are* friends to me. They have nurtured me, instructed me, and helped me survive. At some point, however, I realized that my prodigious accumulation of books was wreaking havoc with my ongoing shift toward greater simplicity. Therefore, I decided to limit my collection to one big bookcase. Everything else would have to go.

With great care, I sorted through a few thousand books, one by one. Those I didn't actually use—or honestly love—were boxed up and recycled to friends, libraries, and secondhand stores. After the initial purging, I committed to a new system: When something new came in, something else had to go. Although this felt brutal at first, I took solace in the fact that my book-friends would probably get more attention in their new homes.

For the next fifteen years, I kept this commitment. Gradually, my bibliophilic compulsions dissipated, and I no longer lusted for books. After that, I playfully allowed myself *two* bookcases and an occasional influx without a corresponding outflow. In the context of this limited library system, I noticed that a core group of books never seemed to leave. The following bibliography is a subset of this core group. More specifically, it's a list of some of my favorite helpmates on the path of compassion.

A few of these helpmates are books I've read and reread many times, savoring every word like a delicious morsel of a sumptuous

Believe nothing, no matter where you read it, or who said it—even if I have said it—unless it agrees with your own reason and your own common sense.

BUDDHA

The things I want to know are in books. My best friend is the man who'll get me a book I haven't read.

ABRAHAM LINCOLN

feast. Others have one or two unique ideas that make them invaluable companions. Still others are my reference buddies—books I can trust to provide reliable information from a compassionate perspective.

In most cases, the relevance of a particular title will be immediately obvious, in terms of its contribution to my thinking for this book. However, a few of the choices may seem puzzling. For instance, why would I include *Demian*, *Safe Uses of Cortisol*, or *Talk Dirty to Me*? The answers are easy. *Demian*, by Hermann Hesse, has been a friend since my early teens. Along with Hesse's other writings, *Demian* planted important seeds of compassion related to spirituality, passion, and the shadow side of life.

Dr. William Jefferies' book, *Safe Uses of Cortisol*, provides extensive medical information and specific protocols for healing adrenal insufficiency and adrenal exhaustion, which had seriously compromised my health for much of my adult life. Dr. Jefferies' book allowed me to overturn years of miseducation perpetrated by mainstream medicine—miseducation that had prevented me from getting the help I needed. I include *Safe Uses of Cortisol* here because its protocols enabled me to finish this book and, more importantly, because it taught me how to be *concretely* compassionate with my body in deeper ways than I'd ever known before.

As for Sallie Tisdale's book, *Talk Dirty to Me*, you might be particularly curious about its inclusion in this bibliography. Aside from the fact that Tisdale's book is one of my all-time favorites, it teaches about *awareness* and *acceptance*, the two components by which I define compassion in the introduction to this book. Tisdale imparts this teaching by examining the twists and turns of her own sexual preferences and prejudices, from within a sea of wildly divergent cultural appetites. The point is, compassion comes in many forms, and sometimes it shows up where you least expect it.

Here, then, is an eclectic group of my special book-friends. Like any group of friends, some are elegant and refined, others are passionately radical, and still others are a little rough around the edges. Their differences will make your explorations juicier; their similarities may give you pause to wonder. In this list, you might discover some of your own favorites, along with new companions waiting to come home with you.

Since many of these books have been with me for ten, twenty, or even thirty years, I've updated the titles (if revised) and the publisher/ publication dates to reflect the most recently available editions. In addition, I've made a note by any books that were out of print or "indefinitely out of stock" at the time of this update. In these cases, you may be able to locate the title at your local library or used book store.

I cannot live without books.

THOMAS JEFFERSON

Amen, Daniel. *Change Your Brain, Change Your Life*. New York: Three Rivers Press. 1998.

_____. *Healing ADD: The Breakthrough Program That Allows You to See and Heal the Six Types of ADD*. New York: Berkley Books. 2001.

_____. *Healing the Hardware of the Soul*. New York: The Free Press. 2002.

_____. *Making a Good Brain Great*. New York: Three Rivers Press. 2005.

_____. *Sex on the Brain*. New York: Three Rivers Press. 2007.

Bass, Ellen and Laura Davis. *The Courage to Heal: A Guide for Women Survivors of Child Sexual Abuse*. New York: HarperCollins Publishers. 1994.

Beck, Charlotte. *Everyday Zen: Love and Work*. New York: HarperCollins Publishers. 1989.

Bee, Helen. *The Developing Child*. Reading, MA: Addison-Wesley Educational Publishers. 1999.

Black, Claudia. *Double Duty: Dual Dynamics Within the Chemically Dependent Home*. New York: Ballantine Books. 1990.

Blum, Ralph. *The Book of Runes*. New York: St. Martin's Press. 1993.

Boone, J. Allen. *Kinship with All Life*. San Francisco: HarperSanFrancisco. 1976.

Boyd, Billy R. *Circumcision Exposed: Rethinking a Medical Cultural Tradition*. Freedom, CA: Crossing Press. 1998.

Bradshaw, John. *Healing the Shame That Binds You*. Deerfield Beach, FL: Health Communications. 1988.

Brezsny, Rob. *Pronoia Is the Antidote for Paranoia: How the Whole World Is Conspiring to Shower You with Blessings*. Berkeley, CA: Frog, Ltd. 2005.

Bryant, Dorothy. *The Kin of Ata Are Waiting for You*. New York: Random House. 1997.

Byock, Ira. *Dying Well: Peace and Possibilities at the End of Life*. New York: Berkley Publishing Group. 1998.

_____. *The Four Things That Matter Most: A Book About Living*. New York: Free Press/Simon and Schuster. 2004.

Cameron, Julia. *The Artist's Way: A Spiritual Path to Higher Creativity*. New York: Putnam Publishing Group. 1992.

Campbell, Joseph. *The Power of Myth*. New York: Doubleday. 1991.

Capacchione, Lucia. *The Power of Your Other Hand: A Course in Channeling the Inner Wisdom of the Right Brain*. North Hollywood, CA: Newcastle Publishing Company. 1988.

Carlson, Lisa. *Caring for the Dead: Your Final Act of Love*. Hinesburg, VT: Upper Access. 1998.

Cassou, Michelle and Stewart Cubley. *Life, Paint, and Passion: Reclaiming the Magic of Spontaneous Expression*. New York: Putnam Publishing Group. 1995.

Castaneda, Carlos. *Journey to Ixtlan*. New York: Simon & Schuster Trade. 1991.

_____. *A Separate Reality*. New York: Pocket Books. 1991.

_____. *The Teachings of Don Juan: A Yaqui Way of Knowledge*. Berkeley, CA: University of California Press. 1998.

_____. *The Wheel of Time: The Shamans of Ancient Mexico, Their Thoughts About Life, Death, and the Universe*. Los Angeles: LA Eidolona Press. 1998.

Chopra, Deepak. *Life After Death: The Burden of Proof*. New York: Harmony Books. 2006.

Clarke, Jean. *Self-Esteem: A Family Affair*. Center City, MN: Hazelden Information and Educational Services. 1998.

Cohen, Lawrence. *Playful Parenting*. New York: Ballantine Books. 2001.

Comfort, Alex. *The New Joy of Sex*. New York: Pocket Books. 1992.

Davis, Laura. *I Thought We'd Never Speak Again*. New York: HarperCollins. 2002.

Davis, Laura and Janis Keyser. *Becoming the Parent You Want to Be: A Sourcebook for the First Five Years*. New York: Broadway Books. 1997.

Dominguez, Joe and Vicki Robin. *Your Money or Your Life: Transforming Your Relationship With Money and Achieving Financial Independence*. New York: Viking Penguin. 1993.

Edwards, Betty. *Drawing on the Right Side of the Brain*. New York: Putnam Publishing Group. 1989.

Estes, Clarissa Pinkola. *Women Who Run With the Wolves: Myths and Stories of the Wild Woman Archetype*. New York: Ballantine Books. 1992.

Fossum, Merle and Marilyn Mason. *Facing Shame: Families in Recovery*. New York: W. W. Norton & Company. 1989.

Garfield, Patricia. *Creative Dreaming*. New York: Ballantine Books. 1985.

Gibran, Kahlil. *The Prophet*. Boston, MA: Little, Brown & Company. 1999.

Goleman, Daniel. *Vital Lies, Simple Truths*. New York: Simon & Schuster. 1996.

Goldberg, Herb. *The Hazards of Being Male: Surviving the Myth of Masculine Privilege*. New York: NAL/Dutton. 1977.

Goldberg, Natalie. *Wild Mind: Living the Writer's Life*. New York: Bantam Books. 1990.

_____. *Writing Down the Bones: Freeing the Writer Within*. Boston, MA: Shambhala Publications. 1998.

Gottman, John and Nan Silver. *The Seven Principles for Making Marriage Work*. New York: Crown Publishers. 1999.

Gurman, Alan and David Kniskern. *Handbook of Family Therapy*. Levittown, PA: Brunner/Mazel Publishers. 1987.

Harner, Michael. *The Way of the Shaman*. San Francisco: HarperSanFrancisco. 1990.

Hay, Louise. *You Can Heal Your Life*. Carlsbad, CA: Hay House. 1999.

Herrigel, Eugene. *Zen in the Art of Archery*. New York: Vintage Books. 1999.

Hesse, Hermann. *Demian*. New York: HarperCollins Publishers. 1989.

Ingerman, Sandra. *Soul Retrieval: Mending the Fragmented Self Through Shamanic Practice*. San Francisco: HarperSanFrancisco. 1991.

_____. *Welcome Home: Following Your Soul's Journey Home*. San Francisco: HarperSanFrancisco. 1994.

Jefferies, William McK. *Safe Uses of Cortisol*. Springfield, IL: Charles C. Thomas, Publisher. 1996.

Jennings, William. *The Ronin: A Novel Based on a Zen Myth*. Boston, MA: Charles E. Tuttle Company. 1989.

Kübler-Ross, Elisabeth. *The Tunnel and the Light*. New York: Marlowe & Company. 1999.

_____. *On Death and Dying*. New York: Simon & Schuster Trade. 1997.

_____. *The Wheel of Life: A Memoir of Living and Dying*. New York: Scribner. 1997.

Lao Tsu. *The Tao Te Ching: A New Translation by Gia-Fu Feng and Jane English*. New York: Vintage Books. 1972.

LeBoyer, Frederick. *Birth Without Violence*. New York: Alfred A. Knopf. 1975.

Lerner, Harriet. *The Dance of Intimacy: A Woman's Guide to Courageous Acts of Change in Key Relationships*. New York: HarperCollins Publishers. 1990.

Levine, Stephen. *A Year to Live: How to Live This Year As If It Were Your Last*. New York: Crown Publishing Group. 1998.

Miller, Alice. *Banished Knowledge: Facing Childhood Injury*. New York: Doubleday. 1991.

_____. *The Drama of the Gifted Child: The Search for the True Self*. New York: Basic Books. 1996.

_____. *For Your Own Good: Hidden Cruelty in Child-Rearing and the Roots of Violence*. New York: Farrar, Straus & Giroux. 1990.

_____. *The Untouched Key: Tracing Childhood Trauma in Creativity and Destructiveness*. New York: Doubleday. 1991.

Millman, Dan. *The Way of the Peaceful Warrior*. Tiburon, CA: H. J. Kramer. 1984.

Mindell, Amy. *Coma: A Healing Journey*. Portland, OR: Lao Tse Press. 1999.

Mindell, Arnold. *Coma: Key to Awakening*. New York: Viking Penguin. 1995.

_____. *Dreambody in Relationships*. New York: Viking Penguin. 1988.

_____. *The Leader as Martial Artist: Techniques and Strategies for Resolving Conflict and Creating Community*. San Francisco: HarperSanFrancisco. 1993.

_____. *The Shaman's Body*. San Francisco: HarperSanFrancisco. 1993.

_____. *Sitting in the Fire*. Portland, OR: Lao Tse Press. 1995.

_____. *Working on Yourself Alone: Inner Dreambody Work*. New York: Viking Penguin. 1990.

_____. *Working with the Dreaming Body*. New York: Viking Penguin. 1989.

Mindell, Arnold and Amy Mindell. *Riding the Horse Backwards: Process Work in Theory and Practice*. New York: Viking Penguin. 1992.

Moody, Raymond. *Life After Life*. New York: Bantam Books. 1975.

Noble, Vicki. *Motherpeace: A Way to the Goddess Through Myth, Art, and Tarot*. San Francisco: HarperSanFrancisco. 1994.

Northrup, Christiane. *Mother-Daughter Wisdom: Creating a Legacy of Physical and Emotional Health*. New York: Bantam Books. 2005.

_____. *Women's Bodies, Women's Wisdom: Creating Physical and Emotional Health and Healing*. New York: Bantam Books. 1998.

_____. *The Wisdom of Menopause: Creating Physical and Emotional Health and Healing During the Change*. New York: Bantam Books. 2001.

Norwood, Robin. *Women Who Love Too Much: When You Keep Wishing and Hoping He'll Change*. New York: Pocket Books. 1986.

Pease, Allan and Barbara. *The Definitive Book of Body Language*. New York: Bantam Books. 2004.

Peck, M. Scott. *The Road Less Traveled*. New York: Simon & Schuster Trade. 1998.

_____. *Denial of the Soul: Spiritual and Medical Perspectives on Euthanasia and Mortality*. New York: Harmony Books. 1997.

Ram Dass and Mirabai Bush. *Compassion in Action: Setting Out on the Path of Service*. New York: Bell Tower. 1992.

Ram Dass and Paul Gorman. *How Can I Help? Stories and Reflections on Service*. New York: Alfred A. Knopf. 1985.

Ray, Sondra. *I Deserve Love*. Berkeley, CA: Celestial Arts Publishing. 1995.

Ray, Sondra and Bob Mandel. *Birth and Relationships: How Your Birth Affects Your Relationships*. Berkeley, CA: Celestial Arts Publishing. 1995.

Redfield, James. *The Celestine Prophecy*. New York: Warner Books. 1995.

Rico, Gabriele. *Writing the Natural Way: Using Right-Brain Techniques to Release Your Expressive Powers*. New York: Putnam Publishing Group. 1983.

Robbins, John. *Diet for a New America: How Your Food Choices Affect Your Health, Happiness, and the Future of Life on Earth*. Tiburon, CA: H. J. Kramer. 1998.

Roberts, Jane. *The Further Education of Oversoul Seven*. Paramus, NJ: Prentice Hall. 1984.

Rodegast, Pat and Judith Stanton. *Emmanuel's Book*. New York: Bantam Books. 1987.

_____. *Emmanuel's Book II: The Choice for Love*. New York: Bantam Books. 1997.

Rubin, Theodore. *The Angry Book*. New York: Simon & Schuster Trade. 1998.

Rush, Anne Kent. *Getting Clear: Body Work for Women*. New York: Random House. 1973.

Safransky, Sy. *Sunbeams: A Book of Quotations*. Berkeley, CA: North Atlantic Books. 1990.

Sams, Jamie and David Carson. *Medicine Cards: The Discovery of Power Through the Ways of Animals*. Santa Fe, NM: Bear & Company. 1988.

Schaef, Anne Wilson. *Co-Dependence: Misunderstood-Mistreated*. San Francisco: HarperSanFrancisco. 1992.

Seabury, David. *The Art of Selfishness*. New York: Pocket Books. 1986.

Siegel, Bernie. *How to Live Between Office Visits: A Guide to Life, Love and Health*. New York: HarperCollins Publishers. 1994.

_____. *Love, Medicine and Miracles: Lessons Learned About Self-Healing from a Surgeon's Experience With Exceptional Patients*. New York: HarperCollins Publishers. 1990.

Smith, Manuel. *When I Say No, I Feel Guilty*. New York: Bantam Books. 1985.

Starlanyl, Devin. *The Fibromyalgia Advocate*. Oakland, CA: New Harbinger Publishers. 1998.

Stevens, Barry. *Don't Push the River*. Berkeley, CA: Celestial Arts Publishing. 1995.

Stone, Douglas; Bruce Patton and Sheila Heen. *Difficult Conversations: How to Discuss What Matters Most*. New York: Penguin Books. 1999.

Sutherland, Amy. *What Shamu Taught Me About Life, Love, and Marriage: Lessons for People from Animals and Their Trainers*. New York: Random House. 2008.

Tisdale, Sallie. *Talk Dirty to Me: An Intimate Philosophy of Sex*. New York: Doubleday. 1995.

Veiny, Thomas and John Kelly. *The Secret Life of the Unborn Child*. New York: Dell Publishing. 1982.

Wilhelm, Richard and Cary Baynes. *The I Ching: Book of Changes*. Princeton, NJ: Princeton University Press. 1967.

Woods, Margo. *Masturbation, Tantra, and Self-Love*. San Diego, CA: Mho & Mho Works. 1981.

INDEX

ABOUT THE AUTHOR

Compassion is the radicalism of this age.

DALAI LAMA

Cat Saunders, Ph.D., has been involved in the fields of psychology and self-help since the early 1970s, when she began studying a wide array of bodywork and breathing techniques, therapeutic methodologies, cross-cultural spiritual disciplines, and creative healing modalities, including art therapy and ecstatic dance. Over time, she integrated this diverse experience into her private practice as a counselor and educator, shamanic practitioner, and nonsectarian minister.

Cat's doctoral research focused on the relationship between functional neurology and eating disorders. She has been interviewed on radio and television regarding her practice, her techniques for working with anger, and her series of articles about death. In addition, Cat's study and practice of interdisciplinary forms of prayer led her to found Rent-A-Monk, which makes certain aspects of her spiritual work available to others.

From a series of 1300 daily drawings completed in 1983-1987, Cat created a deck of healing cards called "Shadow and Light: Images of Change and Transformation for Women in Recovery" (published in 2007). The cover drawing for *Dr. Cat's Helping Handbook* comes from this deck.

To honor Cat's lifelong passion for work with death and dying, she serves as a "death doula" to provide end-of-life care and support for individuals and their families. When people close to death are comatose or otherwise verbally impaired, Cat helps them convey their needs and wishes nonverbally when they are unable to communicate in more conventional ways.

For more information about Cat and her work, please visit **www.drcat.org**.

Made in the USA
Monee, IL
17 November 2022

17960872R00196